COLLATERAL DAMAGE

COLLATERAL DAMAGE

How High-Stakes Testing Corrupts America's Schools

Sharon L. Nichols
and
David C. Berliner

HARVARD EDUCATION PRESS
CAMBRIDGE, MASSACHUSETTS

Library of Congress Control Number 2006939816

Paperback ISBN 978-1-891792-35-9

Library Edition ISBN 978-1-891792-36-6

Published by Harvard Education Press,
an imprint of the Harvard Education Publishing Group

Harvard Education Press
8 Story Street
Cambridge, MA 02138

Cover Design: Alyssa Morris

The typefaces used in this book are ITC Stone Serif—Medium, Medium Italic, Semibold; ITC Stone Sans—Medium, Medium Italic, Semibold; Adobe Caslon—Regular, Bold, Bold Italic.

This book is dedicated
to the remarkable teachers who still influence our lives.

Sharon L. Nichols thanks
T. L. Good and M. M. McCaslin

David C. Berliner is grateful to
B. J. Biddle, U. Casanova, and
N. L. Gage

CONTENTS

ACKNOWLEDGMENTS

We would like to thank our nation's teachers, who faithfully serve the nation by helping the next generation of youth become educated, active, and concerned citizens. They are the reason we wrote the book and why we do what we do. They deserve better from our politicians.

We express our appreciation to the Great Lakes Center for Education Research and Practice for funding the initial report on which this book is based. We also thank Alex Molnar of the Arizona State University Policy Studies Laboratory for providing editorial help and logistical support for our initial project.

The authors are grateful to graduate students James Caldwell and Michelle Lynde for their help with our research and dedication in checking facts. Michelle especially showed great attention to detail, helped track down references and stories, aided in editing, and provided expert formatting skills. Everything we got right is because of Michelle, and anything that we got wrong is our responsibility entirely!

We thank Caroline Chauncey, editor of Harvard Education Press, for her unwavering support and, perhaps even more importantly, for her continued patience with us as we finished the manuscript.

Finally, we also extend our appreciation to the many scholars, journalists, educators, and parents whose insights concerning high-stakes testing and its effects helped shape our thinking. We are grateful for the privilege to have learned from so many wonderful colleagues and citizens and hope that we have done justice to their ideas.

FOREWORD

NEL NODDINGS

As the time nears for reauthorization of the No Child Left Behind Act (2007 or 2008), debate has grown heated. There is still bipartisan support for the law, but there is also strong dissent. Some of us believe that the law has caused such damage to public education that it should be repealed. Others think that its worst defects can be addressed through judicious revision. In the pages that follow, Sharon Nichols and David Berliner show convincingly that one feature of NCLB—the use of high-stakes tests to measure student achievement—is enormously harmful.

Without impugning the motives of those who advocate the high-stakes testing demanded by NCLB, Nichols and Berliner demonstrate that high-stakes testing is wrong—intellectually, morally, and practically. Not only will it "not work" to improve education, it is already doing demonstrable harm. Using Campbell's law—that any indicator to which high stakes are attached will be subject to corruption—the authors provide evidence that a number of important indicators and concepts—for example, proficiency, progress, test scores, and dropout rates—have been corrupted and, worse, in many cases, the people using them have also been corrupted. It is disheartening to read of the increase of cheating among students, teachers, and administrators, and it is frightening to hear how much time is now spent on seeking loopholes to meet the adequate yearly progress (AYP) required by NCLB instead of providing the educational services needed by individual students.

We could have predicted these unfortunate results. Consider what has happened to the SAT over the past few decades. Originally intended to identify academically talented youth who could then be encouraged to enroll in college regardless of their families' economic condition, the SAT came to have high stakes attached to it. Most colleges insisted that SAT scores be submitted with applications for admission. Thoughtful researchers began to question whether the test really measured "scholastic aptitude," and so the name was changed from Scholastic Aptitude Test to Scholastic Assessment Test, which, as Alfie Kohn has pointed out, sounds humorously redundant—the "Scholastic Test Test." Now it is just the SAT, and the letters stand for nothing in particular. But because high stakes are attached to it, wealthier families pay to have their children tutored for the test, and students who can afford to do so often take the test several times. The original indicator has been corrupted, and the correlation between test scores and family income is disconcertingly high.

The declared motivation for NCLB was to improve the academic achievement of poor and minority students—that is, to eliminate or at least reduce the achievement gap between whites and minorities. This is commendable, but there is mounting evidence that our poor and minority students are actually being hurt by high-stakes testing (see, for example, Meier and Wood, *Many Children Left Behind*).[1] Disproportionately, it is these students who are being retained in grade and deprived of high school diplomas because they cannot pass the required tests. In fairness, we must admit that the figures to which I refer are contested. Some policymakers and educators insist that the achievement gap is closing and that NCLB is working for the students it was intended to help. This bears watching.

There is no question, however, that many poor and minority children are suffering from a diminished curriculum. In our zeal to raise test scores, we have corrupted the very concept of education. Children in too many schools slave over worksheets for long hours preparing for the all-important tests that, in reality, are poor reflections of genuine education. Most well-educated, financially able parents would not stand for the practices that masquerade as education in many of our schools. We would object strenuously if our children were deprived of social studies, art, music, drama, and recess in order to prepare for tests in reading and mathematics. Even "reading" has often been corrupted—reduced to pronouncing words and increasing the words per minute pronounced—and there are signs that reading *comprehension* may actually be declining.

Thus, an important objection to high-stakes testing is that it is anti-intellectual. Even if the movement raises test scores (and that is by no means an assured result), it has clearly increased "grade-grubbing"—a habit of disdain for real learning and a concentration on a payoff in terms of higher grades and scores. This attitude will only get worse if we persist in using high-stakes tests. Furthermore, the habit has corrupted teaching. Good teachers who would once have deviated responsibly from the day's learning objective—to explore, to expose students to ideas that might interest them, to wonder, to analyze—are now often constrained to stick to prescribed material. Creative teaching has become suspect.

Neither Nichols and Berliner nor I have strong objections to the appropriate use of standardized tests. The high school mathematics department in which I taught for nearly ten years used them regularly at the end of each academic year. We met later as a department to discuss the results. Could we explain any increases or decreases in scores? Were there topics we were neglecting? But the tests did not count against the kids; the scores did not appear on report cards, and no one failed a course because of a low grade on the test.

I even believe that the SAT *does* measure something of scholastic aptitude, but it does *not* measure perseverance, intellectual curiosity, commitment to worthy goals, openness to criticism, or the level of family support a student may enjoy for academic work. It is, therefore, not a strong predictor of college success, but it does tell us something about academic talent. Well-designed standardized tests have their uses, but we must exercise discretion in using them. There are alternatives to high-stakes tests, and Nichols and Berliner discuss some of these at length in their last chapter. I have suggested others in my own critique of high-stakes testing.[2]

Some advocates of high-stakes testing argue that students will not give much attention or effort to tests if there are not high stakes attached. That people believe this is enormously sad, and it is false. If teachers are encouraged to spend time developing relations of care and trust with their students and succeed in doing so, kids will do almost anything such teachers suggest. Indeed, this potential influence is so great that it places a heavy moral responsibility on teachers. Through relations of care and trust, we encourage our students to internalize and act upon the highest intellectual, social, and ethical ideals. My belief in the efficacy of such relations is not a product of faith but of years of actual experience. If we want kids to take tests seriously, they will do so without threats and penalties.

And most teachers, too, will do a good job without threats, penalties, and rigid controls. In my own work, I have discussed the power of caring relations in teaching,[3] the legitimacy of happiness as an aim of education,[4] and the pressing need for intellectual vigor and critical thinking.[5] As a teacher, I am not alone in treasuring these features of genuine education. Nichols and Berliner point out that the vast majority of teachers are devoted to the well-being of their students. Year after year, when teacher candidates are asked why they want to become teachers, the answer heard most often is "to make a difference in the lives of kids." Too often, when these fine people get jobs in our schools, they find that they cannot do what they hoped to do. They are forbidden to exercise professional judgment with respect to learning objectives for individual students, required to use scripted lessons, and "written up" if they deviate from the standard curriculum. One of the worst results of NCLB and its punitive approach is that teachers are demoralized, and some of the finest are planning early retirement.

There are teachers—perhaps many—who do not know their subject matter as well as they should. Penalties and threats will not help here. Such measures will simply encourage teachers to narrow the curriculum further and concentrate on material directly relevant to the tests. A better response would be to find ways to involve knowledgeable teachers in helping those who need to know more. Such plans would give long-overdue credit to our expert teachers and appropriate help to those who are devoted to kids and the profession but deficient in the content they must teach. This, by the way, is the attitude of real teachers—to encourage, provide substantive help, and deepen the channels of learning. It is not the attitude encouraged by high-stakes testing and NCLB.

Nichols and Berliner have my sincere thanks for making public the harm done by high-stakes testing.

PREFACE

High-stakes tests—those assessments that have serious consequences attached to them—have been imposed on our nation's schools by the No Child Left Behind (NCLB) law of 2002. The scores on such tests are believed by many to be an appropriate way to hold educators accountable for the academic achievement of our country's youth. But the term *accountability* is not just associated with the idea of counting something, like items on a test; it is also associated with the idea of "giving an account," providing verbal and written reports about some matter of importance. In this book we rely primarily on the accounts of journalists, teachers, administrators, and researchers to inform us about the functioning of our nation's schools. Our goal is to give an account of how the high-stakes testing program demanded by NCLB is working in our schools.

A few states were already experimenting with high-stakes testing as a way to increase student achievement in the years leading up to the signing of NCLB. Teachers, administrators, and experts on testing, even then, were beginning to express concerns about the use (and misuse) of high-stakes tests for raising student achievement. The idea for this book originated then, before NCLB, when David Berliner was studying the impact of high-stakes testing and concluded that high-stakes testing not only regularly failed to increase achievement but that it is a theoretically flawed endeavor, as well.[1] In the fall of 2003, after NCLB required high-stakes testing in all our states, we extended the initial study to look further into the intended and unintended effects of high-stakes testing. This effort yielded two reports. One report showed that high-stakes testing does not increase achievement (and in some cases may erode it), while the other report documented how unintended outcomes of the high-stakes testing policy were detrimental to the educational process.[2] Our well-warranted conclusions about the ineffectiveness of high-stakes testing, published in a respected peer-reviewed journal, seem not to have dampened the enthusiasm for high-stakes testing by our legislators. So in this book we go beyond those empirical findings and demonstrate that high-stakes testing is harmful as well as ineffective. Here, we elaborate on our second report, highlighting the distortion, corruption, and collateral damage that occur when high-stakes tests become commonplace in our public schools.

We hope our book will give more exposure to the reports and research about individuals and groups from across the nation whose lives have been tragically and often permanently affected by high-stakes testing. Our nation needs to worry about the environment created by high-stakes testing, since we found hundreds of examples of *adults* who were cheating, costing many of these people their reputations as well as their jobs. The high-stakes testing environment has produced numerous instances of administrators who "pushed" children out of school or did little to keep them in school if their test scores were low, costing too many students the opportunity to receive a high school diploma. We also found school boards that had drastically narrowed the curriculum and who forced test-preparation programs on teachers and students, taking scarce time away from genuine instruction. We found teacher morale plummeting, causing many to leave the profession. The pressures brought about by high-stakes testing seem undeniably to be corrupting our educators and our system of education.

Supporters of high-stakes testing might dismiss these anecdotal personal experiences as idiosyncratic or too infrequent to matter. But these accounts are neither unique nor rare. Moreover, many other respected scholars have documented similar problems, validating the personal, vivid, and often tragic stories we have found in the press. The evidence from journalists and researchers alike continues to provide us with fresh accounts of the problems inherently tied to the use of high-stakes testing. We collected these data on the high costs of high-stakes testing through the summer of 2006, when we finished this book.

Up until that time, we had continually and systematically scoured news outlets and scholarly journals for accounts of high-stakes testing. We amassed a significant collection of evidence that high-stakes testing does more harm than good. But since our work relies so heavily on what journalists report, several caveats are worth mentioning. First, although our ongoing research has been deliberately broad, we did not have the ability to collect all the relevant stories about the corruption of educators. We are quite sure that the stories we present throughout this book do not represent the universe of educational stories available on these topics. We suspect, therefore, that we vastly underestimate the problems we describe.

Second, it is not possible to provide information about rates or frequencies of events. We catalog here only the occurrence of events as reported in the news stories we found using standard search engines. Given our inability to tap all news sources equally, the ambiguity of some of the stories we did find, and the fact that many of the incidents we want to report on are often "hushed up" at the local level, we are strengthened in our belief that our data provide a vast underestimate of the incidence of these problematic events.

Another important caveat about drawing on journalistic sources for stories about high-stakes testing is that some newspaper reports focus on *allegations* of wrongdoing. Follow-up stories to allegations are not always printed, and if they are printed it is often months after the original incidents. This makes it difficult to find and to match these reports with earlier ones. Although we made our best efforts to provide any relevant follow-up information, we must remind readers that we cannot independently verify allegations reported in the news. Again, our goal in including these kinds of news stories is not to point fingers at any particular individual or institution but to indicate the range of ways that reliance on high-stakes testing can distort values and behavior.

Last, readers may notice that some of our stories date back to the years before high-stakes testing was made into national policy by NCLB. We decided to keep these stories in spite of the risk of them seeming "outdated" because they seemed excellent examples of our overall argument. A story of an administrator cheating to secure a large bonus or to make high school graduation rates look better illustrates the same point whether it occurred in 1999 or 2006. The point is that as the pressure on educators to produce certain kinds of school outcomes grows, so too does the pressure to get precisely those outcomes, no matter what and no matter when.

Our goal was to present a cohesive and convincing set of examples of the problems associated with high-stakes testing. We hope this will convince legislators and other supporters of high-stakes testing that the costs associated with high-stakes testing are simply not worth it. We also set out to describe a social-science theory that informs us that high-stakes testing of the type associated with NCLB can *never* be used successfully in our schools. We hope we are successful in explaining this theory, since denying confirmed scientific principles seems patently foolish. We hope also that our brief review of alternatives to high-stakes testing will be taken seriously. We have no doubt that high-stakes testing is corrupting educators and harming our common schools, and so we hope others will join us in demanding an immediate moratorium on high-stakes testing.

CHAPTER 1

A SHORT HISTORY OF HIGH-STAKES TESTING,
Arguments For and Against Its Use,
Its Place in Contemporary Society,
and a Brief Introduction to Campbell's Law

The commission investigating the events leading up to the tragedy of September 11, 2001, found evidence that warnings of the impending violence were clear and numerous. These warnings were unheeded by federal agencies and most of the people who staff them because no crisis seemed imminent. Even then, however, amid the relative peace, some individuals tried to alert the nation that we should not be complacent. These individuals warned us that a crisis was indeed brewing and that the United States would surely be tested.[1]

Once again the United States faces a severe crisis, once again the dangers do not seem imminent, and once again politicians and federal agencies are being alerted to the danger. This time it is not merely a few individuals but literally thousands, particularly teachers, who believe there is danger. Sadly, as in the past, the counsel of these many individuals is unheeded by those who wield political power.

This crisis concerns the corruption of what is arguably America's greatest invention—its public schools. This book joins with others in documenting the damage to education caused by overreliance on high-stakes testing.[2] Our research suggests that the incidence of negative events associated with high-stakes testing is so great that, were we the Centers for Disease Control, we would be forced to declare an epidemic. As will be made clear, because of high-stakes testing, public education is presenting serious and harmful symptoms. Unlike other critics of the high-stakes testing movement, however, we demonstrate that a powerful social science law explains the etiology of the problems we document. Ignorance of this law endangers the health of our schools and erodes the commitment of those who work in them.

A SHORT HISTORY OF LOW-STAKES AND HIGH-STAKES TESTING

For about a century, standardized testing for assessing aptitudes (e.g., intelligence) and achievement (e.g., mathematics) has played an increasingly prominent role in shaping American educational thinking.[3] Today such tests are common. Among the well-known tests used throughout America's primary and secondary grades are the Iowa Test of Basic Skills (ITBS), TerraNova, Stanford Achievement Tests (SAT), and the Metropolitan Achievement Test (MAT). In addition, generations of secondary students have prepared for college entrance by taking the SAT exam administered by the College Board or the ACT exam administered by the American College Testing Program. Applicants applying for entrance to graduate school are often required to take other exams, usually the Graduate Record Examination (GRE) and/or the graduate tests for law (LSAT), business (GMAT), or medicine (MCAT).

These various tests have been used to assess students' aptitudes and achievements, inform decisions about curriculum and instruction, and make predictions about how successful a student may be in the future. Most Americans have had faith that these tests were crafted with the utmost care, with proper concern for validity (does the test really measure what it purports to measure?) and reliability (are the scores students get dependable, were the test to be given again?). For the most part, these tests have been successful. Most citizens are satisfied with the information received from these tests and the uses that are made of them.

Except for the graduate school entrance examinations, these various tests were not often high stakes. That is, they rarely had dramatic and life-changing consequences attached to the scores that were obtained from them. For decades children were not left back a grade or denied a high school degree solely on the basis of their test scores, though that did occasionally happen. On the basis of standardized tests of achievement, however, students were sometimes denied or admitted to gifted programs, and the tests often determined whether or not remedial programs were appropriate for a student. But for most students and their families, achievement tests provided information, not consequences. In recent decades teachers and administrators were rarely given bonuses or fired for the performance of their students on standardized tests, though this too occasionally did happen.

It is true that college entrance examination scores sometimes prevented a student from attending the college of his or her first choice. But rarely, if ever, was a student prevented from going to a public community or public four-year college solely on the basis of his or her score on a college entrance examination. Over the last half-century, regardless of one's test score, opportunities for obtaining a college degree existed. For most Americans, there were very few high-stakes decisions made about young students, their teachers, schools, and curricula on the basis of achievement test scores alone. The times have changed.

The expansion of high-stakes testing

The current emphasis on using tests for making important decisions about students, teachers, and administrators in the elementary and secondary schools—and also for evaluating the schools and school systems those students attend—can be traced back to the 1965 authorization of the Elementary and Secondary Education Act (ESEA).[4] In the post-*Sputnik* era, ESEA was the government's answer to the call for greater attention to the quality of America's schools and the needs of students from less advantaged homes. The concerns emanating from Russia's win in the space race resulted in the development and implementation of minimum competency tests—tests used to ensure all students left school with at least the ability to read and do basic math. Students could be denied a diploma if they did not pass these tests, but there were no consequences for teachers or schools. Eventually the minimum competency tests were criticized for being relatively easy to pass since they were concerned with minimums to be learned: the achievement floor and not the achievement ceiling. Many politicians and citizens alike believed that students were not being stretched enough, that overall U.S. school performance was not improving, and that the terrible achievement gap between white middle-class students and black, Hispanic, or poor students was not being reduced. As discontent grew, the language of minimum competency changed to the language of standards-based achievement.[5]

In the years following ESEA, concern for American education grew. This was fueled, in part, by international data that purported to show that our schools were not as good as those in other nations. More fuel was provided because the international economy was growing at a time when the national economy was performing poorly. A scapegoat for that state of affairs needed to be found. The concerns of the 1970s culminated in the 1983 release of *A Nation at Risk*, a report that predicted that unless public education received a major overhaul and unless expectations for student achievement were raised, America's economic security would be severely compromised.[6] American education became the scapegoat for a host of bad business decisions. As intended, that document sparked a renewed interest in and urgency about how we educate America's students. That sense of urgency set in motion a series of policy initiatives aimed at improving the American education system.

In the years following *A Nation at Risk*, many have eloquently and vehemently challenged the logical and empirical validity of the assertion that American education is badly or fatally flawed. In fact, hysteria about the achievements of our schools was, and continues to be, largely a myth.[7] But the myth lives on, and policies follow from myth as surely as from factual accounts about the way the world works. Despite its mistaken factual claims, after publication of *A Nation at Risk*, many politicians aligned with a growing public demand to improve the "failing" educational system. As a result, the past 20 years have seen a broad range of policy documents and initiatives offering ways of solving America's educational problems; among these was a call for more consequential testing.[8] As we write in mid-2006, we find that the American educational system is being completely transformed from what it was at the time of *A Nation at Risk*.

It is now clear that high-stakes testing holds a prominent place in that transformation, which is the reason for this book.

Some problems with high-stakes testing

The practice of high-stakes testing is not new, having been used in ancient China to hire civil servants after applicants for these jobs had invested years studying for the examination. As one might expect, then, criticisms of high-stakes testing are also not new. For example, the New York State Department of Education made the following comments to the state's legislature as the latter body contemplated establishing what we would today call a high-stakes test:

> It is an evil for a well-taught and well-trained student to fail in an examination.
>
> It is an evil for an unqualified student, through some inefficiency of the test, to obtain credit in an examination.
>
> It is a great and more serious evil, by too frequent and too numerous examinations, so to magnify their importance that students come to regard them not as a means in education but as the final purpose, the ultimate goal.
>
> It is a very great and more serious evil to sacrifice systematic instruction and a comprehensive view of the subject for the scrappy and unrelated knowledge gained by students who are persistently drilled in the mere answering of questions issued by the Education Department or other governing bodies.[9]

In somewhat archaic language, the Department of Education raises concerns about the reliability and validity of its tests, as every testing agency should. But they also are concerned about overtesting and about how testing programs can mislead students (and by implication parents and politicians) into thinking test scores are indicators of sound instructional practice. This Department of Education also expresses its worry about how testing can distort the basic purposes of education by narrowing the curriculum. The enlightened bureaucrats who wrote this report to the legislature were warning the state's politicians that it is possible, even with the best of intentions, for testing programs to corrupt the educational process. The archaic language in this report is better understood after we discover when it was written: 1906!

Another warning about the dangerous side effects of high-stakes testing surfaced when a plan to pay teachers on the basis of their students' scores was offered, making student test scores very high stakes for teachers. A schoolmaster noted that under these conditions, "a teacher knows that his whole professional status depends on the results he produces and he is really turned into a machine for producing these results; that is, I think, unaccompanied by any substantial gain to the whole cause of education."[10] This concern about testing students to judge a teacher's worth first surfaced in the year 1887, but it is as fresh as recent headlines about pay-for-performance in Denver, Colorado; Houston, Texas; Florida; Minnesota; and Iowa.[11]

These worries about what we now call high-stakes testing were made well before modern testing systems had gained admiration for their alleged beneficial effects on education. No crisis seemed imminent, and so the minor worries about testing voiced by an individual or an organization here and there, over the last century, were easily set aside. But high-stakes testing in the United States is now more widespread than ever before in our history, and our nation apparently relies more on ability and achievement testing than most other nations for making important decisions about individuals and schools. Clearly, we live in an era and in a nation where there is strong support for public policies that use test results to compel changes in the behavior of students, teachers, and school administrators. Our president, politicians from both parties, and many citizens, particularly members of the business community, believe that education can be best improved by attaching consequences (i.e., attaching high stakes) to tests. The tests are seen by some as the perfect policy mechanism because they are both *effectors* and *detectors*—they are intended to *effect* or cause change in the system and then *detect* whether changes in the system actually occur. The federal No Child Left Behind Act of 2001 (NCLB) sanctified this approach to school change for every state, district, and school.[12]

As we demonstrate throughout this book, the logic undergirding high-stakes testing policy is unsound. We will show by example after example why strict adherence to this policy does more harm than good. Guided by a little-known but well-documented principle of social science, Campbell's law, we will argue that high-stakes testing, the cornerstone of NCLB, is paving the way for an educational crisis that threatens to leave our *nation* behind.

The present status of NCLB and high-stakes testing

The No Child Left Behind Act, passed in 2001 and signed into law in January 2002, is the reason for the present spread of high-stakes testing. This law is probably the most invasive and complex piece of federal legislation on education in our nation's history. As it has developed and influenced our educational system, we and others have argued that NCLB

- is flawed legislation and cannot work as designed;[13]
- does not produce gains on the National Assessment of Educational Progress (NAEP tests) or other tests of achievement that can be used to audit a state's performance;[14]
- is not closing the achievement gap as it was intended to do;[15] and
- is increasing dropout rates among our nation's youth.[16]

The faults of the NCLB legislation are numerous, but they are *not* the major concern of this book. We are concerned here with only one of the provisions of NCLB, the one requiring that states adopt a system of accountability whereby students, teachers, administrators, and schools are evaluated annually on the basis of students' standardized test performance and that consequences follow when student scores are low or annual gains in school achievement are not made.

Stakes are "high" because of the life-changing significance of the consequences attached to test scores. For example, the consequences of low scores for students include failure to be promoted to a subsequent grade, failure to graduate high school, or denial of college scholarship monies.

Low-scoring students can also switch schools, receive tutoring at school expense, and may also have to attend district-mandated Saturday school, summer school, or after-school programs. Teachers and administrators can receive bonuses for high student scores, or, as is more typically the case, they can be reassigned or fired because of low student scores and poor student gains. Low scores and poor gains allow for schools to be reconstituted as public charter or private schools or simply closed, with the students reassigned elsewhere. The public ratings of public schools also mean that all school personnel receive public accolades or a public scolding as a consequence of school and district test scores. Shaming, an ancient ritual, is a component of NCLB.

Scholars and politicians from divergent viewpoints generally believe that NCLB is legislation badly in need of serious change.[17] As noted, however, our concern is with just one piece of the NCLB legislation required of all the states, sometimes even eagerly accepted by them, that may live on after the inevitable restructuring (or demise) of NCLB. Our concern is with the acceptance of high-stakes testing as the mechanism to effect changes in our schools. In the chapters that follow, we present evidence that high-stakes testing so distorts and corrupts education that their continued use seriously endangers the educational profession and limits the learning outcomes of our youth.

THE LOGIC, ILLOGIC, AND PARTIAL LOGIC USED IN DEFENSE OF HIGH-STAKES TESTING

The theory of action embedded in NCLB is that a system of threats and incentives tied to test performance will energize teachers and their students into working harder and more effectively.[18] Threats and incentives of this type were commonly used to manage workers in the nineteenth century—a workforce consisting mostly of laborers whose intellects were not valuable and who were completely replaceable (pieceworkers in shirt factories, fruit pickers, nonunion laborers). But modern businesses have abandoned this approach as society came to rely more on the intellectual capital of its workers. Computer designers, economists, and market-trend watchers are rarely managed with threats of punishment. Although rewards/ bonuses are sometimes available, rarely are threats relied on as a way to spur these kinds of workers into action. After all, businesses don't want to drive out a labor force that requires years of training and for whom productivity cannot be defined by a single indicator.

The theory of action behind the modern corporation dealing in knowledge and creativity on a global scale is quite different from the one designed to motivate people doing work that is inherently uninteresting and for which replacements are easy to obtain. So incentives and threats seem an inappropriate theory to use with teachers and their students, unless they are considered to be more like laborers than they are like knowledge workers. That distinction seems lost on proponents of this archaic theory of management who argue that carrots and sticks will address problems of low expectations for poor and minority students, will minimize the unequal educational opportunities between the haves and have-nots, and will help establish a clear set of state standards to guide curriculum and instructional decisions. For policymakers and citizens yearning for simple solutions to education's complex problems, a management strategy characterized by reward and punishment is easily embraced.

Let us look a little closer at ten of the many arguments offered by supporters of the NCLB legislation.[19] These arguments are derived from the flawed theory of action that undergirds the legislation.

1. *Students work harder and learn more when they have to take high-stakes tests.* Response: This is true for some students but certainly not for all. Our experience in low-income and high-income schools alike leads us to believe many students don't work harder at all, finding test preparation boring. Intense and lengthy preparation for high-stakes testing reduces most students' motivation for learning and thus reduces their commitment to do the work necessary to score higher on the test. And in many schools, irrespective of the social class makeup of the students, it is not clear that more is learned through implementation of high-stakes tests. A good case can be made that state standards-based curricula (required by NCLB) narrow the curriculum to the subjects in which students will be tested. That is, if graphing is not on the state mathematics test, there seems to be no need to teach anything about graphing. Students too often seem

to learn what is on the high-stakes test, and no more. In addition, it is quite clear that the high-stakes testing movement has reduced the overall curricula choices of students. Where once we saw school time devoted to music, art, physical education, and social studies, now we see a vast reduction in these offerings as more time is spent on the areas of the curriculum that are tested and therefore consequential.[20] So it is not at all clear that students learn more when high-stakes testing is implemented or that they are more motivated to try.

2. *Students will be motivated to do their best and score well on high-stakes tests.* Response: The current version of NCLB does not reward excellent performance on high-stakes tests. Instead, it rewards performance above a certain passing score called "proficient." Once that level of proficiency is set, that is all that counts for federal purposes. So to avoid sanctions by the federal government, many states have apparently set the "proficient" level on their state tests at a relatively low level of achievement.[21] In those states where the standards are low, therefore, there is scant motivation for students—or for teachers to help students—to do their best. There is simply no incentive to go beyond what is minimally necessary to score at the "proficient" level on the test. The testing program we have bought into destroys motivation to excel, rewarding, instead, motivation to get by. Furthermore, our talks with students reveal that many are angry they will be tested by the state and, on the basis of their test score, could be held back or denied a high school degree. They say that if they have done their homework, taken and passed class tests, not been absent or a troublemaker, they should be passed or graduated. They say that their teacher knows what they can and cannot do and that a test imposed from outside is unfair. Although certainly not in their own self-interest, this student anger about the tests often seems to result in lowering motivation to do well on the tests instead of increasing motivation to do well.

3. *Scoring well on high-stakes tests leads to feelings of success by students, while doing poorly on such tests leads to increased effort to learn.* Response: In an ideal world, students attribute their successes on tests and in life to the hard work they did, and they also attribute their failures on tests and in life to their own lack of preparation and laziness. In this ideal world, students would take pride in success on a test and would commit themselves

to work harder after failure. But there is a real world that differs from this ideal world. In the real world, success on a test is often attributed to one's inherent intelligence, one's social class standing and its attendant advantages, or to just plain luck. Students who feel they succeed for these reasons feel little motivation to work hard to pass tests. These students have no reason to believe success is connected primarily to one's effort. Worse, however, is that those who fail at tests often attribute their failure to a lack of intelligence, a belief communicated to them also by schools that see those lower-achieving students as hurting the school's reputation because of their "low ability." A new form of discrimination is apparently creeping into our schools, and it is against the score suppressors, those children who keep the school from looking good on high-stakes tests. These students have little motivation to work harder at preparing for tests since they have learned from the messages they receive from other students and their teachers to accept that they are the "dumb" kids. On the other hand, some failing students attribute their test failure to bad luck or teacher discrimination. Students who attribute failure to low ability, to bad luck, or to teacher discrimination are not likely to make any attempt to study harder the next time the test is given. These students do not make increased efforts to pass the test after failure and, in fact, often choose to drop out of school rather than confront more indications that they lack the academic ability to succeed in a test-oriented environment. Dropping out of school is a perfectly sensible way to protect one's ego when it is under attack, as it always is for the least academically able in an environment that overly values high academic achievement as defined by standardized test performance.

4. *Students and teachers need high-stakes tests to know what is important to teach and to learn.* Response: For decades teachers and administrators have had scope-and-sequence charts at the state or district levels, clearly outlining what is to be taught and at what grade. In more recent years we have had the national professional associations, such as of math or science educators, informing us about what should be learned, and when, and even how these disciplines might best be taught. Textbook publishers responding to these ideas have produced texts that also help teachers and administrators to know what to teach and when. Even more recently,

states have developed their own curriculum standards that inform all teachers, parents, and citizens in the state what is to be taught throughout grades K–12. In each case the curriculum that is adopted by schools should influence the test-makers. The test-makers should not be the ones influencing the curriculum of the schools. Deciding on a curriculum is a difficult and time-consuming job, perhaps the most important in education. There really seems to be no reason at all to have schools if a community cannot answer the (deceptively simple) question: What is it we want the young to know and be able to do? From those answers come the reasons for schooling and the design of curricula. A test must be developed along with a curriculum or after it is decided upon. The test must never dictate what is to be taught and learned. Otherwise, it is a clear case of the tail wagging the dog. Sadly, in high-stakes testing environments, we often see the test overinfluencing teaching, resulting in a narrowing of the curriculum offered to students to just what is on the test.

5. *Teachers need to be held accountable through high-stakes tests to motivate them to teach better and to push the lazy ones to work harder.* Response: Here is the heart of NCLB. This is the theory of action behind the law. This law is designed to push lazy teachers and lazy students to work harder. It is based on the premise that children and teachers are not performing as well as they should, an easy belief to hold and an impossible one to verify empirically. Based on our hundreds of school visits, we have come to believe that the percentage of lazy teachers amid the 3.5 million teachers we have is considerably smaller than the percentage of lazy politicians who do not read the legislation they support. Our visits to schools, as well as some research reports, lead us to believe that NCLB and its reliance on high-stakes testing actually is motivating teachers of poor students to work much harder, though it seems to have little effect on teachers of more advantaged students. Although NCLB is influencing the work of some teachers, primarily those who teach the poor, are we concerned about whether they work smarter, better, and in the best interests of their children? Are they violating their own professional norms of behavior as they engage in preparing their students for high-stakes tests? Are they training their students much more than they are educating their students? Is the work involved in high-stakes testing environments so stressful that teachers

choose to leave the schools they are in for work at schools where the children are more advantaged? Are teachers leaving the profession altogether because of the stress they are under? Although NCLB seems to strongly influence the work of those who teach the lower social classes, it is not at all clear that the increased work is a source of benefit to the students or a source of satisfaction to their teachers.

6. *The high-stakes tests associated with NCLB are good measures of the curricula taught in school.* Response: A typical achievement test might have 50 or 70 multiple-choice items, perhaps with an open-ended item or two, but rarely are such tests much longer. On the other hand, the curriculum in, say, reading and language arts in the fourth grade, or algebra in high school, is quite enormous and varied. The test, therefore, is always a small sample of a much broader curriculum and can never be relied upon to be a completely trustworthy measure of what students know and are capable of doing. Furthermore, while standards-based instruction has narrowed the curriculum a great deal, there is still enormous variation in the implementation of any curriculum in a classroom. The intended curriculum, which the test covers, always differs substantially from the implemented curriculum, the curriculum actually covered in a class by teachers and students. The amount covered per year, the depth of the coverage attempted, the variety of the examples chosen for discussion in class, the use of homework for promoting transfer of learning, and so on: these vary considerably from teacher to teacher and school to school. The only way to control these variations in the implemented curriculum is through scripted lessons by teachers or online, highly controlled exposure to a single teacher and classroom format. In more traditional instructional settings, however, the variations in the implemented curriculum mean that any reasonably brief standardized assessment may not be a good measure of what was actually taught in schools. And this problem of a match between the test and the implemented curriculum is only magnified when it comes to special-education learners or those for whom English is a second language.

7. *The high-stakes tests provide a kind of level playing field, an equal opportunity for all students to demonstrate their knowledge and skill.* Response: The reason that lawsuits against high-stakes testing exist in California, Arizona, and elsewhere is simple: plaintiffs claim they have not had the opportunity

to learn what the tests assess. Imagine a low-income Mexican American student from a small town in an agricultural area of California or Arizona. When compared to a wealthier, white, suburban student, the chances are much greater that the rural Mexican American student had lower-quality teachers, newer teachers, more teachers teaching mathematics and science without mathematics and science majors or minors, less money spent per student per classroom, poor or no bilingual services, fewer opportunities to have advanced-placement courses, less counseling help, access to fewer libraries, and those libraries had fewer books in them. The high-stakes high school exit exams in California and Arizona are predicated on a belief that all who take them have had equal access to a high-quality education. That is patently not true in these cases, and that is why lawsuits challenging the existing exams are plentiful. Until white politicians of the middle class can look poor minority students in the eye and say, "You have had the same high-quality schooling my own children received," there is no level playing field. Legislatively requiring all students to achieve the same level of proficiency, in exactly the same amount of time and under vastly unequal conditions of schooling, appears to us to be more than a pipe dream—it is also immoral.

8. *Teachers use the results of high-stakes tests to help provide better instruction to students.* Response: If tests are formative, designed to provide information about who knows what in a class and whether a teacher needs to reteach a lesson or unit or not, then tests are being used appropriately. Most teachers know how to make adjustments to lessons and to accommodate the individual differences among students as a function of student performance on a test. This is as it should be. But the vast majority of high-stakes tests are given in spring, with results coming back in the summer, and so the testing schedule provides no time to adjust instruction for individual children. Typically, the test informs a teacher about last year's students and provides little guidance about teaching this year's students. Unfortunately, when stakes are high and scores are not at the level desired, the test is used to determine whether more drill or more test preparation is needed. Low scores could mean that more time is needed in the subjects not showing the expected results, thus leading to a decrease in the time teachers spend on nontested subjects. It is questionable, then,

whether receipt of high-stakes test results lead to "better" instruction. Test results may only lead to more efficient instruction that better prepares students for the test.

On the other hand, when test scores go up, it is likely that the inference will be that better instruction is taking place, supporting the argument made by those who approve of high-stakes testing. But this is not necessarily so. Better scores could be a result of more instruction, or more targeted instruction, not better instruction, and a score gain is equally likely to be the result of other forces affecting achievement. Typically, high-stakes testing takes place in an environment where other school reforms and systemic changes are taking place simultaneously. So, along with the imposition of high-stakes testing in every state, the states are also implementing curricular reforms; increasing teacher professional development; changing teacher-education programs and developing mentoring programs for the first few years of teaching; purchasing new standards-oriented textbooks; and increasing the time spent by students in summer school, after-school programs, tutoring programs, and so forth. So even when there are gains on state tests, it is not at all clear that a high-stakes testing program is the reason for those gains. One concrete example of this is that the number of substantive courses taken by high school students went up substantially in the 1990s. The number of years of English, mathematics, history, and science has gone up in every state. And advanced-placement courses have seen huge enrollment increases in the last decade. If scores on a state high-stakes test then go up, is it due to high-stakes testing or because a revised high school curriculum has been put into place? There is no way of knowing the answer to this question without enormously expensive research. Absent such research, we think that the curriculum changes are more likely to lead to higher test performance than the use of high-stakes testing. Actually, the best evidence currently available to answer the question whether high-stakes testing leads to better education comes not from a state's own test but from audit tests. These are tests of similar content, but not the tests for which a state has prepared its students. The National Assessment of Education Progress (NAEP) tests serve this audit function. Currently, there is no evidence that the introduction of high-stakes testing in the states has changed the growth curves on the NAEP assessments.[22] Although the results are mixed, we find no convincing evidence to suggest that increases in students' learning on a state's own high-stakes test generalize to other indicators of achievement.[23]

9. *Administrators use the results of tests to improve student learning and to design professional development.* Response: This rationale is flawed for many of the same reasons we have already discussed. Test results are imperfect measures of what students know and of how well teachers are teaching. Therefore, they do not provide enough information regarding what needs to be changed or how it needs to be changed in order to produce test-score gains. Administrators simply cannot make sensible decisions regarding what the strengths and weaknesses of their teaching staff are on the basis of test scores alone. Administrators require a range of information to make decisions about the personnel they supervise and the nature of instruction at their school, including teacher observations, teacher reports, student reports, and meetings with parents (to name a few). Test scores provide only a small piece of the information administrators need to make the complex decisions they must make. Even when scores on tests go up or down, there is no reason to believe that "good" or "bad" instruction is taking place. What has to be taken into consideration is the demographic makeup of the new class and the old. Two special-education children, two English-language learners, two divorces by the parents of students in the classroom—all make a teacher's classroom from one year to the next highly variable. Even the reliability of scores for a class size of 25 suggests that swings in achievement-test performance from one year to the next could be substantial and unrelated to a teacher's efforts. Moreover, given the known correlation of poverty to school achievement,[24] even when scores do not move up there is no reason to think that teaching is poorly done. Test scores cannot stand apart from these other factors and play only a limited part in judging teachers' performance.

10. *Parents understand high-stakes test scores and can use them to interpret how well their child is doing in school.* Response: Citizens clearly do understand what it means to pass and fail a test, something that is celebrated and admonished over and over again in the press and the subject of conversations in the home. But neither newspapers nor parents understand

the complexity and completely arbitrary nature of determining a cut-off score for a test, the score that is used to determine who will pass and who will fail. Determination of a cut-off score is always difficult to justify, even when done carefully and rationally. No one, not the expert psychometrician, wise business leader, or concerned housewife, has any way to justify that some point on a scale really separates out those who understand something from those who do not. Even among scholars there is no consensus on how to establish a fair way to judge what it means to be proficient and what it means to be less than proficient. There is no way to defend that a test score of 47 indicates proficiency in a subject while a test score of 46 does not. Since experts cannot agree on these things, there is no reason to believe that parents and other citizens will have the knowledge or access to resources to understand the results of high-stakes testing. For example, someone who believes parents are helped by the clarity assumed to be a part of high-stakes testing programs might want to explain to a Pennsylvania parent why their student is a failure (that is, not proficient) when in eighth grade they can do the following:

> An eighth-grade student performing at the Basic Level solves simple or routine problems by applying skills and procedures in the five Pennsylvania Mathematics Reporting Categories. The student performs simple computations on fractions, integers and decimals, including powers; uses the order of operations to simplify basic numeric expressions. The student converts basic customary and metric units of length, capacity and time to one unit above or below (e.g., seconds to minutes); selects and uses correct formulas to calculate basic measures of simple two- and three-dimensional geometric objects. The student matches simple prisms with nets; recognizes properties of angles formed by intersecting lines; identifies or locates points on a coordinate plane. The student extends basic numeric or algebraic patterns; solves simple equations and uses substitution to check the accuracy of the solution; matches a linear graph to a table. The student identifies correct graphical representations for sets of data; calculates simple probability for mutually exclusive events; identifies basic correlations in scatter plots.[25]

A student who fits the above description is a failure, possibly to be retained a grade, because she is not "proficient." But we think this is a description of a quite competent student, and were we a parent, we would wonder why our child and our school was declared to be failing. In fact, there is even empirical evidence that neither subject-matter specialists nor parents can easily interpret the descriptors that accompany some high-stakes tests.[26] We see more of an illusion of clarity than we see genuine understanding by parents and other citizens of what a test score means.

We have now presented many of the arguments supporting the use of high-stakes testing as a lever for improving public schools. They appear to be rational and seemingly straightforward explanations for why high-stakes testing will successfully improve American schools. Closer analysis of all these arguments, however, uncovers many flaws. The arguments often consist of half-truths—that is, truths for some students and teachers but not for most or all students and teachers. Some of the arguments are clearly debatable and likely will always be unconvincing to someone who already has their mind made up. But some of the arguments are simply unfounded. What follows in this book are more reasons to question the use of high-stakes testing as a lever for school change. Although we are sure that high-stakes testing is fatally flawed in theory and in action, these tests have become a part of contemporary American life. Next, we examine why that is so.

WHY HAS HIGH-STAKES TESTING SO EASILY SLIPPED INTO CONTEMPORARY AMERICAN LIFE?

Why has high-stakes testing so easily, so dramatically, and so recently become a part of contemporary American life? We offer five reasons for that change.

First, and the most popular explanation, is one that notes the co-evolution of the prominence of business and accountability in our daily lives. Accountability in education is modeled on corporate efforts to increase productivity. This reflects a larger trend toward seeing society as modeled on the corporation rather than the family. Tax policy, government spending, health care, employment training, and educational policy have all been strongly influenced by the corporate model. Policymakers have

Box 1.1 What Have We Done to Our Students?

From a *Dallas Morning News* editorial, July 2006

When I was teaching sophomore English in 1998, one of my students, a stocky 16-year-old football player, came up to me one day after class to say he wanted to transfer out. His last English teacher, he said, spent much more time preparing her class for the state's standardized assessment test, mostly by having students bubble in sample tests. He had decided my class, where we analyzed poetry and wrote essays constantly, wasn't going to help him pass the test. "If I fail, Miss, it's going to be all your fault."

Macarena Hernandez, "Test Pressure Is Getting to Our Schools: It's Inspiring Cheaters and Stifling Real Learning," editorial, *Dallas Morning News*, July 28, 2006.

applied basic Business 101 models to our schools—namely, to find ways to monitor productivity, then increase it, and to do so without spending any more money. Tests were chosen as the mechanism to measure productivity. Like those in the business community, legislators believed that productivity could be increased without more money needing to be spent simply by holding schools and educators accountable through the practice of high-stakes testing. Lazy teachers and students would be detected and made to work harder. The models of accountability used in business could be applied to the inefficient school systems of America and—voilà!—the schools would improve. For many Americans, the analogy to business seems sensible and worth pursuing, so it was easy to buy into the high-stakes accountability movement.

The analogy doesn't really fit, however. The production of widgets is easier to count than the knowledge and skill possessed by students. Essentially, a widget is a widget but a well-educated student is a good citizen and a caring person, has aesthetic sensibilities, good habits of health, and so forth. These are outcomes our citizens demand that we produce through our schools, but they are never assessed by tests. So productivity for our teachers and our schools means something vastly different than

Box 1.2 What Have We Done to Our Teachers?

From Ann, a first-year teacher

Last year, when I was a college student, I had great ideas for using hands-on activities and cooperative learning in my classroom as a way to get students to be internally motivated for learning. With the testing programs we have in this school, there isn't much leeway for me to be creative or innovative and create excellent lessons. The test is the total goal. We spend every day doing rote exercises. Forget ever doing hands-on activities, science or math games, or creative writing experiences. We do one hour of sit and drill in each of the subjects of math, reading, and writing. We use a basal reader, math workbook pages, and rote writing prompts. It is all step by step; the same thing every week. I have to teach the letters by saying "A, what is A?" I repeat this over and over in a scripted lesson that my principal makes me use. You can't improvise, add, or take away. You read exactly what it says. This is how testing has impacted my school and my teaching. As a first-year teacher I feel like I don't have a choice to deviate from this awful test preparation.

M. Gail Jones, Brett Jones, and Tracy Hargrove, *The Unintended Consequences of High-Stakes Testing* (Lanham, MD: Rowman & Littlefield, 2003).

productivity in a manufacturing plant or productivity in the delivery of routine services. Furthermore, when inputs cannot be controlled, it is difficult to assess outputs. Measuring the production of widgets assumes control over the quality of the inputs needed for the production of the widgets. But in education we have little control over the input side. For example, students from poor and middle-class families, from immigrant and nonimmigrant families, from two-parent and single-parent families, from medically insured and noninsured families, those with and without disabilities, and those with and without English as a native language may all be in the same classroom or school. This represents heterogeneity in school inputs that would drive quality-control personnel from manufacturing crazy! Ordinary ways of measuring productivity appear to be sensible, but they do not work as easily in educational settings. The high-stakes tests, with their threats and incentives, are not well matched to the ways our schools operate. So scores on tests will mislead us about genuine productivity. Nevertheless, it all sounds sensible and thus appeals to many citizens who end up supporting the use of high-stakes testing programs for our schools.

A second and related reason high-stakes testing has slipped into mainstream culture is the emerging belief by both business and government that the future economy depends on a highly educated workforce. This belief took on new urgency after Thomas L. Friedman's book *The World Is Flat* became a best-seller.[27] Large numbers of the citizenry now believe that we need to push all our children to the farthest heights of education, moving most children to high school graduation with a degree indicating that a rigorous curriculum had been mastered. After that, most of those graduates need to be moved into degree-granting two- and four-year colleges. Obviously, the demand for a rigorous curriculum and college-level preparation means a seriousness about testing in our public schools never before required. High-stakes testing is compatible with these national ambitions. High-stakes testing fits neatly into the mindset that Americans have—namely, that to be competitive in the interdependent global economy we need high rates of college graduation, especially in the fields of science and engineering. In fact, this whole theory may be wrongheaded. As Denis Redovich has reported in article after article, the employment profile of the future does not support the need for a big increase in the mathematical and scientific knowledge of our youth.[28] We may well be overdemanding in these areas and already producing enough scientists and college graduates for the needs of the economy. A scientifically sophisticated citizenry is certainly in our national interest, but making advanced mathematics and science a major goal of U.S. education may be counterproductive, producing large increases in school dropouts and contributing to student anomie. In fact, college graduates have recently suffered from the same drop in wages that first hit those who failed to graduate from high school decades ago. That drop was followed only a short time later by a drop in the wages for those who had only a high school education. Now, those with college degrees are suffering the same fate. Earnings for workers with four-year degrees fell 5.2 percent from 2000 to 2004 when adjusted for inflation, according to White House economists.[29] Apparently, large percentages of recent college graduates are taking jobs for which no college degrees are necessary, and the trend may be accelerating. Nevertheless, we continue to demand that the educational system produce ever-increasing rates of high school and college graduates, though we may actually now be near record levels of high school graduation rates.[30]

Despite the fact that our national productivity is much more dependent on our tax structures, relative lack of corruption, and remarkable entrepreneurship, the citizenry believes that we need better schools to be competitive in the world economy. High-stakes tests therefore are a policy mechanism attuned to the mindset of many of our citizens in power and thus slip easily into our everyday life.

The third reason for the ease with which high-stakes tests have become commonplace in our culture is because of changing demographics. We can now clearly see the shape of an emerging gerontocracy. An older citizenry, much whiter than the youth of the nation, relatively well-off financially now but likely to live well beyond their resources, is beginning to act politically in their own best interests.[31] As a powerful political and economic force, these folks want income and services. They will demand medical, pharmaceutical, and social services, full payment of social security, and some form of housing support as their income stays relatively fixed. They may not want to spend, nor will there be much money to spend, on lazy and unappreciative youth, especially youth of color, the offspring of other peoples. For many advantaged people, high-stakes testing separates the deserving poor from the undeserving poor and becomes a policy mechanism to preserve social status more than a policy to improve our schools. High-stakes testing subtly fits the mindset of this growing demographic and thus makes it easier for this policy to gain purchase in our contemporary society.

A fourth reason is based on the same self-preserving, privilege-maintaining quest. Simply put, the power elite in this society, along with the vast middle and upper-middle class whose children now attend good public schools, see high-stakes testing working to their own children's advantage. While they bristle that their own children must suffer through these tests (witness the Scarsdale, New York, mothers' rebellion),[32] the schools their children attend are not much bothered by the tests and the pass rates for their children are very high. When their children are in danger of not succeeding on such tests, they have the intellectual resources to help and can also pay for the tutors needed to ensure their children's success. High-stakes testing blends with their self-interest because it forces a kind of education on the children of the poor that ensures they cannot compete with the children of the wealthy. The drill and test-prep education we see in schools for the poor—and their high failure rate—does not prepare them for knowledge workers' jobs nor for the best universities in the nation. This makes room for the children of the more privileged. Since the status of children from advantaged families is preserved though high-stakes testing, it is easy for these folks to defend their use.

Fifth is the fit between high-stakes testing and other spectacles enjoyed by the public, such as baseball, football, basketball, and hockey. We are a game-playing, competition-seeking nation, and high-stakes testing fits easily into such a culture.

As is true of many sports, high-stakes testing has a tournament-like quality to it, thus bringing seasonal excitement to fans who now can follow the heavily publicized "winning" and "losing" streaks of their local schools, as they have often followed their local teams. Every summer when spring test results are released, there is World Series–like publicity and fanfare around how well (or poorly) our nation's teachers and students did that previous year. And like fanatic fans who delight in watching rivals have a losing season, American media feeds on whatever bad news exists,[33] prompting those who follow the news to ponder endlessly, Why have certain schools/teams failed? How many times has this school/team failed in the past? What is that school's/team's track record? What schools/teams might need to be reconstituted, closed down, or moved? What will we do to get rid of the bad teachers/players, and precisely which ones are they? Is it the science teacher or the first baseman, the English teachers or the defensive line, the coach or the principal? On whom, exactly, can we pin this failure?

Numerous similarities explain the country's preoccupation with testing. After all, the sport of cricket is called a test. Professional athletes in cricket and other sports practice hours and hours repeating the same activities endlessly so that their responses at "test" time will be automatic. In the high-stakes testing game, teachers also engage their students in endless repetitive activities to better ensure students' responses are accurate and automatic come test time. In professional sports, teams with the highest-paid athletes are more likely to have winning seasons. Similarly, schools with more resources and those that serve the most affluent students tend to perform better academically.[34] (Perhaps that is why such inequalities in education are so easily accepted.) In professional sports, fans are immersed in statistics that highlight the successes and failures of their favorite teams and players (e.g., RBIs, shots blocked, touchdowns, assists). In the testing game, parents, politicians, and other community members are immersed in media coverage of academic data showing who is winning and who is losing.

Of course, we know stats say little about a player's many other contributions to the team, such as level of dedication, commitment, morale, and leadership. Similarly, when teachers and administrators are judged by their students' scores, often absent are a teacher's many other contributions such as their nurturance of a love for learning, individual attention given to counseling in a student's time of need, extra time spent meeting with students' families, provision of money from their own pockets for classroom items, and so forth.

High-stakes testing is now a part of our culture and has come to prominence, we think, because it fits easily into contemporary ways of thinking about our nation and ourselves. We are a political and an economic system dominated by the interests of big business, and so business models of accountability for our schools naturally follow. High-stakes testing seems to be a hardheaded business practice brought to bear on the schools, despite the fact that no one uses such a system in knowledge-oriented businesses. And unless we are greatly mistaken, schools fall into that category.

High-stakes testing also seems to help in preparing us for the vicissitudes of a competitive world economy, and so it is easily embraced. The fact that the new American economy may be vastly more service oriented than previously believed—and that it may not require nearly as many college graduates as is now thought necessary—is a point of view that is ignored.

The needs of the emerging gerontocracy and those who already have some status in society are also served by high-stakes testing. And high-stakes testing fits neatly into the gaming and spectacle-seeking culture that so permeates U.S. society. For all these reasons, high-stakes testing has grown to be an acceptable part of the culture. Those who oppose the spread of high-stakes testing are seen as status-quo oriented, against quality in education, against school improvement, obstructionist, anti-efficiency, anti–George W. Bush, and so forth. But we are actually against high-stakes testing for none of these reasons. We are against it because teachers, students, parents, and American education are being hurt by high-stakes testing, and we have, in what follows, the evidence to demonstrate it. We are not against accountability or assessment. We are against accountability systems in education that rely upon high-stakes assessments.

The pages that follow are filled with examples of humiliation, devaluation, deceit, and other illustrations of the tragedies that accompany high-stakes testing. We foreshadow these stories and research reports by sharing a personal story (box 1.3), brought to one of the authors by a real teacher whose livelihood and dignity were threatened as a result of high-stakes testing. This tale illustrates the problem of judging teaching primarily on the basis of test results. Unlike athletes, who are judged mostly on the basis of their own performance, teachers are often held solely responsible for their *students'* performance.

What is problematic about this scenario and thousands of others like this one is not that the principal is monitoring teacher effectiveness. Nor is it problematic to want all teachers to do well. The problem is that these kinds of decisions about the quality of instruction and the success of a school are driven solely by student performance on a standardized test. Just like an athlete who contributes so much more to the team than just his/her statistics, a teacher contributes a great deal more to a student's educational experience, growth, and development than just what is reflected by a test score alone.[35]

CAMPBELL'S LAW AND THE UNCERTAINTY ASSOCIATED WITH TESTS AND TESTING

As the examples presented earlier illustrate, and as common sense informs us, the pressure to do well on a single indicator of performance from which

Box 1.3 A True Story of Problems That Arise from High-Stakes Testing

A dedicated eighth-grade math teacher we know told us that in one year he went from being a celebrated, successful teacher, to being required to attend "remedial" teaching workshops. We asked, "What happened?" In the first year, he said, he taught students who were relatively motivated and interested in the subject. Although these students struggled throughout the year to grasp the mathematics he was teaching, their motivation and his teaching efforts resulted in significant learning, as reflected in his students' "acceptable" test score performance. The teacher was asked to lead workshops to share his techniques with less successful colleagues.

The very next year, however, he saw an influx of students with special learning needs or for whom English was a second language. Still, he went to work doing everything he knew how to do—employing the same tactics that made him a "success" the previous year. He made more home visits than he ever had before and stayed after school to tutor as many students as possible—all without extra support. In the end, all that mattered were the test scores. The principal, seeing practice test scores that were consistently low throughout the fall and early spring terms, actually asked the teacher to attend the same workshops he once taught so he could "improve" his teaching. "How can we recognize good teaching and work to improve it," the teacher asked us, "in an atmosphere of such confusion?"

This story was generously shared with us by a middle school teacher from San Antonio, Texas, who wishes to remain anonymous.

important consequences are derived can be especially counterproductive and destructive. But many of the problems encountered in situations like this are merely illustrations of a well-known social-science law directly applicable to the high-stakes testing associated with NCLB. We refer to this as Campbell's law, named for the well-respected social psychologist, evaluator, methodologist, and philosopher of science Donald Campbell, who brought it to the attention of social scientists in 1975. Campbell's law stipulates that "the more any quantitative social indicator is used for social decision-making, the more subject it will be to corruption pressures and the more apt it will be to distort and corrupt the social processes it was intended to monitor."[36] Campbell warned us of the inevitable problems associated with undue weight and emphasis on a single indicator for monitoring complex social phenomena. In effect, he warned us about the high-stakes testing program that is part and parcel of NCLB.

George Madaus and Marguerite Clarke believed that Campbell had uncovered a kind of social-science equivalent of the Heisenberg uncertainty principle.[37] Named after its discoverer, Werner Heisenberg, the Heisenberg uncertainty principle states that there is always a degree of uncertainty associated with simultaneously measuring the position and velocity of microscopic objects. "The more precisely the position is determined," Heisenberg explains, "the less precisely the momentum is known in this instant, and vice versa."[38] To try to measure a microscopic object inevitably alters the conditions so much as to render the measurement inaccurate—there is inherent uncertainty in the data that is collected.[39]

Madaus and Clarke noted that if Campbell is right, whenever you have high stakes attached to an indicator, such as test scores, you have a measurement system that has been corrupted, rendering the measurement less accurate. Apparently, you can have (a) higher stakes and less certainty about the validity of the assessment or (b) lower stakes and greater certainty about validity. But you are not likely to have both high stakes and high validity. Uncertainty about the meaning of test scores increases as the stakes attached to them become more severe. The higher the stakes, the more likely it is that the construct being measured has been changed. Applied to NCLB, scores on the instruments used as measures of academic achievement become less interpretable as the consequences for not making adequate yearly progress increase.

The ubiquity of Campbell's law

Evidence of Campbell's law is everywhere. Wherever we look, when high stakes are attached to indicators, what follows is the corruption and distortion of the indicators and the people who employ them. In business, economists have long recognized the possibility for corruption when stakes are high. For example, incentives such as big bonuses for increased sales are common in business, but when stakes are attached to sales, then the business of selling could become corrupt. Cars may be sold that are lemons, houses may be sold with concealed defects, guarantees may be made that are not genuine. It is the sale that is important. In California, Sears once stopped paying salaries to its auto mechanics, instead putting them on commission for the repairs they sold to customers. It wasn't long before California authorities had to threaten to close Sears's auto shops because of all the complaints about unnecessary repairs that were being sold.[40] Other businesses have similar problems. Enron, Tyco, and Qwest, to name just a few examples, all needed to keep their stock prices high (their indicator of successful corporate management), and all did so by cheating. Shell needed its stock price high, so it overstated oil reserves. Pharmaceutical companies needed their share prices high, so they lied about the effectiveness of some of their drugs, and people died as a result.

When Russian factory workers in the old Soviet Union were ordered to produce so many tractors or tanks a month or face serious consequences, the requisite number of tractors or tanks were always produced. The fact that the quality of these machines was awful was irrelevant. Many simply did not work. But the quota had been reached and heads did not roll! That was what was became most important to the factory workers.

When police in one city were ordered to clear up the number of unsolved crimes, the rate of solved crimes suddenly went up dramatically. The police simply made deals with newly captured criminals to confess to many crimes they did not commit. For their confessions, the criminals got lighter sentences. Crimes appeared to be solved, politicians were happier, but in fact the public was being fooled—it was all being done by smoke and mirrors.

In baseball, the Olympics, the Tour de France, and in many other sports, steroids have been banned, but they are still used repeatedly. Why? Because the indicators of success have great value attached to them. Monetary rewards and fame go to those that hit home runs, speed through water or over land, and can endure the rigors of many days of bicycling. Losers get little. So some athletes risk their health and their reputations to make themselves look good on the indicators society values. As those indicators take on importance, Campbell's law seems always to come into effect, and corruption of the indicators of success and the athletes themselves follows. Some of the corruption of athletes starts early, as when they are recruited to colleges by being offered sex, parties, and monetary incentives for signing. Then they get all kinds of special privileges after arriving on campus, including high grades in courses specially designed for them. The importance of the winning column corrupts coaches, athletes, and the entire academic enterprise.

Citizens hope that their physicians, like their teachers, will be less corruptible than athletes and businesspeople. We depend on them for so much and generally hold them in high regard. Nevertheless, in medicine, when physicians are rewarded for the number of patients they see, rather than by their patients' perceptions of caring, there is an inevitable corruption of the medical care they give. Value has been attached to the wrong indicator, and thus physicians' caring behavior for their patients inevitably is compromised. Physicians face another problem with another indicator. Physicians are regularly evaluated on the two types of errors that they make. They can diagnose a healthy person as being sick (Type I error) or they can diagnose a sick person as being well (Type II error). Obviously, there are serious consequences associated with either type of error, but the consequences for making a Type II error are much more severe. Type II errors can result in expensive litigation and the loss of reputation by a physician or a hospital. Since the numbers of diagnoses of genuinely sick people as being well must be minimized by physicians, it should not be surprising to find out that physicians have found ways to avoid making Type II errors. So much weight is on that single indicator that physicians have found ways to rarely get caught making mistaken diagnoses.

Physicians avoid Type II errors by overdiagnosing illness among their healthy patients. That is, physicians purposefully inflate their Type I errors to deflate their Type II errors! The result of this is that many people believe they are sick when they are not. Treatments such as invasive surgery and pharmaceuticals are prescribed though they may not be needed.[41] In addition, to keep Type II errors down, physicians also order tests for illnesses that are not likely to be found. Of course, the cost of medicine is driven up enormously by these methods designed to avoid the dreaded Type II error. As Campbell's law predicts, the more importance that an indicator takes on, the more likely *it*, and the people who depend on it, will be corrupted.

We could cite hundreds more cases where Campbell's law seems to explain what is happening. There are military recruiters who must make quotas, and so they lie to young men and woman and their parents. There are scientists who are judged by the amount of grants they get, and so they fudge their data to get those grants. Government officials and businesspeople are sometimes judged by their university degrees, not their competence, so they take degrees from diploma mills. There are corporations that are judged by their safety records, and so many accidents go unreported, endangering the lives of their workers. There are child-protection agency workers who are judged by how many homes they visit per week. When resources are spread thin and the number of visits is given priority over meticulous analyses of a child's environment, children occasionally die.

Despite the sheer number of examples showing negative effects when particular indicators take on too much importance, many people still believe high-stakes testing is a viable way to improve education. By doing so, however, they defy a perfectly valid and ubiquitous social-science principle—at their peril. High-stakes testing is exactly the kind of practice that Donald Campbell warned us about. After all, high-stakes testing places significant value on test scores. Serious, life-altering decisions that affect teachers, administrators, and students are made on the basis of testing. Tests determine who is promoted and who is retained. Tests can determine who will receive a high school degree and who will not. Test scores can determine if a school will be reconstituted, if there will be job losses for teachers and administrators when scores do not improve, or if there will be cash bonuses when scores do improve. Thus, there is no question as to the emphasis and importance placed on a single test score. Under these conditions, we must worry that the process that is being monitored by these test scores—quality of education—is corrupted and distorted simultaneously, rendering the indicator itself less valid, perhaps meaningless.

CONCLUSION

In George W. Bush's state of the union address in January 2006, he proclaimed that America was addicted to oil.[42] He might have noted that America is also addicted to television, fast food, and testing. But these are not real addictions; they are socially created ones, and as such they can be changed through policies that are more sensible than those in place now. Slowly, over the course of the past two or three decades, Americans have been fed the increasingly urgent propaganda that American education is about to collapse. We have been led to believe that if something didn't change soon, we would have a crisis on our hands. It is no wonder our citizenry wants action. We have been led to believe in the "standardized tests as god" religion by the business and test-manufacturing community.[43] In the absence of any visible or viable alternatives, high-stakes testing is presented as the only possible answer to thwart our descent into mediocrity. But opposition to these messages exists.

In the years since NCLB was passed, the number of critics of high-stakes testing and other aspects of the legislation has grown substantially.[44] This growing outcry has prompted federal policymakers to make some changes to NCLB—specifically with respect to special-education and second-language-learner populations. But it isn't enough. In the pages that follow, we argue that the continued use of high-stakes testing as a mechanism for driving school change is fundamentally flawed and that serious damage is being inflicted on schools and our children.

The government did not heed the warnings of 9/11. Neither did they heed the warning of Katrina, the hurricane that wreaked havoc on the people of New Orleans. Now they do not heed the warnings about the social security and medical trust funds that indicate things will surely reach crisis proportions in a few more years. So we are not sanguine about our own warning that the schools are suffering as a function of high-stakes testing. But we do know that we live in a democracy and that concerted action by our citizenry brings about change. We hope this book will spark such action.

CHAPTER 2

THE PREVALENCE AND MANY FORMS OF CHEATING
and the Problem of Absolute and Relativistic Standards for Judging Such Occurrences

Cheating to gain advantages or avoid negative consequences is not new. But some scholars and social critics have observed that, in recent years, cheating has become endemic. The media is saturated with news of lying, trickery, and fraud: corporate leaders stealing pensions, athletes taking steroids, politicians taking bribes, army recruiters lying to would-be recruits. Cheating has become prevalent, visible, and seemingly justifiable. Under these conditions, we become desensitized to the point where cheating is often expected and honesty becomes surprising. Perhaps, as David Callahan has written, we have now become a *cheating culture,* one in which cheating is more acceptable than ever before.[1]

Certainly, a cheating culture seems to describe contemporary American classrooms, as evidenced by the growing number of stories of students and teachers who cheat on high-stakes exams. As Campbell's law predicts, when test scores serve as indicators of great importance, schools and teachers may go to extreme lengths to ensure that the test scores yield favorable results. Some—perhaps quite a few—of these occurrences of cheating and fraud are never discovered. Even so, hundreds of examples now exist of educators who have been caught in the act of manipulating test scores, some through unambiguously fraudulent activities and others through more subtle, less obvious methods. In either case, it is clear that high-stakes testing is compromising our educators, who for generations were looked upon as moral leaders of our country. What kind of a society have we become that requires systems of accountability that too frequently compromise the integrity of professional educators? Do other less hazardous forms of accountability exist? We will answer that question in the concluding chapter.

CHEATING IN AMERICAN SCHOOLS

In reviewing numerous instances of cheating in America's classrooms, we were surprised to find that the bulk of these examples were about adults who cheat. Of course, students were also found cheating—something as old as school itself—but we were shocked to find so many instances of adults engaged in acts of apparent impropriety. What is going on? Are teachers nowadays simply more corrupt? Are they immoral?

Further analysis and reflection led us to two conclusions. First, Campbell's law is busily at work throughout our educational system. The sheer number of examples just from the United States provides ample evidence of how, through the overvaluing of certain indicators, pressure is increased on everyone in education. Eventually, those pressures tend to corrupt the educational system. Educators, like almost everyone else, are tempted to make improper decisions when there is exaggerated emphasis on a single indicator and their jobs or their students' futures are at stake. We believe that teachers are now no more or less moral than they ever have been. Instead, what we believe is that teachers have been placed by our politicians in untenable positions, environments where pressures encourage questionable behavior.

Our second conclusion is a bit more complex. In contemporary educational settings, we have found that our initial repugnance to acts of cheating may be misplaced. In some cases, cheating is difficult to condemn. For example, when a teacher "helps" a struggling student with one or two challenging test items, we may view it as a small and forgivable infraction when compared to the potential motivational and psychological costs of that student failing yet another test. Is that act of cheating as reprehensible as cheating to receive a bonus for having a high-achieving class? Suppose this teacher "helps" a low-ability student in order to save her job? Is the act of cheating still to be judged the same way?

The dilemma of teachers and administrators under NCLB is similar to those posed by Kohlberg in his studies of moral development many years ago.[2] One of those dilemmas posed the question of whether it is right or wrong to steal medicine you can't afford in order to save your own wife or husband. Obviously, this dilemma pushed respondents to deal with whether or not the biblical admonition "thou shall not steal" is inviolable. Under the conditions described, many deeply religious people forgave the theft of the medicine. Teachers are in a similar bind. Teachers are faced with the dilemma of cheating to help a struggling student or to ensure stability in their own family, or not cheating and watching a student falter or their family harmed. Under these circumstances, many teachers may come to the conclusion that cheating on the test, like stealing the medicine, can be justified.

It may be difficult for some people ever to defend acts of cheating, but it became clear to us that more moral ambiguity exists in each act we call cheating than we first imagined. For example, we have no difficulty condemning acts of cheating that improve a teacher's income through bonuses earned for higher student performance. Examples of those self-serving forms of cheating abound, and at first they offer no moral quandary. Even then, however, additional factors add layers of complexity, as in the case of a teacher who cheats to receive a bonus but is a single mother of four children and is not well paid for her 50-hour weeks. Holding absolute standards about acts of cheating became much harder for us as we delved deeper into some of the stories we uncovered.

One purpose of this chapter is to demonstrate the breadth of the cheating problem. A second purpose is to develop readers' awareness that cheating behavior is not always the result of a desire for personal gain but is sometimes considerably more problematic. While we don't condone cheating, we think it's important to understand the context in which it occurs.

Prevalence and forms of adult cheating

As with sexual behavior, it is difficult to ascertain from surveys alone what it is that people do in private and why. Nonetheless, some surveys provide a sense of how widespread cheating has become and the forms it assumes. A survey of teachers and administrators sponsored by a Tennessee newspaper, for example, found that almost 9 percent of the teachers surveyed said they'd witnessed test impropriety on Tennessee's high-stakes exam.[3] Among several of the tactics reported:

- Weak students were seen herded to the school library to watch movies for a week while academically stronger students took exams;
- Teachers were wandering the classroom during the test, casually point out wrong answers to students or admonishing them, saying, "You know better than that";
- Counselors locked their office doors after the state testing was done to "erase stray marks";
- There were suspensions for various infractions of students who were academically at the borderline just before the test;
- Eliminating monitors in testing classrooms, leaving teachers to "do what it takes to get those scores up!"

A national survey revealed that about 10 percent of the teachers admitted to providing hints about the answers during the test administration; about 10 percent of the teachers pointed out mismarked items by students; about 15 percent of the teachers provided more time for the test than was allowed; and about 5 percent of the teachers engaged in instruction during the test.[4] The survey also revealed that about 1.5 percent of the teachers actually admitted that they changed students' answers on the test. This is probably a huge underestimate of the rate of cheating since it is not in the teachers' best interest to report these behaviors.

Another study of the prevalence of cheating was done by economists Brian Jacob and Steven Levitt.[5] They identified a set of Chicago public school classes whose scores on the Iowa Test of Basic Skills (ITBS) seemed unusually high and whose students showed a pattern of answers that seemed statistically unlikely to occur. Those classes were retested. They showed a decline on the retest of a full year's grade-equivalent in scores. These researchers suggest that 3 to 5 percent of the teachers in Chicago were cheating. So whether it is 3 or 5 or 15 percent of the teachers and whether the motive for engaging in certain questionable behaviors was benevolent or self-serving, it seems readily obvious that teachers and administrators are often engaged in test-related impropriety.

It should be noted, however, that the immorality of teachers is often less self-serving than that of the business executives who also cheat. Many of the teachers who admit to cheating or who have been found doing so have as their motive a desire for their students to do well on the tests. Some might be tempted, therefore, to look the other way and let the acts go unreported. But whether such teacher behavior is judged to be either noble or ignoble, a subtle violation of standardization procedures or deliberate and blatant cheating, the result is exactly the same. Cheating of whatever kind decreases the validity of the tests and adds uncertainty to whatever decisions are made on the basis of the test scores. As Madaus warned us, uncertainty about the meaning of scores increases as stakes go up.

TYPES OF CHEATING

In our search for evidence of cheating from across the country, we found many different manifestations of the problem. Cases of cheating were technologically aided or not; creative or pedestrian; engaged in by single individuals or by groups; involving students or not. We chose to organize these cases in the simplest way, by chronology. We organized cases of cheating by whether the incidents occurred before the test (during test preparation), during the test, or after the test. A few of the most common examples of each type are described in box 2.1.

Pretest cheating

Reports of teachers and administrators who cheat by using exam questions to prepare students for the test are too numerous for complete cataloging. These activities ranged from blatant acts of malfeasance (stealing the actual test, making a copy of it, and then passing it out to students) to

Box 2.1 Types of Cheating Identified*

Pretest activity

1. Hand out copies of the test to teachers to use in preparing students.[1]
2. Hand out copies of test or test items to students to prepare for test.[2]
3. "Peek" at test.[3]

During-the-test activity

4. Coach/encourage students as they take the test.[4]
5. Give out "tip" sheets.[5]
6. Ask students to change or elaborate answers/thinking.[6]
7. Whisper answers to students.[7]

Post-test activity

8. Erase test answers/Change wrong answers to right answers.[8]
9. Change student ID numbers for students of lesser ability—causing many low test scores to be thrown out.[9]
10. Scrubbing—used when scoring English examinations; subjectively "raise" scores on essay exams.[10]

** Notes appear on pages 210–11.*

more subtle acts (using a "close" version of the actual test as a study guide). In all cases, teachers' or administrators' efforts were designed to help increase students' test scores—scores that would be used to judge the school, administrators and teachers, and the students themselves. In many cases, allegations of cheating were directed at the school's principal, as in Massachusetts, where an elementary school principal resigned under suspicion that she helped students by passing out copies of the test days before the test was administered.[6]

We found it common, as in the Massachusetts case, for charges of impropriety to be met with resignations rather than having formal charges brought against a violator of test security. It seems that these incidents are hard to prove and costly to prosecute, so they are often "brushed under the rug," becoming incidents to get past as rapidly as possible with as little publicity as possible. While that makes some sense, it also means that punishment for impropriety occurs infrequently. The commonness of such improprieties is illustrated in box 2.2 and elsewhere in this chapter.

In some cases, a teacher or group of teachers was involved. This is what happened in Nevada, where two high school teachers allegedly copied test questions and handed them out to students to use as a study guide.[7] Another high school teacher in Nevada had his teaching license revoked after evidence was found that he shared with students a handwritten math study guide that contained 51 of the actual exam questions. The test was a high school exit exam where a passing score was needed to receive a diploma.[8]

Box 2.2 Cheating by Passing Out Tests and Answers

- In Greensboro, North Carolina, three teachers and one central office testing coordinator resigned after being accused of sharing copies of the physical science and U.S. history end-of-course test questions with students before taking the exams. At their high school, teachers can receive performance bonuses based on students' achievement on the state exams.
- In California, more than 200 teachers were investigated for helping students on the state exam. Allegations included that teachers had handed out copies of the test booklets so students would know the vocabulary words that would be on the test.
- One elementary school principal and two teachers were accused of giving students answers to questions on the statewide assessment (the Wisconsin Knowledge and Concepts Examination and TerraNova), both taken in November 2003. The school in which the alleged cheating occurred had low test scores. The article notes that the stakes attached to the Wisconsin assessment were possible motives for the alleged impropriety. The allegations were that the teachers "had students memorize the sequence of answers" on a multiple-choice section of the test in the third, fourth, and fifth grades.

Bruce Buchanan, "Teachers May Earn Bonuses Despite Scandal," *News and Record*, Feb. 21, 2003, A1; Erika Hayasaki, "One Poor Test Result: Cheating Teachers," *Los Angeles Times*, May 21, 2004; Sarah Carr, "MPS Looks into Claims Staff Helped on Tests, Tipster Alleges Student at Palmer Saw Answers," *Milwaukee Journal Sentinel*, Jan. 31, 2004, 1A.

During-the-test cheating activity

There are numerous stories of inappropriate behavior by teachers and administrators during the test. These are especially problematic, because, in most cases, the act involved the collaboration of students. For example, some teachers blatantly told students the correct and incorrect answers and then asked them to keep these "tips" a secret.[9] In Massachusetts, after the test, one principal entered a fourth-grade classroom and asked the teacher to leave—after which the principal instructed the students to change their incorrect answers to correct ones. The pressure not to be labeled as a "low-performing" school was allegedly to blame. According to one student, "Ms. Brady said that our school had low performance and we need it to be higher."[10] When students are asked to collaborate in cheating, it is especially worrisome. It may be the reason some believe we are developing a culture that condones and justifies instances of cheating.[11]

Other examples of cheating during the test are much harder to identify and therefore harder to judge. When students take a standardized test, teachers are bound by an honor code that they will adhere to test-administration protocols that typically require them to maintain a silent classroom and adhere strictly to a rigid test-taking time allowance. These protocols prohibit teachers from coaching, guiding, or prompting students. But, as we found, there are a great number of examples where teachers modify these instructions and end up in violation of the standardization procedures to which they had agreed to abide.

In Maryland, for example, an elementary school principal coached students during the test—giving them the answers and extra time to finish.[12] In Kentucky, among 80 violations identified at one school, one included an accusation of the principal, who encouraged students to seek help from teachers as they took the test.[13] In Pennsylvania, a fourth-grade student complained to his mother that he was tired of tests and tired of his teacher putting Post-it notes on his exam telling him to go back and revisit answers that are "wrong."[14] And in California, teachers helped students at a school that has historically won national recognition for its education of minority and poor students. Eleven former students reported that teachers gave students test answers or at least strongly hinted at them.

Box 2.3 Cheating in Houston

From 1994 to 2003, Wesley Elementary School in Houston won national accolades for teaching low-income students how to read and was featured in an *Oprah* segment on schools that "defy the odds." But it turned out that Wesley wasn't defying the odds at all: the school was simply cheating. The *Dallas Morning News* found that in 2003, Wesley's fifth-graders performed in the top 10 percent in the state on the Texas Assessment of Knowledge and Skills (TAKS) reading exams. The next year, however, as sixth-graders at the M. C. Williams Middle School, the same students fell to the bottom 10 percent in the state. Obviously, something was amiss! In the end, Wesley teachers admitted that cheating was standard operating procedure. But the school wasn't alone. The newspaper found several statistical anomalies in nearly 400 Texas schools in 2005.

Jason Spencer, "Schools Accused of Cheating: Three Low-income Acres Homes Elementaries Had Big TAKS Gains," *Houston Chronicle*, Jan. 1, 2006, B1.

According to one former teacher, "You do whatever you need to do to get those scores up!"[15]

There is a significant difference between blatantly helping students during a test—giving them answers, directing them to change wrong answers—and more subtle acts of encouragement—encouraging them to keep going or to use their "thinking" strategies. One directly informs the student that the test is perceived by the teachers themselves as valueless and that passing is the only thing that matters—even if it means that teachers give students the answers. The second, however, recognizes that students who take a test with so much at stake often experience anxiety that can impede successful performance. Subtle reminders/cues would seem to help students demonstrate more fully what they know at test time. Of these two violations of standardization procedures, the cheating is much easier to condemn than the use of encouragement. But what is not understood well is that one is as much a problem for test interpretation as the other. Both violations of standardization procedures make interpretations of the test more difficult. The inferences we can make from scores that have been changed or scores that have been raised through pep talks during the test are compromised: uncertainty has increased. Each violation has reduced the validity of the test, clouding the meaning we give to a score.

Post-test cheating activity

We found after-the-test indiscretions as well. In Arizona, one principal was suspected of changing students' test scores—an action that would have given teachers access to incentive money, resulting in a raise in their pay.[16] Could this administrator be rebelling against using the test as a credible measure of a teacher's worth? Could this administrator be angry over the relatively low pay teachers receive? Did the administrator want to enhance her own reputation? Each of these reasons for cheating may elicit slightly different degrees of condemnation for what clearly was an act of blatant cheating.

In another problematic case in New York, a particularly clever and somewhat subtle form of cheating may be occurring when teachers grade English exams. The procedures of interest are called "scrubbing." Essay exams (English and history) in New York are often graded by two teachers who naturally must make subjective decisions when scoring these exams. If it is found that a student is just a few points shy of some critical cutoff score, the exam is given to a third party who then tries to "find" extra points to help push that student over the top.[17] Given what we know about the subjectivity of grading, is "finding" a few points cheating? Or is it just a responsible reaction to the problem of subjectivity in scoring? The teachers themselves are conflicted. One teacher says, "I'm sorry if it's shocking for layman to hear [about]. Scrubbing is something we do to help the kids get their asses out of school." Another says it's just about diplomas and merit pay: "The students of the school benefit because they pass. The school benefits because the pass rate is up . . . but it is grade inflation. It's cheating. You're falsifying exams. It's totally corrupt."

In all of these examples, it is clear that administrators' and teachers' behaviors were always about raising test-score performance. Whether

Box 2.4 Statistical Anomalies Reveal Likelihood That Someone Cheated

As of summer 2006, the Texas Education Agency is suspending a plan to reward teachers at 14 schools across the state pending an investigation into cheating on the Texas Assessment of Knowledge and Skills (TAKS). The money, the result of an initiative by Governor Rick Perry to reward high-performing schools, was to range from $2,000 to $10,000 per teacher.

Local school-district officials were instructed to investigate whether cheating may have occurred—virtually guaranteeing that the investigations will be less thorough than if an outside audit agency investigated the allegations. But the coincidental appearance of the same 14 schools on both the bonus list and the list of possible cheaters spurred the TEA to take action of its own. The possibility of $60,000 to $220,000 going to schools that cheated finally prompted serious investigation of the allegations. Using 2005 test results, analysts from the firm Caveon identified suspicious results in 609 schools (8.6 percent of the state's campuses).

Caveon's analyses looked at four types of possible "cheating":

- Answer sheets with unusual numbers of wrong responses that have been erased and replaced with correct ones
- Inexplicably large jumps in students' test scores from the previous year
- Students who answer the harder questions on a test correctly but miss the easy ones
- Answer sheets that are unusually similar to those of other students in the same classroom

At one high school, the following was found:

- 91 students took the eleventh-grade math TAKS test.
- 55 percent of test takers got an unusual number of hard questions right but an unusual number of easy questions wrong (statistically expected number: 4 percent).
- 98 percent of answer sheets were identical or nearly identical to another answer sheet in the group (statistically expected: 6 percent).
- 49 percent of students showed unusually high gains from the previous year's test (statistically expected: 5 percent).
- According to the report, "The probability value that these identical answer sheets occurred by chance is so small as to approach the realm of impossibility." Caveon says that chance is less than 1 in 1,000,000,000,000,000,000,000.

Joshua Benton, "Analysis Suggests Cheating on TAKS," *Dallas Morning News*, May 23, 2006. See also Jenny LaCoste-Caputo, "Hold Slapped on TAKS Bonuses," *San Antonio Express-News*, June 17, 2006.

Box 2.5 Student Cheating at Military Academies

Cheating has rocked the U.S. military academies throughout the decades, in spite of their prestige and reputation for moral integrity. At West Point, the Cadet Honor Code states that a cadet will not lie, cheat, or steal nor tolerate those who do. A cadet who violates the honor code shall be expelled from the U.S. Military Academy. Such students are not exempt from Campbell's law when enrolled in an institution where the pressure to succeed is high.

During the 1950s, cadets on Army's football team shared answers to quizzes with one another, and later they were found to have stolen tests and shared answers. Tutors were involved—passing information at training tables in libraries and cadet rooms where there were study sessions. In the end, 94 cadets were found guilty of violating the honor code; of those, 83 resigned, including 37 Army football players. In that group, those discharged included 25 of the 27 returning lettermen. During the previous season (1950), Army was the number two team in the nation. Twenty-five years later, in 1976, after thorough investigations, 134 cadets had resigned or been expelled in some manner from the academy for cheating on take-home problems given by the Department of Electrical Engineering.

The Air Force has similar problems. In 1965 over 100 cadets were found cheating; in 1967 more than 60 cadets were found to be cheating; in 1972, 39 more cadets were found to be cheating; and in 1984 another 19 cadets were found guilty, though twice that number was thought to be involved. More recently, in 2005, a cheating scandal happened again. The pattern seems repetitive because the pressure never ends. In fact, another incident occurred in the fall of 2006 when Captain Rhonda McDaniel was found guilty of wrongfully possessing and sharing contents of a secured test. The Weighted Airmen Promotion System (WAPS) test is required for any person seeking promotion in the Air Force, and more than 100,000 take it every year. Investigations into probable cheating began in May 2005, and as of October 2006, 14 people had been charged with cheating on the test.

The Naval Academy is not exempt either. In December 1992, 133 cadets were accused of cheating, and in 1994, 24 midshipmen were dismissed from the academy, six of whom were on the Navy football team.

John Harry Jorgenson, "Duty, Honor, Country and Too Many Lawyers," *American Bar Association Journal* 6 (1977): 564–657; "New Scandal at Air Force Academy," Associated Press, Apr. 28, 2004, *http://www.cbsnews.com/stories/2004/11/13/national/main655536.shtml*; Iver Peterson, "Cheating Prompts Air Force to Halt Cadet Honor Boards," *New York Times*, Sept. 20, 1984, A1; "Allegations of Air Force Academy Cadet Cheating Investigated," Associated Press, May 25, 1983; Paul Valentine, "Two Dozen Expelled in Naval Academy Cheating Scandal," *Washington Post*, Apr. 29, 1994, 2; Lisa Burgess, "Another Conviction in the Air Force Promotions Test Cheating Ring," *Stars and Stripes*, Oct. 8, 2006.

blatant or subtle and whether it was done for self-preservation or altruistic purposes, the end result seems painfully clear. Undue emphasis on tests as the sole measure of students' and teachers' worth puts them in morally complex dilemmas where "cheating" is viewed as a viable, if not a morally acceptable, option.

As we end this section, we must note that an equally vexing problem related to cheating is the problem of going after cheaters. Since we have created a system that seems to increase cheating behavior, we obviously must be more vigilant about its occurrence. This can lead to witch hunts like those Senator Joseph McCarthy led in pursuit of communists in government. McCarthy and the House Un-American Activities Committee saw threats to America everywhere. In their zeal to protect America, they ignored basic rules of decency. The hunt for cheaters may undermine the profession as much as cheating itself.

STUDENT CHEATING

In 2004, a movie titled *The Perfect Score* showed how important college entrance tests can be in the lives of some students, so in the movie the students set out to steal the test. They justify their theft because they know that the tests could not ever come close to defining who they are or what they will be, and that the tests should never be used to do so. They were sure that the tests could not assess what they actually did know. They resented the importance of the tests in their lives, and many in the audience become sympathetic to their argument. These fictional students have their real-life counterparts in true stories that document student cheating and students speaking out against the test.

By far the saddest issue that emerges from our analysis is that we have designed a system that encourages our children to cheat. Legislators and state department of education employees around the country recognize that the pressure to do well on tests is associated with increased cheating. So they have developed policies for securing tests and establishing auditing procedures to look for suspicious patterns of answers indicative of cheating.[18] Nationwide, there appears to be the assumption that cheating is inevitable: an ordinary activity under the conditions of schooling that we have designed.

In response to the incidents of cheating, of course, schools and state departments of education take steps to deter them. It is not clear how much time and money are being invested in policies and technology to detect and thwart cheating, but it is surely substantial. Yet reactive approaches to controlling behavior seldom work.[19] As building more prisons does nothing to change criminal behavior, it is likely that better detection and prosecution for cheating will not deter it. Instead, we need to invest proactively in schooling practices that help us raise children less tempted to transgress. Using Campbell's law to analyze our educational practices might be a good first step in structuring a national dialogue about the design of such practices that compromise those who attend and work in our schools. Through dialogue we can ponder one of Einstein's remarks, tailored perfectly to our high-stakes testing era: "Not everything that counts can be counted, and not everything that can be counted counts."

As student cheating becomes more visible, likely due to the increasing incidents of cheating, so does the level of suspicion associated with test performance. For example, it was reported in the spring of 2004 that a single school raised a great deal of suspicion after two years of strange test-score trends. As reported by the *Washington Post*, Moten Elementary School near Washington, D.C., posted significant gains on the Stanford 9 test during the 2001–2 school year, only to be erased by the next year's dramatic dip in test performance. Many, including some of the teachers at Moten Elementary, strongly believed that cheating must have occurred during the year the school posted significant score gains—but no one ever came forward and no evidence was found. Even an expert of educational measurement weighed in, claiming "my hunch is there's some point in the handling of these documents that they've been altered. . . . I'm trying to think of any other plausible explanation, but I'm just not able to come up with one."[20]

It is hard to know for sure what happened that led to this anomaly. As many statistical experts would argue, a significant jump in one year of testing is most likely due to something other than true performance gains, because such a jump is statistically unlikely to have happened in such a short time period. What we find astonishing in this incident is the complete absence of hypothesizing that students actually *may* have learned a great deal in one year. Citizens expect cheating to be the reason when such statistically unlikely events take place. This was made obvious in the movie *Stand and Deliver*, a fictionalized account of a true event. The movie documented how Educational Testing Service refused to believe that a group of barrio Latinos/Latinas could score well on a calculus test. What they imagined to be a clever scheme of cheating was in actuality an exemplary teacher named Jaime Escalante. The students were forced to take the test again to prove that they had not cheated. Such humiliation probably never would have occurred had the students been white and middle class. But ETS seemed unable to believe that poor Latinos/Latinas could score well without cheating. We cannot help but wonder if such powerful expectations of cheating results in self-fulfilling prophecies for some students. That scenario seems likely and cannot be healthy for our youth.

Box 2.6 Student Cheating in Georgia

Marissa Harding, 18, a senior at Cross Creek High School, has seen students take cheat sheets into vocabulary quizzes, sometimes even putting the answers on the back of chairs they sit behind. "They spend a lot of time thinking of ways to cheat rather than trying to study," Marissa said. "I don't know if they don't want to learn it or like to see if they could get away with it." Many students cheat because of the increased pressures to do well. One senior said that "with so much emphasis on grades and so much riding on academic excellence, students resort to cheating." She goes on, "There's so much pressure on students today—especially upperclassmen—they start to think: 'I want to pass this class; I want to get into Georgia; I need a good grade.' The pressure is overwhelming sometimes."

Kamille Bostick, "Cheat Tricks/Failing Grades: Punishments Are in Store for Students Who Get Caught," *Augusta Chronicle*, Dec. 16, 2003, D3.

THE DIFFICULTY OF STANDING UP TO CHEATS AND CHEATING

Cheating seems to be an integral part of the high-stakes testing movement, but so is resistance to it. We found many examples of adults and youth standing up to the kind of test-related improprieties that commonly occur. In some cases, however, the "whistleblowers" lost their jobs or were forced to resign. We discovered that there is a high price to pay for standing up against the pressure to cheat when many of one's colleagues see cheating as a reasonable response to an immoral system. Holding an absolute value that cheating is always wrong makes one a pariah if others in your professional community take a much more relativistic position.

Montgomery, Alabama, provided an example of this phenomenon. At least 100 students were involved in a cheating scandal that caused a suspicious "jump" in student performance among Sumter County High School students, with some students' scores increasing from the 38th percentile to the 97th percentile. Bob Armstrong, a teacher at Sumter County for nearly ten years, was fired by the county after aiding the investigation.[21] A principal in Camden, New Jersey, was fired by the school board after alleging that he had been pressured by a district official to cheat on the state high school proficiency exam. The principal, Bob Carruth, stated that he was directed by an assistant superintendent to open a test booklet and create an answer key to later change students' wrong answers.[22] In Pennsylvania, a Philadelphia teacher was fired after reporting that an administrator was helping students cheat on the assessment test. She had witnessed the administrator encouraging third graders to "stop and check their work."[23]

In Columbus, Ohio, fifth-grade teacher Barbara McCarroll was castigated by her principal for her students' test scores being so low in comparison to their scores from previous years. When she asked her students for an explanation, they were all too frank: it was "because they gave us the answers and you didn't."[24] McCarroll ended up on disability leave after developing sleeping and eating problems, and she was eventually forced out of the school for complaining about the coaching for the tests that other teachers were doing at the school.

Mitch Dorson, an American studies teacher, felt obligated to resign after reporting a student who had cheated under his watch yet received no support from the district.[25] During the 2003–4 academic year, Dorson granted one of his students the opportunity to take a test one day early, after which the student e-mailed all of the test answers to 50 other students. The alleged offender in this incident never apologized or explained his/her actions. However, a year later, the same student applied for a prestigious scholarship awarded by the Flinn Foundation, an application Dorson could not reasonably support given the immoral actions of the student from the previous year. Students in contention for the scholarship are judged on strong moral character as well as academic achievement. Dorson asked administration officials to speak up against this particular student's attempt to garner a scholarship. The administration, however, encouraged Dorson to keep the incident quiet, resulting in his resignation.

These are egregious examples of outright bullying of whistleblowers, and it is too often reinforced in schools. When test scores constitute the only measure of teachers and teaching, it puts school leaders in the precarious position of having to do whatever it takes to preserve jobs even if it means sacrificing others or sacrificing doing the "right" thing.

Origins of the beliefs that cheating and resistance may be justified

The punishment of whistleblowers puzzled us. We would like to think educators are moral and decent professionals. Why, we wondered, were so many of them so unforgiving of those who publicly speak out against cheating? The answer, we think, is that many teachers believe the high-stakes testing system is itself grossly unfair to their students and themselves. Many teachers and administrators, perhaps the majority, hold this belief, though certainly others find much to commend in NCLB and its requirement of high-stakes testing. But for those who do not believe that high-stakes testing is fair, cheating may become a form of resistance: a way around a testing program seen as inappropriate, harmful to students and themselves, limiting of their professionalism, and so forth.

Some of these beliefs in the inappropriateness of high-stakes testing are echoed in the research community, and the negativism of prestigious scholars is perhaps a source of justification for both cheating and the nasty treatment of those who protest cheating. For example, the former president of both the National Council on Measurement in Education (NCME) and the American Educational Research Association (AERA), Robert Linn, has argued the testing systems we use cannot do what the politicians want them to. "Assessment systems that are useful monitors lose much of their dependability and credibility . . . when high stakes are attached to them," he writes. "The unintended negative effects of the high-stakes accountability . . . often outweigh the intended positive effects."[26]

Robert Brennan, director of the Center for Advanced Studies in Measurement and Assessment at the University of Iowa and also a past president of the NCME, said recently that "the accountability provisions of [NCLB] and its regulations are *outrageously unrealistic and poorly conceived* from a measurement perspective. . . . For the most part, I would argue that a more accurate title for the Act might be 'Most Children Left Behind'" (emphasis added).[27]

Stephen Raudenbush, one of the leading statisticians in the nation, is a professor of education and statistics at the University of Michigan and also a member of the prestigious National Academy of Education (NAE). In a recent speech to the Educational Testing Service (ETS), one of the developers of tests that have high stakes attached to them, he said: "High-stakes decisions based on school-mean proficiency are scientifically indefensible. We cannot regard differences in school-mean proficiency as reflecting differences in school effectiveness. . . . To reward schools for high mean achievement is tantamount to rewarding those schools for serving students who were doing well prior to school entry."[28]

None of these critics of testing is advocating that teachers or students cheat. But when so many prestigious scientists say the system is not working, is unfair, punishes people who should not be punished, and rewards people who should not be rewarded, teachers and students may feel they have the grounds for resistance, passive aggression, or civil disobedience. Segregated facilities in the South may have been legal, but they were wrong. Changing that system required courage and the willingness to suffer the punishment that often follows acts of disobedience. We seem to be witnessing the same phenomena in some of the violations of testing procedures

Box 2.7 Monitoring the Cheats and Discouraging Whistleblowers

In New Jersey, education officials didn't notice that standardized test scores from three Camden schools had risen in 2005 at a seemingly inexplicable rate—and thus might be worth investigating—until prodded by reporters. As of summer 2006, officials were investigating dramatic rises in 2005 test scores at H. B. Wilson and U. S. Wiggins Schools and Dr. Charles E. Brimm Medical Arts High, where the recently fired principal has said he resisted a supervisor's pressure to change scores. At H. B. Wilson, 100 percent of fourth graders passed the math test last year, but only 23.2 percent this year. At U. S. Wiggins, 96.6 percent of fourth graders passed the language arts test last year and 55 percent this year. Scores dropped 17 percentage points to 74.6 at Brimm.

No one keeps track of the extent of cheating on standardized tests in this country, whether orchestrated from the top or done by individual students. Experts rely on media reports, and those reports suggest that irregularities are on the rise. In New Jersey, the Department of Education does not routinely analyze results to look for irregularities, even though there is a ten-month lag between the time the tests are given and their scores made public.

A number of states, including Illinois, South Carolina, and Pennsylvania, rely on the firms contracted to write and grade the tests to look for evidence of foul play. Officials in states that don't routinely review the data—among them Alabama, Connecticut, Massachusetts, Missouri, Montana, Nebraska, Tennessee, Utah, and Virginia—say they haven't seen evidence to suggest that cheating is widespread in their areas.

Texas, Ohio, and North Carolina have hired consultants to conduct statistical analyses looking for unusual year-to-year gains, high numbers of erasures, and students who get easier questions wrong and harder ones right.

Kellie Patrick and Larry Eichel, "Education Tests: Who's Minding the Scores? A Poll Shows Less Than Half of States Look for Cheating," *Philadelphia Inquirer*, June 25, 2006. See also Monica Yant Kinney, "Camden School Scandal Has Reached a New Low," *Philadelphia Inquirer*, Aug. 3, 2006; and Melanie Burney, "Knox Got Bonuses Without Board's OK," *Philadelphia Inquirer*, June 4, 2006.

we described above. We can blame teachers or administrators for moral lapses if we want, but blame must also be apportioned to our politicians and bureaucrats, who have produced through laws and regulations a climate in education that encourages illicit behavior and also threatens the very livelihoods of individuals willing to stand up to corruption.

A sense of unfairness and resistance to testing

Teachers report that high-stakes testing is unfair, that it hurts children and compromises their professional integrity, and these beliefs find great support from many popular school critics and distinguished educational researchers. Among the voices raised in criticism are Gerald Bracey; Robert Brennan; the Center for the Study of Testing, Evaluation and Educational Policy; FairTest; Robert Linn; Jay Heubert and Robert Hauser writing for the National Research Council/National Academy of Sciences; Lyle Jones; Alfie Kohn; the National Board on Educational Testing and Public Policy; Susan Ohanian; Gary Orfield and Mindy Kornhaber of The Civil Rights Project at Harvard University; and Stephen Raudenbush.[29] So it is not surprising that some teachers and administrators engage in passive aggression against the system by cheating in one way or another. Others are more forthright in expressing their resistance. Among those is the North Carolina principal who will not test what she calls "borderline kids," her special-education children, despite the requirement to do so.[30] She says, "I couldn't. The borderline children experience enough failure and do not need to be humiliated by a test far beyond their abilities." By not testing all the children in the school, the principal is cheating. But this is also an act of human kindness. And it is at the same time an act of resistance to laws made by faceless bureaucrats in some other community. It is not easy to judge this principal harshly.

Box 2.8 also tells the story of an educator who would not compromise. In British Columbia, teachers are upset with the testing program and have called for a boycott. The teachers' federation of the province urged parents to withdraw their children from standardized province-wide tests for fourth- and seventh-grade students, which were scheduled to be given in May 2006.[31] The provincial government has used the Foundation

Box 2.8 Story of Teacher Resistance

In January 2001, a middle school teacher in Greeley, Colorado, refused to administer the Colorado Student Assessment Program tests to his students—the first resistance of its kind in Colorado at the time. Donald Perl, who teaches eighth-grade Spanish, reading, and language arts, refused to administer the test on grounds that it conflicts with his beliefs as an educator. "I've anguished over this for a long time, and I cannot administer these tests, knowing the population here and seeing how discriminatory the test is." Perl also said the test cultivates competition instead of cooperation and test-taking skills over "true stimulation of our children's curiosity." "These high-stakes standardized tests violate my egalitarian values of what the public school system is supposed to be about." For his protests, he was suspended for six days without pay. In 2004 the school board reviewed Greeley's proposal for a statewide ballot initiative to get rid of the Colorado Student Assessment Program.

Percy Ednalino, "Teacher Won't Administer CSAP," *Denver Post*, Jan. 27, 2001, A1, *http://www.alfiekohn.org/standards/boycotter.htm*; Percy Ednalino, "Teacher Gets Suspension Over Test Flap," *Denver Post*, Feb. 10, 2001, A1; "City Briefing," *Rocky Mountain News*, Mar. 4, 2004, 11A.

Skills Assessment since 2000 to evaluate reading, writing, and math skills. But the teachers' federation wants parents to write letters to have their children excluded from taking the test. "We are opposed to a one-shot snapshot test," they say, "that seems to have gained an unwarranted level of attention in our system." The teacher federation argues that the test is not useful educationally, and the results are misused to compare schools, causing "considerable harm" to poorer communities.

The federation has stated that "teachers believe these tests have negative effects on teaching and learning. Teachers . . . are now seeing the same negative effects of testing already documented by researchers in several countries." Teachers have reported feeling pressured to teach to the test, spend instructional time on test practices, and ignore other aspects of the school curriculum. They note that teachers see students who "suffer from test anxiety, value tests more than learning, and lose their motivation to learn if they do badly on tests." For all these reasons, the federation is fighting the imposition of high-stakes testing.[32]

Sam Esmiol, a Spanish teacher in a middle school in Colorado, refused to serve as a translator for a standardized test, arguing that foreign-language students are severely handicapped when asked to take an orally translated version of the test. Part of the problem, he argued, is that not all translators have the same skills, thus students taking the test in this way may be taking radically different versions. The translated test, according to Esmiol, "just doesn't represent their [students'] abilities. It's not an accurate way to judge their performance." According to the director of the assessment unit at the Colorado Department of Education, there are no firm requirements for translators on the tests. Therefore, they have no way of "knowing who would be translating or not translating."[33] Still, for his resistance, Esmiol was suspended without pay for the six half-day testing sessions.

Students have also learned to resist. For example, in the spring of 2005 John Wood, ranked sixth in his high school class, was denied a diploma because he refused on moral grounds to take the Ohio proficiency tests—a test students must pass in Ohio in order to receive their diploma. According to Wood, who wrote to the *Athens News*, "I did this because I believe these high-stakes tests are biased, irrelevant and unnecessary."[34] In Texas, high school student Kimberly Marciniak, a high honor roll AP student, decided to boycott the Texas Assessment of Knowledge and Skills (TAKS)—another test students must pass in order to receive their high school diploma. In spite of receiving a great deal of pressure and condemnation for this resistance, Marciniak was accepted to her top three college choices and offered scholarships from each one for her strong convictions. Kimberly would have passed the test easily, but she resisted on the grounds that the test was unfair. Her seventh-grade civics teacher would be proud: "Civic responsibility is something I learned about in my seventh-grade year. You have no right to complain about the president if you don't vote. Well, I look at TAKS the same way. I would have no right to complain if I know there is something I can do to change it."[35] Box 2.9 provides more student voices of resistance.

Parents, too, are involved with protests. The Scarsdale, New York, protest, in which two-thirds of the district's eighth-graders boycotted the state's standardized tests, was among the biggest and best publicized, but many more are occurring across the nation. Resistance to unfair practices

Box 2.9 The MCAS Is a Waste of Time: Students Resist

Student #1

Annabel Gill Groton is a tenth-grader at Parker Charter School in Fort Devens, Massachusetts, responding to a May 4, 1998, editorial, "Don't Worry about the Tests." About the MCAS, she says, "These tests are an enormous waste of 17 hours of my time. The only thing accomplished by these tests will be the standardization and institutionalization of what we focus on in school. By forcing schools to conform to the arbitrary standards set by the test, the creativity and innovation of what and how we learn will be eliminated in the pursuit of high test scores. I am glad I will be out of high school by the time MCAS counts toward graduation, because I will hopefully be able to avoid the sterilization it will force upon my school and others like it."

Student #2

Jake Wachman attends Pierce Middle School and also weighed in on the MCAS. "I wrote this letter during my MCAS test today because I was so infuriated with what I was having to do. The MCAS epitomizes the stupidity of government bureaucracy. I should know, for I am an eighth-grader who has to take this behemoth of a 'test.' In the la-la-land of educational reform the MCAS is a great test, but where I reside—in reality—it fails miserably. Homework, or any type of work for that matter, has become all but extinct over the past week. The MCAS is simply too time-consuming. It has taken what would have been three weeks of normal learning and transformed them into what amounts to a giant party.

"Putting aside all of the stupidity of the test's logistics, the actual questions are horrid. One question, as I recall, asked how one could tell that a lady in a story was born in Norway. It gave the choices: (A) her speech, (B) her mannerisms, (C) her special clothing, or (D) her preference for coffee. What a question! Seeing as that you cannot derive her mannerisms and clothing type from a story that did not describe either, (A) her speech would be the only choice. I learned about how to generalize and stereotype! Instead of taking this test in class, we should be learning from mistakes. It is not an overstatement to say we can learn more from the generalizations, grammatical errors, stereotypes and other mistakes that appear in MCAS questions than we can from the information about which MCAS supposedly tests us."

Annabel Gill Groton, "MCAS Exams Are a Waste of My Time," *Boston Globe*, May 18, 1998; Jake Wachman, "Testing 1-2-3: Is This MCAS Working?" *Boston Herald*, May 17, 1998.

is as American as the Boston tea party. The number of protests against high-stakes tests—acts of resistance by educators, students, and parents—has become more common. Perhaps our legislators will listen to these voices of protest, anger, disappointment, and professionalism, and these little acts of defiance will result in changes to NCLB and the removal of its most corruptive requirement, high-stakes testing.

CONCLUSION

Let us be clear. We are not trying to castigate administrators and teachers by identifying the unsavory practices in which some of their colleagues engage. About three and a half million teachers and hundreds of thousands of administrators are practicing the profession honorably. As stated at the beginning of this chapter, the more engaging question is: Why have we created a system that seems to unnecessarily pressure people whom we expect to be moral leaders of our youth? Every sensible adult understands that large incentives and threats of punishment and humiliation push honest people to do bad things. So why do we design systems that we know will result in bad things happening, especially when other ways to improve education exist? That is the important question for our nation's policymakers.

We should be asking why so many competent and decent professionals think the system they are in is so unfair to their students, their schools, and themselves and, as a result, feel justified in doing direct test preparation, violating standardization procedures, and cheating. We should also ask, What sort of educational system have we developed in which some teachers and administrators worry so much about their jobs that they would cheat to be sure they have work in the future? Management through fear seems archaic, repudiated by virtually every business school in the country. Yet it appears to be the case that management by fear is precisely the kind of system we have adopted for our schools when we passed NCLB. Is this what we want? These are the questions that ought to be debated. The conditions fostering the corruption of students, teachers, and administrators should receive a great deal more attention.

CHAPTER 3

EXCLUDING STUDENTS FROM EDUCATION BY DESIGN AND BY NEGLECT,
the Crisis of Caring in Our Schools, and the Special Case of the "Bubble Kids"

In our analysis of cheating, we discovered that events that at first seem simple often turn out to be much more complex than they first appeared. But there are other manifestations of Campbell's law that are less nuanced. These reprehensible acts, which are more easily condemned, have to do with denying students their place in American public school classrooms. As Jonathan Kozol has argued, high-stakes testing in America makes important contributions to maintaining an educational system he characterizes as a system of apartheid.[1]

It is widely known that if the disaffected or weakest students can be pushed out of schools or allowed to drop out, then the test scores at the school or district that lose these students will go up. There is considerable evidence that some educators have shaped the test-taking pool in their schools or districts through such exclusionary practices as withdrawing students from attendance rolls. Others have purposely demoralized students, causing them to give up in the face of what they accurately perceive to be a hostile school environment. High-stakes testing creates conditions in which a great number of our most vulnerable and less advantaged students are denied a chance at a productive life.

How does this happen? When stakes are high, students sometimes are administratively withdrawn from school. This is just another way adults try to manipulate scores to which consequences are attached. When they want to, administrators seek and always can find "reasons" to drop low-scoring students from school rolls. In this way, come testing day, only the higher-performing students are present to take the test. We found instances in which students were withdrawn from school even without their knowledge and without any notes to their parents or guardians. Even when the students petitioned to be allowed to take classes, they were told that they had shown "insufficient interest" in school. An equally sinister trend is that educators have become complaisant toward students who want to drop out. Since these students are usually (though not always) low scorers on the test, there is little incentive to convince them to stay in school. In fact, the schools fare much better if those students leave. So those more challenging students who are more apt to give up, reject schooling, and drop out are gleefully allowed to go. A Florida superintendent noted, "When a low-performing child walks into a classroom, instead of being seen as a challenge, or an opportunity for improvement, for the first time since I've been in education, teachers are seeing [that child] as a liability."[2] The ethical and moral problems associated with this type of attitude are even more serious than they might appear because those most affected by self-serving professional behavior are our most vulnerable populations—those who are poor, migrant, have special learning challenges, or for whom English is a second language. In this chapter, we reveal what we regard as contemptible instances in which the future of many of our nation's youth are compromised and sacrificed in the quest to leave "no high-scoring child" behind.

EXCLUDING STUDENTS FROM THE TEST

In the age before high-stakes tests, it didn't take long for students to "know" who was smart and who was not, simply on the basis of how they did on classroom exercises and quizzes related to literacy and mathematics. For generations, schools narrowed their view of what constitutes competence to these two primary areas. That was unfortunate, but not intolerable. Now, however, our K–8 students are not merely classified on the basis of their academic performance, they may be stigmatized for it! Low scorers in reading and mathematics may impede a school's capacity for making

"Adequate Yearly Progress" (AYP), preventing bonuses and accolades and making punishments and public humiliation inevitable. A low-scoring student, a score suppressor, thus has little value in a school that is judged through high-stakes testing. It is the score increasers, not the score suppressors, who have value for a school. Students learn quickly if they are score suppressors or score increasers, where once they were just children named Bill or Maria. Because of high-stakes testing, it probably takes much less time today for our K–8 children to develop their academic self-image than in the past, and that image is probably more rigidly held than ever before. Although it is our youngest and lowest-achieving students who are likely to be subject to a crisis of confidence in their talents, it is our low-scoring high school students whose lives are being most seriously compromised—whether they drop out or are pushed.

If students do not finish high school, their chances for an economically productive life are in serious jeopardy. In Chicago, one of many urban areas with high dropout rates, 22 percent of all residents between 16 and 22 were out of work and out of school in a recent year. That constituted about 80,000 young people in Chicago alone.[3] Across the nation, it has been estimated that we have upward of 5.5 million young people out of school and out of work.[4] Such youth were once metaphorically called "social dynamite," energetic, unstable, angry, and ready to explode. So it is always in the best interests of society to keep students in school and help them to get degrees. We do not do that now.

Because of failure, or expectations of failure on high-stakes tests, student dropout rates are increasing.[5] Thus, we can expect society's costs to rise as well. Recent economic analyses reveal not just the usual costs of dropping out before high school completion, such as earning $260,000 less in lifetime wages than a high school graduate or lower payments of taxes. The new data suggest that if high school completion rates were to increase by 1 percent among adult men, $1.4 billion a year would be saved by reductions in crime. That slight rise in graduation rates would also promote a reduction of murder and assault rates by 30 percent. Rates of car theft would drop by 20 percent, rates of arson would drop by 13 percent, and rates of burglary and larceny would decrease by 6 percent. Health-care costs would also be reduced by billions of dollars as a function of a simple

1 percent increase in high school completion rates.[6] High-stakes testing has simply exacerbated the traditional problem of keeping disaffected youth of all ability levels in school. But it particularly erodes the spirit of students whose only barrier to high school graduation is a high-stakes test.

In New York City, the encouragement of "difficult-to-teach" youth to drop out was so bad in 2002 and 2003, and so obvious, that the chancellor of the system was embarrassed. He was forced to admit that for many years the New York City schools engaged in the systematic dumping of thousands of children onto the streets.[7] At New York City's Boys and Girls High School in Brooklyn, a lawsuit revealed that the school had been "warehousing" struggling students in the school's auditorium during the tests, where they "fill out worksheets for three hours a day and attend no classes."[8] As a result, these students "fail" and therefore are denied promotion, then dropped from the school.

Birmingham, Alabama, seems to have been caught in a particularly egregious violation of youth rights so they could game the testing system.[9] Just before administering the annual high-stakes tests, Birmingham officials had 522 young people "administratively withdrawn" from high school. By doing so, scores on the state test went up and the district superintendent received a substantial bonus and pay raise, while several schools avoided being taken over by the district. This problem was brought to the public's attention by a teacher at an adult education facility who noticed an alarming pattern of high schoolers coming to his classes after finding out their high school had dropped them and was denying them reentry. One student explained, "I showed up for class and my teacher told me that my name was on a list, and he sent me down to the office. When I got there I saw my name was on a list, and they told me that I had to be withdrawn." Another student offered this further indictment:

> About two to three months ago, there was a school assembly. The principal spoke to us and said that he didn't want any students to interfere with the SAT scores. He said that the SAT scores were already low, and that the state was going to take over. He said that he would try to get . . . the students out of the school who he thought would bring the test scores down. He also gave us this same message over the intercom a couple of

> times after that. On the last day that I went to school, I was told to report to the principal's office because my name was not on the roster. I was given a withdrawal slip that said "Lack of interest." I did miss a lot of school days. I had family problems. I had allergies.[10]

As these examples illustrate, adults engage in unprofessional, indeed unscrupulous behavior when testing becomes the only measure by which they are judged and evaluated. The tragedy is not only that adults are modeling immoral behavior but that students are caught in the crossfire when they are unsubtly informed they are not valued and that schools do not believe in their potential.

Nevertheless, bullying students to leave school or dropping them from the school rolls without their knowledge, as in New York City and Birmingham, are not the only tactics used to increase scores. Some educators make the "effort" to keep youth in the game by encouraging them to enter GED (general education degree) programs. Arenson notes that this program has been growing and removes weak students from the NCLB school accountability programs:

> Nationally, teenagers accounted for 49 percent of those earning GEDs in 2002, up from 33 percent a decade earlier. The growth has been especially pronounced in New York City. Last year, more than 37,000 school-age students were in GED programs run by the school system, up from 25,500 two years earlier.
>
> Experts attribute the flood of young people in part to . . . the increased difficulty of earning a traditional high school diploma in many states. New York, for example, has made passing five Regents exams a condition of graduation, and no longer offers a lesser diploma for weaker students.
>
> Under the federal No Child Left Behind law and state efforts to hold schools more accountable, schools have more incentive to discourage weak students from staying. Students who transfer to GED programs are usually off school rolls but in many states are not counted as dropouts.
>
> Mr. Chaplin, of the Urban Institute, said he had "found pretty strong evidence that the GED option has been encouraging kids to drop out of high schools nationwide. The rules governing the GED have become more lenient over time," he said. "Under No Child Left Behind, we're holding schools very strictly accountable for test scores, but barely holding them

> accountable for students who drop out or go into GED programs. It is like holding hospitals accountable for the condition of patients who leave, but ignoring the number who die. It's a perverse incentive system."[11]

Yet another tactic used by morally corrupt school personnel is to temporarily restrict a student's schooling experience through expulsion or suspension in the days leading up to and during test taking. In North Carolina, figures from some school systems showed a spike in suspensions as the end-of-grade tests approached. One teacher was quoted as saying, "What I hear is that they believe a lot of kids who aren't making it academically are becoming more vulnerable to becoming suspended and expelled so they don't weigh down the test scores."[12] At Oak Ridge High School in Orlando, Florida, 126 low-performing students were "purged" from the attendance rolls just prior to state testing and without parent's permission.[13] According to the *Orlando Sentinel*, in 2004 approximately 160 Florida schools assigned students to new schools just before standardized testing began.

In Houston, several districts lied about their academic success by playing with the data and through selective reporting. For example, Lisa Snell from the Reason Foundation reported that at Austin High School in Houston, 2,757 students were enrolled during the 1997–8 school year. At the same time, it was reported that about 65 percent of students had passed the tenth-grade math test. Three years later, the school reported a 99 percent passing rate. Curiously, however, the enrollment had simultaneously shrunk to 2,215—raising the question of whether this pass rate was "real" or simply a function of a manipulated test-taking pool (i.e., the lower scorers had simply dropped out). At the same time, the school also reported that the dropout rate had plummeted from 4.1 to 0.3 percent. However, as Snell pointed out, their strategy for calculating these dropout rates was to "hold back low-scoring ninth-graders and then promote them directly to eleventh grade to avoid the tenth-grade exam."[14] The problem here is that somewhere along the way, students are being lost from the school system. Tragically, we see Campbell's law at work when well-intentioned adults prioritize ways to make the data look more favorable instead of helping struggling students see their education through.

One 17-year-old African American student in Florida was told not to return to school after his junior year because he had failed the Florida Comprehensive Assessment Test (FCAT). In spite of being a B and C student with aspirations to go to college, the school pushed him out—telling him he would be better off attending a GED program. Only after his aunt brought the media to the school for a meeting with the principal was he readmitted.[15] In Illinois, state law allows school officials to "disenroll" 16-year-olds who can't be expected to graduate by their 21st birthday. Not surprisingly, this law offers administrators opportunities to manipulate their test-taking pool by withdrawing any student they feel won't graduate. This was precisely the case with two 17-year-old students, Jennifer and John. Jennifer began missing school due to academic difficulties and because she could not get the help she needed. John was missing school because of family problems and an ill sibling. When both students returned to school, they were told they were no longer on the school rolls.

Box 3.1 Suspending Students When They Fight: High Scorers Get Shorter Suspensions

Since 2001, when the No Child Left Behind Act tied federal school funding to performance on annual tests for students in grades three through eight, critics have charged that the law encourages schools to boost their test scores artificially. A new study of one potential score-padding maneuver—suspending probable low scorers to prevent them from taking the test—provides grist for this argument. Researchers examined more than 40,000 disciplinary cases in Florida schools from the 1996–7 school year (when Florida instituted its own mandatory testing) to the 1999–2000 school year. They found that when two students were suspended for involvement in the same incident, the student with the higher test score tended to have a shorter suspension. This isn't in itself surprising: high achievers are often cut some slack. But the gap was significantly wider during the period when the tests were administered, and it was wider only between students in grades being tested that year!

Taken from David N. Figlio, *Testing, Crime and Punishment* [NBER Working Paper No. 11194] (Cambridge, MA: National Bureau of Economic Research, 2005), *http://www.nber.org/papers/W11194.*

In New York, 15-year-old Tanya was told she could not remain in high school because her grades were too low and that she would have to enroll full-time in a GED program. Yet what is shocking about this and so many other stories is that students are expelled from school because of "academic" reasons, even when they are not given *any tutoring or counseling* to try to get them back on track. Instead, they are just told to leave. Even when Tanya's mother argued with school officials that she had a right to be in school until the age of 21, school officials argued she was simply too far behind and would never be able to catch up to justify her staying enrolled. In a perfect Catch-22, when Tanya tried to enroll in the GED program, she was denied because the counselor said she was too young. Although lawsuits have been filed in New York on behalf of thousands of students like Tanya who have been pushed out of school, community-based adult educators say the numbers of students—especially very young students—entering their programs is growing. There is some evidence that they are not completing the program, however. According to one report, the number of students enrolled in GED programs rose from 18,000 in 2000–1 to 28,000 in 2002–3 while the number of GED diplomas granted stayed constant.[16]

THE PLIGHT OF SPECIAL POPULATIONS

The tragedy of this trend is not just *that* it is happening but to whom it is happening. Students who fail the test often come from poverty, have special learning needs, and represent our most ethnically and linguistically diverse populations. These groups of students are being shortchanged by NCLB in many ways, despite the claim that they are the ones who are not to be left behind. Based on Campbell's law, we predict that the students least likely to be score increasers, and most likely to be score suppressors, would be those most likely to be denied an education. These are perfect examples of Michael Apple's argument that accountability shifts the emphasis from "student needs to student performance, and from what the school does for the student to what the student does for the school."[17]

Special education

Under NCLB, students with learning disabilities are required to take the same test as peers their age. Districts can allow students with severe cognitive challenges to take a special version of the test, but only if these students constitute 1 percent or less of the student body.[18] This means that schools are put into the position of picking and choosing which students qualify for the special assessment and which special-education students must be forced to take the regular version. Not surprisingly, any school with a special-education population over 1 percent is likely to show less annual progress than other schools. Thus, special-education students are punished when they cannot pass the regular version of the test. In Florida, third-graders with disabilities failed the state assessment at twice the rate of their nondisabled peers—which means they all would be held back a grade. It is estimated that for approximately 8,300 of them, they flunked the test two years in a row. One anguished administrator remarked, "I just don't know how many times you can hit somebody over the head and say, 'You're not good at this, you're not good at this.'"[19]

At the high school level, this is especially troublesome because too often high school diplomas are on the line and, consequently, so is entry into postsecondary academics or vocational training. As of spring 2006, 23 states require students to pass an exit exam to receive a diploma.[20] For special-education students, this hurdle may be too great to overcome, thereby setting up a situation in which they never receive a high school diploma. In California, the projected passing rate on the state's high-stakes exam for 2004 (based on 2003–4 testing results) was 48 percent for nondisabled students and only 13 percent for disabled students. Not surprisingly, students feel pushed out because, even though they work hard and fulfill all other requirements, the exit exam is an obstacle many of them simply cannot overcome. And it changes their lives in drastic ways.

- After Justin Pierce, an eleventh-grader with dyslexia, failed the math portion of California's new graduation exam for the second time, he left his family in Napa and moved in with Texas relatives to attend high school there.

- Philip Cacho, 17, has cerebral palsy, cannot talk, and is nearly blind. He worked for 11 years to graduate on time from Berkeley High but found the "exit exam" an insurmountable barrier. He quit school in October.
- Anthony Lau-Segarra felt proud to earn As and Bs in special education at Washington High in San Francisco and planned to go to college. But after failing the exit exam four times, Anthony gave up his goal.

Not surprisingly, the high-stakes "few exceptions" environment is demoralizing. "I didn't feel like this before, but after the test, school feels worthless," said Lau-Segarra, age 17, who took extra classes to prepare. "I had my mind set to go to college and get a job. Then the exit exam popped up. I'm not capable of doing it. It makes me sad because I'm pretty smart."[21]

In Massachusetts, a student with Down's syndrome was denied entry into a local culinary college because she hadn't passed the state's MCAS exam—a requirement to receive a diploma. The college could not bend the rules for a student who had worked hard throughout high school and had completed all other requirements for graduation. What is especially astonishing is the district's refusal to give the student an official diploma even though they acknowledge they had failed to provide her the support she needed to graduate.[22]

The problem extends throughout the country. In California, approximately 20,000 special-education students have not been able to pass the state's high school exit exam—a test they must pass to receive a diploma.[23] This dire outcome prompted California legislators to revisit their testing policies concerning special-education students. As we write this in 2006, California has put a stop to the provision that students must pass a test to be eligible for a diploma.[24] That decision is being appealed.

In Tennessee it was estimated that about 15,000–16,800 special-needs students across the Memphis city school district were forced to take the regular version of the state exam.[25] In San Antonio in one middle school alone, 15 percent of the 1,100 students are designated as special-needs students. Under federal guidelines, 1 percent of special-education students with severe cognitive deficits are exempt from accountability, which means that in this case, 154 special-needs students had to take the regular version of the state exam.[26]

Box 3.2 More Students Get Special-Education Label Under High-Stakes Testing

In *Accountability, Ability and Disability: Gaming the System*, David Figlio and Lawrence Getzler study the effect of the introduction of the Florida Comprehensive Assessment Test (FCAT) in 1996 in six large counties in Florida. Examining data from as many as 4.1 million students, the authors find that the schools did "game the system" by reshaping the test pool. Schools reclassified students as disabled, putting them into "special education" programs exempt from the state tests, and therefore ineligible to contribute to the school's aggregate test scores.

Figlio and Getzler conclude that the introduction of the FCAT test is associated with an increase in the likelihood that a student will be classified as disabled by 5.6 percentage points. All together, 8.9 percent of the sample of students is identified as having a test-excludable disability. So the introduction of high-stakes testing resulted in more than a 50 percent higher rate of disability classification in these six counties. Moreover, schools are more likely to switch low-performing students from a test-included category to a test-excluded disability following the introduction of the testing regime. Those schools with a higher rate of poverty, indicated by how many students are eligible for free lunches, tend to be more aggressive in reclassifying previously low-performing students as disabled, apparently hoping to avoid being classified as a failing school.

The reclassification of students as disabled "profoundly affects the student's individual educational experience," the authors note. It also reduces the accuracy in the grades or classifications given to schools based on the accountability exams and thereby reduces the potential effectiveness of a public policy aimed at improving the educational system. Some students may end up in special education but would be better off in traditional classes. The trend also has an impact on total school costs, since special education, on average, costs 1.9 times as much per student as regular education in Florida.

David Francis, "How School Administrators Cheat the Accountability Rules," *National Bureau of Economic Research Website*, June 2003, *http://www.nber.org/digest/jun03/w9307.html*; report cited is David N. Figlio and Lawrence S. Getzler, *Accountability, Ability and Disability: Gaming the System* [NBER Working Paper No. 9307] (Cambridge, MA: National Bureau of Economic Research, 2002), *http://papers.nber.org/papers/w9307*.

Box 3.3 The Fate of a Score Suppressor

Martin B., the 16-year-old son of a friend, came home from high school one day and asked his mother if he should quit school. Mrs. B., of course, asked what prompted this concern. Martin explained that in his English course the teacher said to the students, "Why are you still here? Don't you know that no matter how well you do here you will all fail the AIMS test" (the Arizona Instrument to Measure Standards, the high school exit exam that must be passed to receive a diploma). He told the students they should quit and get jobs; since they would never get a degree anyway, they might as well go out and make some money.

The high school class was a special section of English for kids like Martin, kids who are not retarded but who are slow in academic areas. For reasons we may never know, thousands of Martins are in our schools. But does that make Martin any less valuable as a citizen? Martin was active in his church, a 4-H club member and prize-winner, on a school sports team, and emerging as popular with his friends, particularly girls! He could read all the instructions that came with his computer, his iPod, and the model race cars that he made. He could keep track of his money and liked welding, which he was good at. He hoped to get into the Army and be trained to improve his welding, perhaps making that his trade. He had every likelihood and qualification for becoming a productive citizen, except for the fact that his teacher and his school wanted to dump him, keep him from a diploma, and negate his chances to serve his country and learn a trade. Martin is a good kid, but unfortunately he happens to be a score suppressor.

Of course, special education includes the gifted, the score increasers, as well as the more academically challenged, the score suppressors. High-stakes testing distorts their lives as well. As box 3.4 makes clear, Campbell's law applies to the quickest as well as the slowest students.

Language and cultural diversity

No Child Left Behind represents an aggressive attack against students who have limited English proficiency or are not fully bilingual.[27] According to Title III of NCLB, states apply for federal funding based on the proportion

Box 3.4 The Peculiar Fate of a Score Increaser

The *Wall Street Journal* reported on an Ohio sixth-grader who was in a gifted program but whose scores on the state's high-stakes test were never counted in the school he attended, a school for the gifted. Instead, his scores were credited to the neighborhood school he does not attend so the average score of that school could go up. The logic is as follows: if no "credit" was given to the local schools, the local schools might not identify any students as gifted, fearing that they might lose the student to a school with a gifted program. Apparently, such "credit" systems also exist in Missouri and Iowa, where schools fear losing their high scorers to other schools. As we see with the least able students, the score, not the child, has become more important.

But the gifted are not just coveted, they are sometimes asked to suffer for the good of the school they are in, as well. It was revealed that in some Arizona schools and districts, their most talented students were talked into taking the high-stakes high school exit exam over and over again, after they had passed it. This, of course raises school and district scores, though it wastes students' time. Again, in a high-stakes testing environment, the students themselves are less important than their test scores.

Pat Kossan and Mel Melendez, "Schools Hoping to Boost District Rankings," *Arizona Republic*, Apr. 22, 2004; see also Daniel Golden, "In Era of Scores, Schools Fight Over Gifted Kids," *Wall Street Journal*, Feb. 4, 2004, A1, A9.

of students identified as Limited English Proficient (LEP). In turn, districts apply for these funds to support instructional programs geared toward the LEP students. Once it is determined how much in Title III funds a state will receive, it must design programs geared toward two main goals. The state must demonstrate that LEP students are making adequate progress toward proficiency in (a) English skills (reading, writing, speaking) and (b) subject-area content domains (math and science in particular). The manner in which the states are to accomplish these goals varies widely. But common to all states is the pressure to demonstrate academic proficiency in English quickly, which in turn has created a climate that is often insensitive and marginalizing to students from different linguistic and cultural backgrounds.

Wayne Wright, a language policy analyst, has described the ways NCLB disadvantages LEP students—two of which are especially fitting for our discussion: (1) *the pressure to increase scores forces instructors to narrow curriculum and to move away from consideration of the unique needs of LEP students*, and (2) *educators have huge incentives to find creative ways to keep LEP students from being tested and therefore lowering school averages.*[28] Indeed, our review of examples from across the country confirms Wright's analysis. We also discovered how LEP students—who tend to be low scorers on high-stakes tests—become disenfranchised from a full public education. Their unique cultural needs, perspectives, and experiences are removed from curricula that have become overly narrow and unidimensional, perhaps even culturally insensitive. If and when students are pushed aside, exempted, or bullied out of an educational system, those with diverse linguistic skills are apt to be disproportionately affected.[29]

If students can't understand the test question, it is absurd to think they will be successful on the test. Too many of our LEP (or English-language learner, ELL) students are forced to take standardized tests in English before they are ready. A quick look at passing rates illustrates this point poignantly. In Texas in 2003, the ELL eleventh-grade TAKS passing rate was 15 percent, compared to 49 percent for all other students.[30] In 2004, the passing rate on math was 91 percent for white students compared to 59 percent for ELLs. In reading, the passing rate was 92 percent for white students compared to 42 percent for ELLs. In North Carolina, passing rates on the 2002 reading and math exams were 87 percent for white students and 38 percent for ELL students. In New Jersey, the 2003 passing rate in math was 77 percent for white students and 22 percent for ELL students.[31]

State passing rates reveal a disturbing trend, where mostly white, mostly middle-class Americans do okay and those from poverty or for whom English is a second language do poorly. The categories "ELL" and "poor" contain a disproportionate number of minority youth, and high-stakes testing has a large and adverse impact on these minority children. In Massachusetts, Hispanics drop out of high school at the second highest rate in the country, and only half of African American students graduate.[32] By some estimates, 36.1 percent of Hispanics graduate in Massachusetts, falling far below the national rate for Hispanics of 53.2 percent. Massachusetts is a state with high stakes and high pressure on its educators and citizens to perform well on tests. Thus, many blame the pressure to do well on rigorous tests as a reason why so many students end up dropping out of school. In Alaska, minority students also struggle with the high school exit exam more than their white peers.[33] A larger proportion of LEP and/or ethnic minority students fail the test. In Texas, the eleventh-grade passing rate was 15 percent for limited English students, 38 percent for Hispanics, 33 percent for African Americans, and 59 percent for white students.[34] In Arizona, where state legislation outlawed the use of bilingual education, passing rates on high-stakes testing are even more discouraging. For example, an overwhelming majority of English-language third-graders in Arizona failed that state's exam (AIMS) from 2002 to 2004.[35]

A report sponsored by the Center on Education Policy published passing rates of students who took and passed their high school exit exam on the first try. The results show that, by far, white students have an easier time in their first try on these tests (see table 3.1). What seems missing in every state we have examined, in a nation with millions of students whose first language is not English, is the simple realization that any test *in* English is a test *of* English! Thus, we probably underestimate the academic abilities of millions of our youth with English-only high-stakes tests.

For some ELL students, high-stakes testing makes education a cruel endeavor, as when students fail a test by just a few points. In Florida, one high school senior, Leah Hernandez from Mexico, had been in the United States for five years and posted a 3.5 GPA. Still, after taking the state reading exam six times and ending six points short of the cutoff, she was denied her diploma.[36] When President Bush has difficulties using the English language properly but expects leniency, shouldn't we consider giving the same to our students?

Curriculum insensitivity

The curriculum imposed by high-stakes testing for Native Americans seems to be especially damaging. Not only is the curriculum narrowed to

Table 3.1 Percentage of Students Passing an Exit Exam on the First Try for All Students and by Subgroups

Student Subgroups	INDIANA 2003		NEW JERSEY 2003		NEVADA 2004		WASHINGTON 2003	
	Math	ELA	Math	LA	Math	Reading	Math	ELA
ALL	67	69	66	80	43	77	39	60
White	73	75	77	88	54	86	44	65
Black	33	39	33	61	22	62	14	37
Hispanic	46	44	42	63	25	62	16	35
Asian	85	78	83	87	53	81	47	64
Native American	54	57	57	74	29	72	22	43
ELL	41	27	22	18	13	34	8	12
Free or Reduced Lunch	46	48	36	57	25	60	24	43
Students with Disabilities	27	22	22	35	6	30	4	12

Note: ELA = English Language Arts; LA = Language Arts

Source: Keith Gayler et al., *State High School Exit Exams: A Maturing Reform* (Washington, DC: Center on Education Policy, Aug. 2004), *http://www.ctredpol.org/highschoolexit/ExitExam Aug2004/ExitExam 2004.pdf.*

focus on the tests, an issue we discuss in chapter 5, but the curriculum is culturally irrelevant to the students it is supposed to educate.[37] In an era in which we are trying to teach teachers to use culturally relevant pedagogy with Native Americans, African Americans, and Latinos, teachers feel forced by high-stakes testing pressures into designing curricula that are boring and alien to many of their students. What we are doing, then, is driving out these students with a test-oriented curriculum and abandoning the kind of culturally relevant curriculum that might keep them in school. This will have the effect of driving up the already high dropout rates for students from other cultures. The flip side, of course, is that the scores in the schools and districts go up when these kinds of students leave, making it especially difficult to persuade school personnel to address this issue.

A crisis of caring and compassion

Another ominous trend playing out under high-stakes testing illustrates a different kind of problem—that the need to test has replaced the need to care, a corruption of the traditional role of teachers. In these unsettling cases, students are not forced out of school; rather, they are forced to stay in school and endure a system that is indifferent to them. What we have observed are cases of apparent injustice that occur when laws are written by faceless bureaucrats a long distance from the places where the laws must be administered. Under high-stakes testing programs, teachers and administrators become complicit in these acts of unfairness.

For example, the interpretation of the rules for testing seems particularly harsh and bureaucratic in Florida. An article in the *South Florida Sun-Sentinel* highlights the state's zero-tolerance policy for children who *must* take the test in spite of emotional trauma or face being held back a grade.[38] No flexibility in test procedures was allowed for a 14-year-old child who lost her brother to a shooting and was still mourning; or for the 15-year-old whose father had hung himself in their home, causing the son to suffer anxiety attacks afterward. In fear that students and their parents would take advantage of any leniency in the rules, the school system and all the personnel in it become oppressors of some of the children.

Stories such as these are numerous. In Louisiana, one student who was in a car accident that claimed the lives of a brother and sister—leaving her paralyzed from the chest down and afflicted with a brain injury forcing her to relearn basic math and how to hold a pencil—was forced to take the regular state exam. This practice frustrates educators who are forced to be complicit in acts of cruelty against their own students. In the words of this student's principal, "It's unfair and it's mean. We are hurting the children we are supposed to be helping the most."[39]

Bubble kids

High-stakes testing is forcing educators to pay most attention to the "bubble kids" or the "cusp" kids, which ultimately punishes the high and

Box 3.5 High-Stakes Testing and a Crisis of Caring for Our Schoolchildren

The following interview with philosopher of education Nel Noddings took place in 2000 and was posted online at Teachers.net.

Question: Is there a way high-stakes testing can be considered caring?

Noddings: This is just the right question. No, I think this is what might be called fake caring. People claim to care and institute these tests in the name of caring and equality, but the kids do not feel cared for and teachers are demoralized. Caring requires a response of recognition for the cared-for. Politicians are making names for themselves [with these high-stakes tests], but the end result so far seems to be an undermining of care and trust—and not much by way of real improvement in learning either.

To care we have to know the cared-for. Time spent in building relations of care and trust are vital to teaching. When those relations are established, everything else goes better, and the teacher has a chance at helping the student to find meaning in what is being taught. I make a distinction between caring as a virtue and caring as a relation. Caring as a virtue means that we act from our own framework and try to do what we think the other needs. In caring as relation, we work with the needs expressed by the cared-for. And we judge what we do, not from the perspective of our own virtue, but by the response of the cared-for. This accounts for the widespread claims by teachers who care and the corresponding claims by kids that "nobody cares."

When we live with kids, work with them daily, we should be able to make well-informed judgments in much the way good parents do. That means less, not more formal evaluation. I travel the country giving talks and listening to people. Teachers are sick of the testing and disgusted with the pernicious comparison of kids, schools, districts, and states. Teacher educators are ready to rebel. I really wish parents would refuse to send their kids to school on test day and that teachers would back them up on this. We need to reclaim the strength of our professional judgment.

Adapted from a discussion with Nel Noddings sponsored by Teachers.net and moderated by Marty Kirschen, available online at *http://teachers.net/archive/testing032300.html*. Noddings is the author of two books relevant to this discussion: *The Challenge to Care in Schools: An Alternative Approach to Education* (New York: Teachers College Press, 1992) and *Caring: A Feminine Approach to Ethics and Moral Education*, 2nd ed. (Los Angeles: University of California Press, 2003).

low achievers. This problem was made obvious in a recent story in the *Los Angeles Times* that discusses the "cusp" kids—those almost at the point of passing the high-stakes test, perhaps needing a little extra teaching time to help them to pass.[40] In some schools that are trying to make adequate yearly progress to avoid sanctions, these students get all the school's attention, including special tutoring. The students who are performing less well academically are score suppressors—they get little in the way of attention and no special resources. The schools have effectively written them off. The story makes clear that the increased importance of achievement indicators has taken away some of the humanity of these educators.

A study by Jennifer Booher-Jennings of Columbia University found evidence that teachers and administrators mobilize and divert all their resources to the bubble kids—those on the cusp of passing the test. Their approach is not unlike what British researchers refer to as "educational triage":

> In the service of increasing a school's aggregate test scores on the English national secondary school assessment, students are divided into three groups: non-urgent cases, suitable cases for treatment, and hopeless cases. Schools then effectively ration their resources by directing them toward students believed to benefit the school's aggregate performance most: the suitable cases for treatment.[41]

Booher-Jennings found evidence that these "hopeless" cases were sacrificed in the name of focusing all resources and instructional attention on the bubble kids. Some of the methods used to do this included (1) time in class focused on giving bubble kids extra help either one on one or in small groups; (2) literacy teachers having special sessions with the bubble kids throughout the school day; (3) after-school and Saturday tutoring targeted to the bubble kids; (4) summer school programs for K–2 students serving the bubble kids; (5) music, gym, and library teachers, in lieu of teaching their assigned subjects, engaging in test-preparation activities with small groups of bubble kids.

BES is a prekindergarten through fifth grade school located in the Brickland Independent School District in Texas. At BES, approximately 90 percent of students qualify for free or reduced-price lunch, and all the students are Hispanic. At BES, as with elementary schools across the state of

Box 3.6 Teach the Bubble Kids—Forget About the Rest

Teacher, Beck Elementary School, Texas (pseudonym)

I guess there's supposed to be remediation for anything below 55 percent, but you have to figure out who to focus on in class, and I definitely focus more attention on the bubble kids. If you look at her score [pointing to a student's score on her class test-score summary sheet], she's got 25 percent. What's the point in trying to get her to grade level? It would take two years to get her to pass the test, so there's really no hope for her. . . . I feel we might as well focus on the ones that there's hope for.

Another teacher explains, "If you have a kid who is getting a 22, even if they improve to a 40, they won't be close—but if you have a kid with a 60, well, they're in shooting range. Bush says that no child should be left behind, but . . . the reality in American public schools is that some kids are always going to be left behind, especially in this district, when we have the emphasis on the bubble kids. Some are . . . just too low."

Jennifer Booher-Jennings, "Rationing Education in an Era of Accountability," *Phi Delta Kappan* 87, no. 10 (2006): 756–61; Jennifer Booher-Jennings, "Below the Bubble: 'Educational Triage' and the Texas Accountability System," *American Educational Research Journal* 42, no. 2 (2005): 242.

Texas, third-graders must pass the state test in order to be promoted to the next grade. School-level aggregate scores also determine the success or failure of the school. One month before the last administration of the third-grade reading test, BES purposely directed all of their attention to the bubble kids—effectively leaving all other kids out. Any student who had scores between 45 percent and 55.6 percent on the next to last administration of the test was the focus of these special activities. Teachers were cajoled into giving these students the most attention. Because the state mandates that students who failed the First TAKS administration receive reduced-class-size instruction during the school's literacy block (a 10:1 ratio), the school had to get creative in order to meet this requirement. College students were hired to monitor the "regular" classrooms while teachers left the room to tutor students who had failed. They tutored for about

1.5 hours a day. The teacher assigned "seat work" to the students who remained in the regular classroom to complete quietly, under the supervision of their "baby-sitters." All teachers opposed this policy:

> My thing is that the kids who failed shouldn't take the time away from the other kids. They failed because they weren't ready, and they weren't going to be ready. I would have retained them anyway. Out of the four [in my class] who failed, three of them should have been retained in second [grade]. There's just too much emphasis put on these kids who failed, and it's taking time away from everything else.[42]

As one educator put it, "To say that hope is absent for a ten-year-old child is a particularly telling comment on how dramatically the accountability system has altered the realm of imagined possibility in the classroom."[43]

CONCLUSION

It appears to us that the most important problem emerging from reading these stories is the loss of humanity that high-stakes testing produces: not just in the treatment of the special-education students and those with special psychological problems, but also in the treatment of poor, immigrant, and minority children who are likely to be score suppressors, not score increasers. Teachers and administrators are beginning to treat the score suppressors and the score increasers in the same way that children on the playground treat them. When forming teams in baseball, basketball, and track, the score increasers (the best hitters, shooters, and runners) are the ones who are picked first. Those perceived as the score suppressors are picked last or not picked at all. They endure public, often daily humiliation on the playing fields of the school. Now the same incentive system is found inside the classroom. Some schools and districts are treating the academically weak among their students as pariahs. They are to be gotten rid of or labeled in some way so as not to take the tests and bring down the average.

We must emphasize that the source of the problem lies in the policy, not with individual teachers or administrators. The models we have for public education and for the roles to be played by teachers and administrators throughout the country have become corrupt. When rigidity replaces flexibility and cruelty replaces compassion, we see our educational system in decline. This decline is not due to the promotion of accountability but the promotion of a faulty accountability system. As Campbell's law would predict, the pressure to demonstrate progress in educational achievement using test scores makes corruption inevitable. We see LEP students ignored, pushed aside, or at the mercy of a curriculum that has become culturally insensitive, rigid, and cold. We see special-education students and others who may score low on academic tests reviled, and we even see gifted children handled in unacceptable ways.

It is true that since NCLB was first passed, the laws regarding testing of special-education and English-language learners have been adjusted. And it is also true that there is some benefit in drawing attention to the education of special education and LEP students. They have not always been given a high-quality education. When high-stakes testing is the mechanism chosen to bring about school change, however, unintended and mostly negative effects for those groups of students still exist. Because low-ability but perfectly normal children, special-education, and LEP children are the most likely to have difficulty passing tests—tests used to determine sanctions and rewards at the school and district level—we can expect these children to suffer the most from the inevitable workings of Campbell's law.

CHAPTER 4

STATES CHEAT TOO!
How Statistical Trickery and Misrepresentation of Data Mislead the Public

Another form of cheating or educational distortion that emerges in a high-stakes testing environment is the act of manipulating data at the district or state level. When so much rides on a few solitary data points (e.g., test scores, dropout rates, high school completion rates), then Campbell's law predicts that humans become human, not surprisingly. Not unlike other animals, humans seek to avoid pain and are drawn to pleasure. It is disappointing, perhaps, but not surprising that humans will engage in activities that will make data related to their job performance look as favorable as possible. Just as someone selling advertising in a magazine might distort the truth about its circulation, state or district administrators might distort and manipulate test scores or dropout rates to avoid sanctions and to obtain rewards.

While the departure of "weaker" students raises test scores (as we discussed in chapter 3), their rates of high school completion are also monitored and used as another indicator of school success (or failure) for a school or a district under NCLB. The stakes attached to this evaluation parallel those assigned to achievement: good graduation rates means large bonuses and/or public accolades for superintendents or state officials, whereas lower graduation rates lead to public shame or even termination. Thus, as Campbell's law might predict, because the indicators have assumed great significance, they are quite likely to become corrupt. We discovered that when it comes to reporting the number of students who have dropped out or have completed high school (and obtained a high school diploma), school districts have simply fudged the data or lied in order to look more favorable.

HIGH SCHOOL COMPLETERS AND DROPOUTS

Under NCLB, all high schools are mandated to include—as part of their accountability reports—a measure of how successful they are at "finishing" students. Although the federal government requires that states report their graduation rates (number of students who complete high school within an "average" period of time), lax oversight and inadequate student tracking systems essentially assure that, by design or by accident, the states will misrepresent how well they're doing. Not surprisingly, they err on the side of looking more favorable.

On the surface, the definition of a high school graduate seems pretty straightforward—anyone who completes all the requirements and obtains a high school diploma within the average time span of four years (if starting in ninth grade) is a high school graduate. But a closer analysis reveals it just isn't this simple. Although a large majority of students fit this definition of high school graduate (some estimates suggest approximately 70 percent of students nationwide graduate "on time"), we know that if we allow a longer time span for graduation, say five or six years, this estimate hovers around 82 percent on average (and when broken down by ethnicity, 85 percent for whites, 95 percent for Asians, 75 percent for Blacks, and 74 percent for Hispanic).[1] Regardless of the time frame, however, there are debates about how best to account for those students who "disappear" and do not graduate (i.e., the remaining 20–30 percent). For example, many students move around from school to school, and district to district, as family fortunes wax and wane. Others, particularly those of Mexican origin, move in and out of the country. In the case of African American students, too many end up incarcerated. Inadequate tracking systems mean that the schools students leave have no way of knowing where they went. They cannot determine if a student dropped out or simply changed schools. Under these circumstances, it is easy and tempting to paint a positive picture of what happened to the disappeared students.

In spite of the challenges involved in tracking students, states have usually tried to provide a reasonable estimate of how well they are doing "finishing" their students. But because there is no federal oversight or guidelines, the states (and the districts upon whose data they rely) vary widely in how they track, monitor, and report on their students. In a recent audit, the Education Trust analyzed all the states' documentation submitted to the federal government in January 2005. Among other things, they documented the states' progress toward an improved graduation rate. They found that almost every state inflated the number of students they reported as having graduated (we report on these discrepancies later).

Another indicator that becomes corrupt when systems are lax and incentives are high is the school, district, or state dropout rate. According to the federal government, a dropout is officially defined as someone who leaves school before graduating.[2] Students who transfer to another school or leave to pursue a GED are not considered dropouts. States that have inadequate tracking systems often do not count students who leave school because they cannot track where these students go. By not counting them as completers or as dropouts, schools eliminate them from calculations altogether. Thus, dropout rates look more favorable.

Fudging the number of high school dropouts

The ongoing problem of how to account for dropouts always provided states an opportunity to fudge or mask real dropout rates. NCLB now provides the motivation for states to actually engage in such deception. When so much is riding on this single indicator, it is even more likely that educators will opt for an accountability method that paints the most favorable picture possible—even if that method involves lying.

Dropout data is itself an indicator of a district's productivity. So when a district increases its dropouts and pushouts to influence its test scores, it then has the problem of presenting its dropout rate for public scrutiny. In Houston,[3] a Sharpstown High School dropout and his mother noticed that the high school he should have been attending had no dropouts recorded for that year. Since that was obviously not true, the mother, with the help of a local newspaper, began an investigation. She found that 462 students had left Sharpstown and were reported to be in charter schools or other schools, even though Sharpstown administrators had not asked these students where they were going and had no knowledge of what they were doing. None was recorded as having dropped out! Sharpstown had started out with some 1,000 ninth-graders who, by the time they were seniors, numbered about 300, even though the school had recorded no dropouts.

In 2000–1, the year that Houston said it had a 1.5 percent dropout rate, about 5,500 left school and over half should have been counted as dropouts, but were not. For his leadership of the Houston school district, superintendent of schools Rod Paige was honored by McGraw-Hill and, on the basis of his record as a school leader, was elevated to the highest educational position in the land, secretary of education, under President George W. Bush. For their outstanding urban education programs, Houston received $1 million from The Broad Foundation. And prior to the announcement that it was not telling the truth, the Sharpstown high school staff received bonuses based on good attendance, low dropout rates, and *increased test scores*. Sharpstown and Houston are models of the applicability of Campbell's law.

Houston also had another indicator of success that it was quite proud of—the rate of college attendance by its high school graduates:

> At Jack Yates High School here, students had to make do without a school library for more than a year. A principal replaced dozens of experienced teachers with substitutes and uncertified teachers, who cost less. And yet from 1998 to 2002, Yates High reported that 99 percent to 100 percent of its graduates planned to attend college.
>
> Across town, Davis High School, where students averaged a combined SAT score of 791 out of a possible 1600 in 1998, reported that every last one of its graduates that year planned to go to college.
>
> Sharpstown High School, a high-poverty school that falsely claimed zero dropouts in 2002, also reported in 2001 that 98.4 percent of its graduates expected to attend college.[4]

These reports were completely false. As with the dropout scandal, Secretary of Education Rod Paige refused to comment. One of Houston's principals, who asked not to be identified for fear of reprisals, made the following comment:

> Lower-level administrators inflated their figures in the hope of attracting the children of active, involved parents. More students also mean more money from the state. On paper, her school claimed that almost all of its graduates were headed for college. In fact, the principal said, most of them "couldn't spell college, let alone attend."

Houston is not alone. Tall tales emerge from all over Texas. A 2003 analysis by *Education Week* found that half of the 108 schools throughout Texas that they studied, where 70 percent or more students were considered at risk of academic failure, claimed a dropout rate of 1 percent or less. A closer examination, however, revealed that many schools' enrollment actually decreased by 30 percent or more by the time ninth-graders reached twelfth grade.[5] Texas, of course, is not alone. In Freeport, New York, as revealed by a state probe, the actual dropout rates ran more than five times higher than those reported by the district. In November 2003 a state audit found that as many as 255 students (or 10.4 percent) of the high school's enrollment dropped during the 2000–1 school year. In contrast, the district had reported to the state only losing 46 students during that time. The state department of education found that 175 students, not 46, should have been counted as dropouts.[6] And in California, by some estimates, the dropout rate hovers around 11 percent of all students; if one looks at graduation rates, however—the difference between student graduation rates and the number of students enrolled in ninth grade—the rate rises to 32 percent.[7]

In Chicago, although public records suggest the city's dropout rate has been falling over time, an independent analysis suggests that it has actually been going up. The discrepancy is explained by the fact that the city excludes approximately 27 special or alternative schools from their reporting—a practice that is entirely antithetical to the goals of accountability. As William Leavy, executive director of the Greater West Town Community Development Project, notes, "You can't just throw your hands

Box 4.1 Not Counting Those Who Need to Be Counted Most

NCLB provides some flexibility to districts for determining which test scores are to count toward accountability and which can be considered "unaccountables." In the Houston Independent School District, the largest in Texas and the seventh largest in the nation, the average school excludes 8 percent of its students from its "accountables." Almost one-third of Houston schools (31 percent) exclude more than 10 percent of their students from scores used for accountability. By any measure, this is not an insignificant number of students.

Moreover, some demographic groups have much higher numbers of mobile—and thus unaccountable—students. In Houston, an average of 16 percent of special-education students and 11 percent of African American students are not counted in schools' scores because they have not been enrolled in a school for a full academic year. Ironically, the very students NCLB was designed to target are often those least likely to be counted.

Jennifer Booher-Jennings and Andrew A. Beveridge, "Who Counts for Accountability? High-stakes Test Exemption in a Large Urban School District," in *No Child Left Behind and the Reduction of the Achievement Gap: Sociological Perspectives on Federal Education Policy*, ed. Sadovnik et al. (New York: Routledge, forthcoming). See also Jennifer Booher-Jennings, "Rationing Education in an Era of Accountability," *Phi Delta Kappan* 87, no. 10 (June 2006): 756–61.

up about the high-risk kids and say they don't count if you want an accurate picture of what's going on."[8] According to his report, one of the most severely troubled neighborhoods has produced more dropouts than graduates. In 2001–2 this one school system graduated 15,653 seniors while 17,404 students in grades 9–12 dropped out.

Playing with numbers and manipulating the results

In Massachusetts, there is strong (and vocal) opposition to the high-stakes testing of student performance on the Massachusetts Comprehensive Assessment System (MCAS). There, the stakes are very high for teachers and students, and thus the potential for manipulating data is great. Because of previous problems with data reporting, when state passing rates were released in 2004, they were examined closely.[9] It was certainly in the state's self-interest to have such data reassure the public that the testing system was working.

Anne Wheelock and colleagues on the National Board on Educational Testing and Public Policy at Boston College noted that the state claimed that 96 percent of the class of 2004 had passed the MCAS and thus would graduate high school. What the state failed to disclose, however, was the dropout rate. The class of 2004 had lost 18,232 students from grades 9–12. That represents a 23 percent dropout rate and makes the actual passing rate of the 2004 graduating class 74 percent, not 96 percent.[10] Moreover, if you look at the cohort beginning at grade 9, instead of just the survivors at grade 12, then the pass rate for African Americans and Latinos was 59 percent and 54 percent, respectively. This way of reporting the data paints a different picture.

Massachusetts state officials did the same thing when reporting the numbers of special-education students who passed the state tests. Their press release of May 7, 2003, reports that 5,268 out of 7,307 grade 12 special-education students had passed the MCAS and would graduate that spring.[11] The state declared the passing rate of these students to be 72 percent. But once again the state left out the nonsurvivors, the many pushouts and dropouts who left along the way. Using ninth-grade special-education enrollments, the pass rate was recalculated by Anne Wheelock and her colleagues as 42 percent, not 72 percent. Less than half the class of 2003 managed to graduate, thus inflating the MCAS pass rate substantially.[12]

As Campbell's law predicts, indicators that take on inordinate value are corrupted. It appears that the Massachusetts State Department of Education was not presenting all the data to the public. They did not engage in a conspiracy to deceive the public, as appears to be the case with the administrators in Houston. Nevertheless, they did not tell the entire story, telling only the piece of the story that made them look good on the indicator of interest.

These are not isolated cases. Most states are in the business of inflating numbers when it comes to high school completion. For the year 2001–2, states had to submit to the federal government their graduation-rate data.

According to the Education Trust, most states are making themselves look good by manipulating how they calculate graduation rates. For some states, they simply calculated the percentage of twelfth-grade students who graduated. By using this formula, states can "honestly" portray how many students received a high school diploma. But again, what is not factored into this equation is the number of students who were lost, expelled, pushed out, or dropped out along the way. So a school might enroll 1,000 students in ninth grade, only have 500 in twelfth grade, graduate 475 out of that 500, and then report a graduation rate of 94 percent when in fact it is probably closer to 50 percent.

New Mexico, for example, did exactly that when they reported a graduation rate of 90 percent.[13] North Carolina also used the same formula and reported an incredible 97 percent graduation rate for the year 2002–3.[14] When compared with an independent calculation of graduation rates, the Cumulative Promotion Index (CPI), created by Christopher Swanson of the Urban Institute,[15] the "success" of these two states was a more alarming graduation rate of 61 percent and 64 percent, respectively.

Table 4.1 shows huge differences between some states' own calculations of graduation rates versus the CPI rates estimated by Swanson and his colleagues. Yet we are unsure whether even Swanson has it correct. As we write, an intense debate is going on in the literature related to the recent publication of Mishel and Roy's computations of contemporary dropout and graduation rates.[16] Their work appears to be the most accurate yet, and it suggests that high school graduation rates actually are at historic highs.[17] Although racial and ethnic differences exist, it may be that the current dropout crisis in America is confined to about 10 percent of America's high schools and that, in other schools and districts, the rates of graduation are, indeed, quite high. Clearly, graduation rates and dropout rates are not easy to calculate. But they are also subject to distortions by bureaucrats and researchers who are self-interested. Thus, data associated with these indicators are particularly susceptible to the effects of Campbell's law.

We should also keep in mind that some groups wish to see high dropout rates in order to remind people of how "awful" our public schools are and, therefore, to promote privatization. Others hope for data that show public schools in a better light. On one thing only do all researchers

Table 4.1 Comparison of State-Reported Graduation Rates and CPI Calculated Rates

State	State-Reported Grad. Rate 2002–3 (percent)	CPI 2000–1 (percent)	Difference (percent)
Alabama	N/A	61	N/A
Louisiana	N/A	65	N/A
Massachusetts	N/A	71	N/A
North Carolina	97	64	33
New Mexico	89	61	28
South Carolina	78	51	27
Mississippi	81	58	23
Nevada	75	55	20
Delaware	83	64	19
Indiana	91	72	19
Texas	84	65	19
California	87	69	18
Tennessee	76	58	18
South Dakota	96	79	17
Oklahoma	86	70	16
Colorado	84	69	15
Maine	87	72	15
New York	76	61	15
Hawaii	80	66	14
Kentucky	79	65	14
Wisconsin	92	78	14
Florida	66	53	13
Ohio	84	71	13
Connecticut	89	77	12
Iowa	90	78	12
Kansas	86	74	12
West Virginia	83	71	12
Arkansas	82	71	11
Illinois	86	75	11
Michigan	85	74	11
Missouri	84	73	11
New Hampshire	85	74	11
North Dakota	91	80	11
Pennsylvania	87	76	11

(continued)

Table 4.1 (*Continued*)

State	State-Reported Grad. Rate 2002–3 (percent)	CPI 2000–1 (percent)	Difference (percent)
Maryland	85	75	10
Minnesota	88	79	9
Nebraska	86	77	9
Virginia	82	74	8
Arizona	74	67	7
Georgia	63	56	7
Montana	84	77	7
Oregon	81	74	7
Rhode Island	81	74	7
Utah	85	78	7
Vermont	84	78	6
Wyoming	77	72	5
Alaska	67	64	3
New Jersey	89	86	3
Washington	66	63	3
Idaho	81	80	1

Source: Daria Hall, *Getting Honest About Grad Rates: How States Play the Numbers and Students Lose* (Washington, DC: Education Trust, 2005), *http://www2.edtrust.org/NR/rdonlyres/C5A6974D-6C04-4FB1-A9FC-05938CB0744D/0/GettingHonest.pdf.*

agree—namely, that poor and minority students, particularly from inner-city schools, are not graduating at high enough rates.

Misleading indicators are endemic to a system with no oversight, no accountability, and no support for creating sensible tracking systems. Furthermore, in the United States, there is no consistency across states in how students are tracked.

As Daria Hall of the Education Trust notes,

> some states used questionable graduation-rate definitions, while others provided no information at all about the graduation rates of the students who are facing the biggest challenges in high schools—low-income students,

> students of color, students with disabilities, and students with limited English proficiency. Not only did the [U.S.] Department [of Education] allow states to report inaccurate and incomplete data with no consequence, it actually made the problem worse by communicating the NCLB graduation-rate requirements differently in different places.[18]

The real story of dropouts

Reports of inaccurate or misleading data are certainly part of what Campbell would predict and are alarming in and of themselves. What is more alarming to us, however, is what such reports mask: a real national crisis in which a growing numbers of students—especially poor and minority students—are leaving school. For example, The Civil Rights Project at Harvard University highlights a distressing trend that reveals discrepancies in dropout data and the tragedy of lost educational opportunities for minority and poor students:[19]

> When graduation rates for each racial group were calculated for each state, the racial gap between whites and most minority groups was pronounced. However, closer examination of the data for each minority group revealed that across 50 states, there were a few states where the gap was non-existent or reversed. For Blacks the gap averaged 24.7 percentage points nationally and ranged from 0.0 (Alaska) to 41.3 (Wisconsin) percentage points. For Hispanics, the disparity average for the nation was 21.7 points and ranged from being 6.2 points (Louisiana) higher than whites to 43.4 (New York) points below. For Native Americans the average was 23.8 below whites nationally, but had the largest range from 2.8 (Alabama) above to 56.4 (Pennsylvania) below. Despite these wide ranges, in every state (except Hawaii) that had disaggregated data for at least one minority group, there existed a large (5 or > points) and negative gap compared to whites.[20]

This dramatic variation among ethnic groups in graduation rates across the nation is found regardless of the method used to calculate those rates. This is what is so alarming. High-stakes testing does not appear to be any kind of solution to the real problem of unequal education and unequal opportunities offered to our poor and minority student body. Moreover, a recent report by John Warren and colleagues unveiled the disturbing research finding that high school exit examinations lower the graduation rate. An analysis of data spanning 1975 through 2002 finds that the institution of exit exams—particularly those that are difficult to pass—is significantly associated with lower public high school completion rates and higher rates of General Educational Development (GED) test-taking. They find that these relationships are even stronger in states that have higher concentrations of racial and ethnic minority students and those from poverty.[21] Thus, it seems that one significant effect of consequence-based testing is to deny students—especially poor and minority students—an official high school diploma and, therefore, the chance for a more productive life.

Our research on high-stakes testing and progress through high school

In our own research, we have created a scale that quantifies the amount of pressure felt by students, teachers, administrators, and parents as a function of each state's high-stakes testing system. We call our scale the Accountability Pressure Rating (APR).[22] To date, we think it is the best instrument for looking at the impact of high-stakes testing pressure on student outcomes.[23] We developed our scale by first identifying states with complete sets of NAEP data over a long period of time. We found 25 such states. Then, using a procedure to sample fairly from news stories, we compiled articles about testing from the leading newspapers in each state. This gave us 25 thick portfolios of articles and commentary that we gave, two at a time, to over 300 educators. We asked each educator for a simple judgment: Which of the two states you are judging exerts more pressure on students, teachers, and administrators to perform well on the state's high-stakes tests? This allowed us to scale the states from lowest to highest in pressure related to test performance. Once we had the states ordered from lowest to highest in pressure, we could correlate the Accountability Pressure Rating with many other things, such as NAEP performance and rates of progression through school.[24] We found an alarming, but not surprising, outcome (see table 4.2).

Table 4.2 Correlation of Accountability Pressure Rating (APR) and Progression Through Various School Grade Levels

	CORRELATIONS WITH APR				
Grades	American Indian	Asian, Pacific Islander	Black, non-Hispanic	Hispanic	White
8–9 (1999–2000) Progress	−0.377	0.167	0.282	0.25	0.078
8–12 (1999–2003) Progress	−0.359	−0.043	−0.101	−0.348	−0.155
9–12 (2000–2003) Progress	−0.149	−0.143	−0.274	−0.434	−0.146
10–12 (2001–2003) Progress	−0.159	−0.118	0.01	−0.309	−0.053

Source: Sharon L. Nichols, Gene V Glass, and David C. Berliner, "High-Stakes Testing and Student Achievement: Does Accountability Pressure Increase Student Learning?" *Education Policy Analysis Archives* 14, no. 1 (2006), *http:epaa.asu.edu/epaa/v14n1.*

As can be seen, the great majority of these correlations are negative—indicating that the greater the pressure to achieve on high-stakes tests, the *less* likely it is that students will stay in school through twelfth grade. The progression rate for grades 8–12 or 9–12 is negative for every ethnic or racial group. The higher the pressure, the lower the progression rate. A simpler way to say this: As the pressure to pass tests goes up, so do dropout rates. This is especially true for Hispanic students. These data add to a growing body of literature that suggests high-stakes testing, particularly high school exit exams, may disproportionately disadvantage minority youth.

Data trickery: Keep your eye on the indicator

A spring 2006 report by Education Sector[25] examined states' data reporting and uncovered some interesting ways states manipulate their

Box 4.2 How Students Are Racially Transformed Before Our Very Eyes and Split Up into Tiny Pieces, Too!

NCLB requires that when scores are reported, ethnic/racial test performance be disaggregated so we can see how various groups are doing. These scores must be reported if there are 30 or more students in a category. And at least 95 percent of the students in each ethnic/racial category need to have been tested, so that we get a reasonable fix on the scores of students in each group. Arizona has chosen five groups to report on: white, black, Asian/Pacific Islander, American Indian, and Hispanic. But students don't always fall neatly into these categories since there are many children of American Indian and Hispanic parents, or of white and black parents, or who believe themselves to be a different racial group (South Asians, for example). The test forms, therefore, have an "other" category that students can check if they choose to.

Arizona came up with a unique way to use these "other" students. If 95 percent of one of the five ethnic/racial categories had not been tested at a school site, they simply changed some children's self-identified race! For example, if a student who is half Asian and half white selected "other" as her ethnicity on the AIMS test, the ADE could count her in the black subgroup to help meet the 95 percent tested requirement. A student from the Middle East who selected "other" may become a Native American if need be to make sure the Native American subgroup meets the 95 percent requirement. Even students who select one of the five ethnic/racial groups that Arizona had chosen to report on could be reassigned if their group had an overcount compared to the state's database. For example, if the state database showed 78 white students enrolled in the school but 80 students self-identified as white on the AIMS test, then the Department of Education could count the two extra white students as black, Asian, Native American, or Hispanic.

Children could be split into pieces, too. Fractions of students could be counted so a high-scoring white child in a school with an overcount of whites can be split up, with half assigned to one ethnic/racial category and half to another. We haven't a clue how that gets done, but chances are this guideline was used to make data look better. When the stakes are high, creative ways to avoid censure and obtain rewards will always be found.

Arizona Department of Education, *Adequate Yearly Progress*, vol. 2 of *Arizona's School Accountability System Technical Manual* (Phoenix, 2004). See also Wayne E. Wright, "Intersection of Language and Assessment Policies for English Language Learners in Arizona" (PhD diss., Arizona State University, 2004).

accountability measures.[26] One such indicator is student achievement. Under NCLB, schools must demonstrate that, over time, more of their students are achieving a level of "proficiency" across all state curriculum standards as measured by the state's own achievement test. Because NCLB allows for some flexibility in how proficiency is calculated, not surprisingly, many states take advantage by setting low standards of test performance to achieve the designation of "proficient," giving the appearance that their students are achieving at very high levels. For example, Mississippi claims that 89 percent of their fourth-grade students scored at or above proficient on the state's reading exam. However, if you look at how Mississippi fourth-graders performed on the "audit" test, the NAEP, it shows that only 35 percent of Mississippi fourth-graders scored that well. The reverse situation happens as well. Massachusetts has the highest fourth-grade NAEP reading scores in the nation, and yet ranks fifth from the bottom of all states in the number of fourth-grade students who were proficient on the state exam (the MCAS). Thus, Mississippi seems to set their standards too low and Massachusetts too high, though there is no way to know if that is true. Who among us is wise enough to proclaim that a certain score means you are more proficient, but one point less means you are not?

Figure 4.1 illustrates the dramatic differences between state-level proficiency and NAEP performance for fourth-grade math.[27] This kind of statistical gymnastics is enough to make one's head spin, but it illustrates a very deep problem embedded in the high-stakes testing game—when significant consequences are tied to a single indicator, corruption, manipulation, and distortion are likely to follow. As Kevin Carey from Education Sector notes, this kind of flexibility in a high-stakes environment sets up a "perverse" system where low standard-setting gets rewarded and high standard-setting gets punished.

Principals and teachers in states that establish high standards under NCLB are under intense pressure to improve, while similar educators in states with low standards are told that everything is fine and they're doing a great job. Students in states that set the bar high for school performance have access to free tutoring and public school choice when their schools fall short; students in identical circumstances in other states

Figure 4.1 2005 State vs. NAEP Results, Fourth-Grade Math

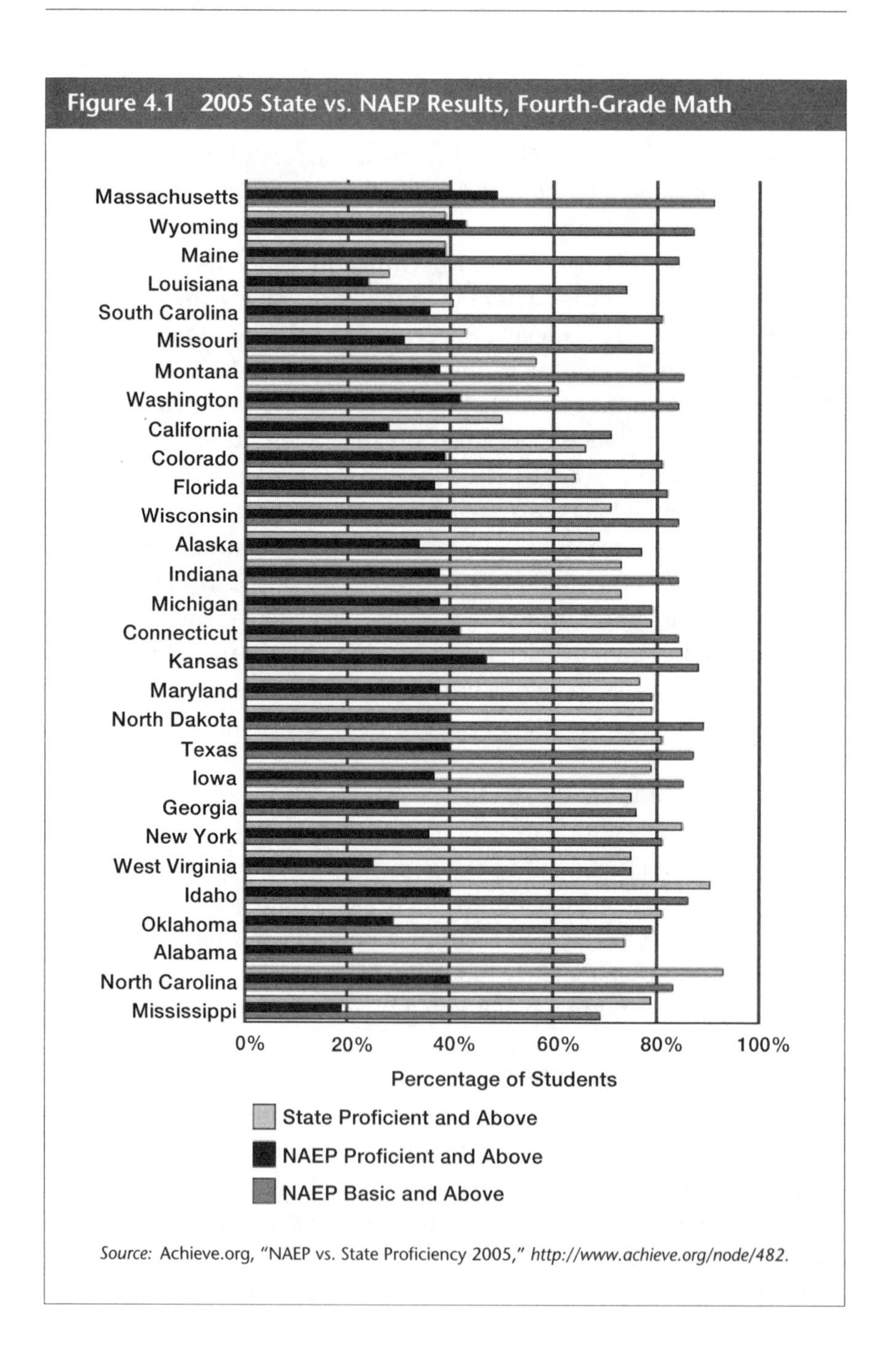

Source: Achieve.org, "NAEP vs. State Proficiency 2005," *http://www.achieve.org/node/482.*

must do without. The result is a system of perverse incentives that rewards state education officials who misrepresent reality. Their performance looks better in the eyes of the public and they're able to avoid conflict with organized political interests. By contrast, officials who keep expectations high and report honest data have more hard choices to make and are penalized because their states look worse than others by comparison.[28]

Setting the cut scores on standardized tests is also an activity that is highly susceptible to Campbell's law—especially since it is an arbitrary endeavor in the first place.[29] As an example, think about driving tests. Suppose there are 40 items on the driving test derived in a sensible manner from the rules for driving in a particular state. Then, how many of these items does an examinee need to answer correctly before we say that person can have a license to drive? Do 26 or more items correct make for a proficient driver? That would be 65 percent correct. But if applicants for a license got 25 items right, one less than our passing score of 26, should they be prevented from driving because we are quite sure that they cannot do so competently? Is there really a difference between the driving skills of someone who gets 25 right out of 40 rather than 26?

Let's say we're "tough" and have high standards, setting the passing rate at 90 percent correct. At this cutoff, there are still four items that a test taker could get wrong. Might there still be some items on the driving test that are so important that getting such an item wrong *ought* to be grounds for an automatic failure? Would you ever want a driver on the road who cannot answer a question like this correctly: What should you do when you see a sign that says School X-ing? Even with a cut score at 90 percent, there is still the possibility for a test taker to get this item wrong. Is this acceptable? And if you set the tougher standard for passing, would English-language learners be able to pass the test in the same numbers as native speakers? Would that be okay?

What this example illustrates is that the decisions about what level of performance constitutes passing and what constitutes failing on a standardized achievement test are arbitrary. It is not surprising, then, that some states have played around with these cut scores in order to pass more students and avoid the consequences of NCLB. A perfect example of this comes from Arizona. In the spring of 2005, after high school students' abysmal performance on the state AIMS test (used to determine whether a student can receive a diploma), the state board decided to lower the acceptable pass rate on the test from 71 percent to 60 percent on the math test and from 72 percent to 59 percent on the reading test. State schools' chief Tom Horne was against this move, arguing that if the cut score was not changed, 55 percent of students still would have passed and those who failed would have two more tries.[30] He wanted tougher standards, the state board chose easier ones, and there is no way of judging who is being more sensible. Cut scores on tests, determining who is proficient and who is not, are political decisions. They are not scientific or psychometric decisions.

Box 4.3 Playing Around with Cut Scores: Historic Gains or Data Illusion?

Chicago public school students produced stunning double-digit gains on their state reading and math tests this year (2006)—results Mayor Daley hailed Tuesday as "historic" but others said could be illusory. For the first time, more than half of the city's public school students passed their state tests in third-, fifth-, and eighth-grade reading, math, and science. In eighth-grade reading, almost three-quarters of the students passed, up from just under 60 percent last year.

The jump in eighth-grade math—once the hardest test to pass—was astronomical, from roughly 33 percent passing to 66 percent. However, that increase came after state officials lowered the passing score from the 67th to the 38th percentile!

Monty Neill of FairTest said the gains are so big, "they could be an illusion for several reasons. The test may be easier, there's probably more teaching to the test . . . and the extra time produces gains that you wouldn't have seen earlier."

Rosalind Rossi and Kate N. Grossman, "'Historic' School Test Results," *Chicago Sun-Times*, July 12, 2006.

Another label states must apply to their schools in order to receive federal funding is "persistently dangerous school." Some states are bold enough to say they have no persistently dangerous schools. Well, that is probably true if you define "persistently dangerous" in terms of shootings, which happen very rarely. But in order to secure positive reputations and significant financial support, some states trivialize definitions of "dangerousness." For example, in Arizona's definition, they ignore "rape, gang violence, readily available illegal narcotics, and many other indisputably dangerous things."[31] Obviously, defining "persistently dangerous" is not any easier than defining "proficient." Does one include instances of theft? Assault? Physical threats? How often must it occur to qualify as a "persistent" situation? Should there be different definitions for elementary schools and high schools? If so, what are those distinctions? But as long as significant consequences (such as large financial resources) are tied to determinations of whether a school is safe or not, it will continue to encourage administrators to mislabel, undercount, and trivialize acts of violence. Just as academic accountability asks teachers to focus on test scores at the expense of the process of learning and academic growth, so too does safety accountability ask schools to focus on violence rates at the expense of understanding the potential causes of and treatment for such violent behaviors as bullying, assault, and other types of serious violence. Students become the collateral damage in this game when they attend schools labeled as "safe" although there actually is a pervasive culture of bullying, intolerance, and lack of adult support.

ERRORS IN DATA REPORTING

Errors of omission and deceit are sometimes blatant attempts to lie and cheat the public while making the school, district, or state look "better." If a state fudges its high school dropout numbers, as Massachusetts has done, or a district lies about its college entrance figures, as Houston has done, or a test is made patently easier, as Arizona has done, the public is deceived.[32] But there are also errors that are less devious, even unintentional, but no less harmful—especially when life-altering decisions are

Box 4.4 What Does It Take to Be a Persistently Dangerous School?

On March 17, 2005, 15-year-old Delusa Allen was fatally shot while leaving Locke High School in Los Angeles. Four months before that, several kids were injured in a riot at the same school, and last year the district had to settle a lawsuit by a student who required eye surgery after he was beaten there.

Violent crime is common at Locke. According to the Los Angeles Police Department, in the 2003–4 school year its students suffered 3 sex offenses, 17 robberies, 25 batteries, and 11 assaults with a deadly weapon, which was actually an improvement over past years. In 2000–1 the school had 13 sex offenses, 43 robberies, 57 batteries, and 19 assaults with a deadly weapon.

Sounds unsafe, doesn't it? Not in the skewed world of official education statistics. Under the No Child Left Behind Act, states are supposed to designate hazardous schools as "persistently dangerous" and allow their students to transfer to safer institutions. But despite Locke's grim record, the state didn't think it qualified for the label.

Lisa Snell, "How Schools Cheat," *Reason Online*, June 2005, *http://www.reason.com/0506/fe.ls.how.shtml.*

being made. In the rest of this chapter, we share the unbelievably large number of errors made by test companies—errors that not only alter the life of the students who take these tests but which should raise serious concerns regarding the validity of the tests in the first place.

In any large-scale testing system, three kinds of errors are possible: errors of *test construction* (test items with more than one correct response), errors of *scoring* (items marked wrong when they are right), and errors of *reporting* (reporting that 50 percent of students passed when actually 75 percent did). Typically, everyone concerned with testing does everything they can to avoid these types of errors. Nevertheless, errors occur, though in the past the consequences of such errors were less dire. In today's high-stakes testing environment, however, any such errors can be life-changing.

Errors in test construction

There have been many instances in which students, teachers, administrators, and even test designers identified test items that were incorrectly written or keyed. In some instances, it is even worse—the questions contain misleading or inaccurate data. For example, in Georgia teachers found significant flaws in the state's science exam:

> [High school physics teacher] Maley estimated [that] about 10 percent of the questions on the science section, which about 30 percent of students fail each year, had no best answer because of errors in information provided to students; had multiple correct answers; were ambiguous or were misstatements of science. Department officials acknowledge [that] the acceleration formula and periodic table were wrong, because of a printing error, and two questions were thrown out in scoring because of those mistakes.[33]

A similar situation occurred in Hawaii, where testing errors were brought to the attention of officials after teachers, students, and others found errors in the test.[34] In the *New York Times*, Diana Henriques reported:

> During a tutoring session last December, Jennifer Mueller, a high school student in Whitman, Mass., came up with a second correct answer for a question on the state's high school exit exam; an answer that the giant company that designed the test had never anticipated. When statewide scores were adjusted to reflect Ms. Mueller's discovery, 95 dejected seniors who had failed the test by one point suddenly found they could graduate after all.[35]

Students in Massachusetts also reported two right answers to an item in the eighth-grade science exam, leading to changed and higher scores for 1,367 students.[36] And in New York, 200,000 fourth-graders took a test with an item that might have "confused" the students.[37]

In Arizona, James Middleton, a mathematics educator and researcher at Arizona State University, analyzed items on the AIMS test, Arizona's high-stakes high school exit exam, released in 2001.[38] Middleton was looking for mathematical accuracy, the potential for multiple interpretations (which tends to cause confusion in children in a high-stakes situation, unrelated to their degree of understanding of the content), and contextual realism, in terms of any pragmatic context within which an item might have been embedded. Of the 38 core items released, 17 (45 percent) had some problem associated with them that could have caused a consistent measurement error, meaning that the score students received for that item might not have reflected their actual level of understanding of content or skill in problem-solving. Of those 17 items, 10 had problems significant enough to warrant their removal from the assessment. Here is an example of Middleton's analysis of the test and two of the items from the test designed by CTB/McGraw-Hill in 2001:

> The trouble begins on page 1, the AIMS Reference Sheet, on which are placed potentially useful formulas and theorems for the students to use in taking the test. Unfortunately, the students cannot trust the Reference Sheet as the formula for the volume of a sphere is incorrect. Instead of 4/3 pi r^2, the stated formula, the actual formula should be 4/3 pi r^3. Moreover, even if the student caught the mistake, they may not remember the value of pi, since the key on page one suggests that students use 3.14 or 22/7 as the value for ρ, [which is] the Greek symbol for rho, not pi.
>
> It gets worse from there.
>
> Problem 16: Alex is building a ramp for a bike competition. He has two rectangular boards. One board is 6 meters long and the other is 5 meters long. If the ramp has to form a right triangle, what should its height be?
>
> (A) 3 meters
> (B) 4 meters
> (C) 3.3 meters
> (D) 7.8 meters
>
> In this item, none of the answers is correct. The student is expected to use the Pythagorean Theorem ($\text{Hypotenuse}^2 = \text{Side1}^2 + \text{Side2}^2$). So, $(6\text{m})^2 = (5\text{m})^2 + (\text{EF})^2$. To maintain a right triangle, the only correct answer is the square root of 11 meters, one that is cumbersome in real life, and so requires rounding off to an acceptable level of accuracy. Depending on the convention for rounding, a reasonable height could be 3 meters (if the convention is rounding to the nearest meter), 3.3 meters (if the convention is rounding to the nearest decimeter), 3.32 meters (if the convention is rounding to the nearest centimeter), and so on.

> The answer marked as correct, 3.3 meters, is actually about 1.2 centimeters off (about $\frac{1}{2}$ inch). Any carpenter worth his or her salt would not make an error of $\frac{1}{2}$ inch given a tape measure that is precise to $\frac{1}{32}$ inch.
>
> Moreover, as a male, I cringe at the thought of a bike competition that requires riders to jump off 3.3 meter heights (between 10 and 11 feet, ouch!). Or if the rider is to ride down the ramp, a slope of 66 percent (33.5 degrees) is steep enough to scare the bejeebers out of me.
>
> Lastly, a 6-meter board? Come on! When was the last time you found a board of 20 feet at Home Depot? In short, the context within which the problem is embedded shows a lack of the everyday sense for numbers that is required in the *elementary* standards for Arizona children.
>
> If the released items are a representative sample, then this analysis indicated that over one-fourth of the State's mathematics assessment provides incorrect data to the state department of education, school districts, parents and children anxious to graduate.

Things did not get much better over time. The Arizona State Department of Education released 18 more items from the spring 2004 administration of the AIMS test. Now, only one-sixth of these items appears to be wrong or misleading.[39] But if 1 out of 6 items on the AIMS test is mathematically flawed, it could mean that up to 17 percent of a student's responses are marked incorrect when they should not be. For many of Arizona's students, just a few poorly written problems of this sort can cause them to fail the test and not graduate from high school.

Badly constructed tests do not just exist in Arizona. Here is the editor of the *Orlando Sentinel* weighing in:

> As a *Sentinel* editorial revealed last week, third-graders are likely to be tested on material written at a seventh-grade level or higher. Sentences in the state's sample test were too long-winded and complex for the average young reader.
>
> A look at the state Department of Education's Web site shows that fourth-graders fare no better. The average fourth-grader is likely to encounter FCAT essays that are better suited to much older readers. What's more, one essay contains a spelling error.
>
> An essay about silver ants from a sample fourth-grade test is written at the seventh-grade level, according to the well-known Flesch-Kincaid

> readability index. The index measures readability based on the length of words and sentences.
>
> Another essay from a previous fourth-grade FCAT also was written at the seventh-grade level, according to the index. The state posts only select items from FCATs given several years ago.
>
> The latter essay, about a butterfly farm, contains challenging words, such as chrysalis and hydrangea and hibiscus. It also refers to gulf "frittilary" butterflies and asks a question about the "frittilaries" in the essay. That word is so tough that it is frequently misspelled—including on this test. The correct spelling, according to *Webster's New World Dictionary* and scientific dictionaries and encyclopedias, is "fritillary."[40]

A report by the National Board on Educational Testing and Public Policy has identified many more examples of these and other types of errors.[41] Releasing a test with so many bad items is inexcusable. It means that test companies are spending too little on item-review panels and on item field-testing. But then, their incentive is money, and as is so often the case when money is the major objective, quality suffers. States are also at fault. States usually have commercial companies bid to get these contracts and often must pick the cheapest of those bids when awarding contracts. Because of this, states contribute to the process of having too many bad items on too many high-stakes tests.

Test-scoring errors

There are also many examples of scoring errors. As a consequence of being under pressure to get scores back to states, scoring companies oftentimes rush through the scoring process, which increases the possibility of making scoring errors. In Minnesota, about 8,000 students were unjustly denied a high school diploma because it was determined that they "failed" the test when in fact they did not. Subsequently, many of these students who were "wrongly" failed participated in a suit against the scoring company (NCS Pearson), which they won. The judge in the case was severe, writing "a scathing opinion" that said the company "continually short-staffed the relatively unprofitable Minnesota project."[42] Compensation did not

Box 4.5 Who Is Grading Our Children?

Dozens of this year's graders of Florida's FCAT exam were graduates of foreign universities who provided little more than copies of their college degrees, often written in a foreign language, to get a temporary job scoring Florida's high-stakes public school assessment test. Only a couple of the applicants provided transcripts of their college work showing they had taken math, science, and English courses.

Among them was a tourism major's transcript from the United States International University in Nairobi, Kenya, which revealed grades of A in beginning French and the principles of marketing but a D in composition and a C in algebra. A graduate of the University of the Andes in Bogotá, Colombia, earned Cs in two English classes.

It appeared there was no background check conducted to verify the educational information on the application and no indication which part of the state exam the individuals were hired to evaluate. The newspaper revealed that hundreds of the temporary FCAT evaluators had no apparent experience as educators or degrees in fields related to the academic subjects they were grading.

Senate Democratic leader Les Miller of Tampa, a candidate for Congress, sued the state and CTB/McGraw-Hill (responsible for the test scoring) to get the employment applications and background documentation of more than 2,500 individuals hired to grade this year's FCATs. According to Miller, "I have nothing against anyone who graduated from a foreign school, but if they got a D in composition, suppose they are grading the English test? We're talking about the most important test of a child's career. There is no accountability and it is shabby work."

Only some of the applications include a recent work history. Among these, there's a Romanian who majored in world and Romanian history and works as a cosmetologist, a physical education major from Hungary who sells jewelry, a science major from Colombia who paints houses, a biology and chemistry major from Sierra Leone who bags groceries.

Linda Kleindienst, "Critics Cite Lack of Documentation, Call for Overhaul of Hiring System," *Orlando Sun-Sentinel*, June 16, 2006. See also David Glovin and David Evans, "How Test Companies Fail Your Kids," *Bloomberg Markets*, Nov./Dec. 2006, *http://www.bloomberg.com/news/marketsmag/education.pdf.*

change the fact that Pearson's placement of profits before quality denied thousands of students the opportunity to participate in the once-in-a-lifetime tradition of walking across the stage at graduation. In another incident, in the fall of 2005 the Ohio State Department of Education reported that Measurement, Inc., had failed to correctly translate raw scores on the state's high school test into scores on a publicly reportable scale. The "scaling" mishap resulted in new scores for 5,000 of the 5,400 students who had taken the test the previous summer, including 900 students who had been told they could not graduate because they had failed the test, when they hadn't.[43] Errors like these in Minnesota and Ohio have changed lives forever.

The stories of simple human error and avoidable error are almost endless. In New York, 2,400 students in grades three, five, six, and seven were asked to retake a test (after they were mistakenly given the wrong practice exam), using a test booklet with a key that didn't match the answer booklet. "At one school in Brooklyn, teachers clarified the issue by writing on the blackboard that 'A=E,' 'B=F,' 'C=G,' and 'D=H.'"[44] Were students given extra credit for accurately decoding the adult-created problem with the answer key? Probably not.

Another example comes from the College Board, which admitted to scoring errors when they scanned the October 2005 SATs.[45] The scores of more than 5,000 students were inaccurately reported. As of March 2006, the College Board had notified colleges of the corrections for 4,411 students whose scores were too low—in some cases by as much as 450 points out of a possible 2,400.[46] Although many believe college admission decisions were not unduly affected by these errors, it seems as if a significant number of student scholarship amounts have been negatively affected. In New Jersey, students are offered scholarships on a sliding scale that is purely based on SAT scores. In-state students can earn anywhere from small stipends through full tuition, room and board, plus a laptop computer for combined scores of 1500–1600. At Franklin and Marshall, SAT scores are taken into account when scholarship decisions are made. For one applicant, a corrected score of 300 points meant the difference between a $5,000 scholarship and one worth $12,500.[47] For another student looking at schools with strong lacrosse programs, he was told his SAT scores were too low by about 100 points, causing him to apply to lower-division programs. After the corrections were made raising his SAT scores by 170 points, it was already too late, since he had already been accepted by New York Institute of Technology, a Division II school.

Test-reporting errors

There are also examples of reporting errors. These kinds of errors have all sorts of consequences. To students, it is likely a humiliating—and confusing—experience to first be told you failed a test, only to be told later that you passed. How does a student recover? To teachers and schools, being wrongly labeled "failing" is demoralizing and difficult to recover from, as illustrated in Nebraska, where the state had to apologize for incorrectly labeling seven schools as failing.[48] In Pennsylvania, it happened not once but twice that a school's publicly released report cards contained erroneous information, including bad achievement data that affected school-level ratings. There are literally hundreds of examples of all three of these types of errors.[49]

The U.S. Government Accounting Office (GAO), as part of its investigation into the functioning of NCLB, has also looked at this problem.[50] One of their major findings was that the problems of unreliable tests and test scoring are common. The report notes:

> Concern about the quality and reliability of student data was the most frequently cited impediment to implementing student proficiency requirements. . . . For example, officials in California indicated that they could not obtain racial and ethnic data—used to track the progress of designated student groups—of comparable quality from their school districts. Officials in Illinois reported that about 300 of its 1,055 districts had problems with data accuracy, resulting in those schools' appealing their progress results to the state. Similarly, officials in Indiana acknowledged data problems but said addressing them would be challenging. Inaccurate data may result in states incorrectly identifying schools as not meeting annual goals and incorrectly trigger provisions for school choice and supplemental services.

We are not surprised that many of the larger testing companies are involved in many of these cases, though we are sure they did not set out to deliberately and negatively impact the lives of students and their families. But they are the ones that bid low on test-development contracts and then they have to find ways to make profits, which they apparently do by sacrificing quality. Harcourt Assessment is implicated in several of these cases. For example, in California in 1999,[51] they were named in a $1.1 million lawsuit for mismanaging the statewide assessment system. What is disturbing is that such companies, and the states that hire them, don't seem to learn. Later, in 2003, they were also responsible for distributing exams and answer booklets that did not match up in New York[52] and for distributing tests that contained errors in Hawaii.[53] Other well-known testing companies that have had similar problems include NCS Pearson and CTB/McGraw-Hill. Everyone is compromised when legislation such as NCLB requires millions of new standardized tests to be developed, scored, and used in decisionmaking in just a few years. The testing companies are overwhelmed fighting for competent personnel and searching for more efficient mechanisms for scoring tests. At the same time, the integrity of the decisions made about these high-stakes testing programs is in the hands of bureaucrats and budgetary analysts rather than educators. This is not a healthy situation.

Student errors, honest mistakes

Students can err, rendering their test score invalid. For example, students may miss a line when marking their test booklet, throwing the remainder of their test answers off by a line. The College Board estimates that only a fraction of test takers encounter this problem (about 100 test takers out of 1.5 million).[54] We cannot help but believe that this error rate is quite different for fourth-graders than it is for college-bound high school seniors. There seems to be no mechanism to catch such errors. And when stakes are high, we think there should be.

So how does Campbell's law relate to errors of testing? In these stories we focus more on the problems of test companies rather than those of teachers and students. We find in these stories evidence of companies trying to maximize profits. But what we don't know is if the best psychometrics and business practices are being sacrificed for the sake of those profits. Campbell might worry about that, and we do too. The dual concerns of timeliness and cost put testing companies under great pressure to produce products that may not be as good as they should be. When such indicators as tests scored per minute, essays read per hour, or profits earned from test development take on undue value, as they sometimes do, Campbell's law enters the picture. When important decisions are to be made about students, teachers, and schools, those individuals and institutions have a right to demand high-quality tests and trustworthy data. Despite a cost to taxpayers of hundreds of millions of dollars annually to implement NCLB, the high-stakes testing systems common across the nation do not all meet the standards of quality that the public deserves.

CONCLUSION

Bureaucracies do what they can to perpetuate their organizations. So it is no wonder that districts and states have fudged, manipulated, or otherwise used data to make themselves look good. We need to keep, therefore, a sharp eye out as we monitor the effects of NCLB on our schools and youth.

The particular problem we focused on in this chapter is that because of high-stakes testing, poor and minority students are disproportionately more likely to drop out. Though the figures are disputed, some suggest that nationally, about 68 percent of students who enter ninth grade will graduate "on time"—or four years later. Currently, the graduation rate for white students is probably hovering somewhere between 75 and 85 percent, whereas in many parts of the country, only half of the black, Hispanic, and Native American students earn their diplomas. Newer data suggest that higher rates of graduation hold for all ethnicities, particularly if the window for completion of high school is extended from four years to six and if earning a GED is counted as completing high school. Regardless, there are dramatically lower rates of graduation for certain minorities and for poor children, some of which is connected with the imposition of high-stakes testing.

What is most moving about stories of testing errors is the harmful consequences for test takers and their teachers. These harmful effects occur simply as a function of living in high-stakes testing environments. Without high stakes being attached to the tests, they could be produced more cheaply and quickly because we could use more authentic assessments and live with less reliable measures of the complex phenomena we wish to assess. Absent the high stakes attached to the scores on these tests, the nation might be more tolerant of errors in test construction, scoring, and reporting. Our nation could easily muddle through with not-so-perfect tests and arbitrary cut scores for defining proficiency if the consequences attached to those scores and standards of performance were not so serious.

Students, teachers, administrators, parents, and community members have a legal and moral right to the highest-quality tests if the scores on those tests are being used to make important decisions. If we cannot afford the time and the money to give the public that kind of data, we cannot continue to insist on high-stakes testing. On the other hand, if such important decisions were not based solely on test scores and a wider spectrum of performance indicators were used to make decisions about the performance of students and schools, we might get along with much less costly and perhaps even more valid accountability systems.

CHAPTER 5

WHAT HAPPENS TO VALIDITY WHEN INDICATORS ARE DISTORTED AND CORRUPTED,
the Many Ways That High-Stakes Testing Promotes Such Distortion and Corruption, and How Those Practices Lead to Confusion About What Test Scores Mean

In his 1975 paper on planned social change, Donald Campbell stated that undue emphasis on a single indicator would distort the very process the indicator is meant to evaluate. If, to avoid sanctions or receive rewards, you do things to make an indicator move in the desired direction, then you probably won't be measuring the entity that you originally set out to measure. In psychometrics, this is called a validity problem. Validity concerns the *interpretation* you make from all the evidence you have about an indicator that you use. It is the ambition of all who work with indicators to be able to say, "From the evidence I have accumulated I am pretty sure that I am actually measuring what I want to measure." Validity is the most important characteristic of a test.

FOUR KINDS OF VALIDITY TO WORRY ABOUT

A simple way to think about validity is to think of its four commonest forms, the four Cs: content, construct, criterion, and consequential validity. The most difficult form of validity to determine is usually construct validity, and some consider it the most important of the four. But we think it is hard to specify which form of validity is most important. Each type of validity contributes to the overall judgment about a test's meaningfulness, so each has weight when trying to assess if a test is actually working as it should.

Content validity

When an instrument appears to be measuring what it purports to measure, we say it has content validity (or content-related evidence of validity). Teachers, for example, must be sure that when they put together, say, a geology test, they are really measuring geology knowledge and skills. They must ensure that test questions pertain to what they have taught through various classroom presentations, videos, textbooks, and field trips to which the class had access. Whether we are judging a short weekly test, a longer end-of-course test, or a high-stakes standardized test, questions on the test should be about the content that students had an opportunity to learn. If questions on a geology, reading, or mathematics test reflect the actual curricula that students were supposed to learn, then the test can be said to have content validity. Years ago in a famous court case involving the use of tests for personnel selection, applicants for a "linesman" job at a power company were administered a difficult test involving reading comprehension. The content of the test had nothing to do with the skills needed to do the job. The test lacked content validity and, as a result, other kinds of validity too.

Content validity of the standardized (high-stakes) tests that accompany NCLB should be relatively easy to establish because these tests are required by law to reflect the curriculum standards each state has chosen to teach. Content validity is determined by the judgments of one or more experts who simply compare the intended content at some grade level with questions on the test. These judges decide whether the test is made up of a reasonable sample of questions covering the curriculum students were to have learned. If test questions reasonably map onto the intended curriculum, then it has content validity.

It is relatively easy to ensure that content validity exists, and when it

Box 5.1 Content (and Construct) Validity Problems: Who Chooses the Content for the Standardized Test? Does the Test Really Measure the Achievement of Poor Children in Arizona?

In the following comments, teachers of young children talk about the high-stakes standardized test their poor and minority students in Phoenix, Arizona, had just taken:

> *Mrs. H.:* I think these tests are made by people who live only in the central part of the country.
>
> *Mrs. S.:* I don't think they are teachers. The questions are worded so poorly that you know that this is not written by a teacher in the classroom who knows her children at their level. In the section on compound words, the sample question gives you three different choices, and the kids are supposed to read them and pick which one of them is the compound word. Well, the one that is in the sample is "peanut."
>
> *Mrs. M.:* They [the students] are all giggling because they are second-graders, and they can't get over the fact that their teacher just said "pee."
>
> *Mrs. S.:* Even as a grownup, you don't think of "peanut" as being a compound word ("pea" and "nut"). A teacher would put "bed-room" or "base-ball," something that students would know [is] definitely a compound word. You think, "Who in the world thought to word it this way or to put this example in there?"

One question on the test mentioned a blizzard, something Mrs. H. thought would be hard for students from Phoenix to comprehend. Another example showed a picture of a bus along with a question asking where the child was going. Most of the students picked grocery store as the response because in their real life they go to the grocery store by bus (they are poor and have no cars). However, the "correct" response was school. Teachers felt that these kinds of questions were simply not pertinent to the experiences of their students.

Annapurna Ganesh, "Bubbling In: Standardized Testing in Second Grade" (PhD diss., Arizona State University, 2004).

does, you have part of the evidence you need to interpret the score a student gets as a valid indicator of what has been learned in some curriculum area. The items on the test are then seen as trustworthy indicators of the domain of knowledge you set out to assess. Unfortunately, a recent report suggests that high-stakes state tests of student achievement, designed to comply with NCLB, do *not* assess state standards as well as they should.[1] The researchers examined standards and systems for aligning tests with those standards in every state. Only 11 states appeared to have done this well, while 9 had no documentation at all that this was even attempted. The other 30 states were in various stages of documenting the alignment of their tests with their standards. The concern, of course, is that if teachers teach to the standards, but the tests aren't aligned to the standards, then the test will underestimate the amount of content actually learned by students.

If the current tests do not represent state standards well, what are they measuring? We don't know, and we doubt whether anyone else does either. Without content validity, you have no chance at building a case for other types of validity that, when present, give confidence that test scores are meaningful indicators of students' knowledge and skills.

Construct validity

This type of validity deals with the question of whether a test measures the abstract attribute or characteristic it claims to measure. Questions about content validity ask if the items on a test come from the curriculum that was available to be learned. For instance, in a test of geometry, are the items drawn from the textbook or lectures to which students were exposed? Questions about construct validity (or construct-related evidence of validity) ask a far more difficult question: Is the test we use measuring the underlying characteristics we hope to measure, or is it measuring something else? That is, does the test actually assess students' knowledge of geometry?

A "construct" such as geometry knowledge, intelligence, or creativity is an abstract quality. We don't see constructs. But we try, nevertheless, to measure them through testing. Testing is a way to make these hypothetical constructs visible. We invent tests of geometry, intelligence, or creativity, and we collect evidence about how each of those tests works so we can decide if they really do seem to measure the constructs they claim to measure. For example, if we claim to measure the construct of intelligence, we expect that persons who test high will succeed more often at complex jobs, successfully solve more problems which they are confronted with at work and at home, cope better with the environment they are in, and so forth. Someone who scores low on intelligence should show the opposite characteristics if the test is successful at assessing the underlying but hidden construct of intelligence. Similarly, a person who scores high on tests of geometry ought to be able to apply geometric knowledge in the real world, like determining the area of carpet needed for a room they are remodeling, the shortest distance from point A to point B in a city, the cubic footage of their house so they buy the proper air-conditioning unit, or the way a two-dimensional drawing of a house would look in three dimensions. The hidden constructs that states are required to assess under NCLB are such things as reading ability in the third grade or knowledge of mathematics in the eighth grade. The latter construct might include geometric and algebraic knowledge among the many hidden mathematical constructs we also want to test at the eighth-grade level.

So we never see a person's intelligence or creativity, or their reading and mathematics abilities, directly in a test. Those are all constructs that are hidden from us. Our assurance that we are accurately measuring the constructs in which we are interested would most likely come from assessing those skills in natural settings as people go about their lives. But skills and abilities demonstrated in the real world are usually too expensive and time-consuming to assess. Thus, we invent tests to stand in for the skills and abilities we really want to assess. Test scores are the guesses we make about how much and how little of the construct a person possess.

The tests we invent to comply with NCLB are designed so we can make inferences about such constructs as ability to read and comprehend, skill at mathematical computation and thinking, and scientific knowledge. If we measure the constructs sensibly, we might also compare students within a state with one another, asserting that students in this school or district have more or less of this thing we measured than do students in another school or district.

When we build our tests for use in low-stakes testing environments, assessing achievement after students have had ordinary, typical classroom instruction, we usually feel confident that the achievement test scores tell us something about students' mastery of the underlying constructs of interest. But things change quite a bit when the stakes get high. The inference we make about the score reflecting the construct of interest is suddenly suspect. Here is how it works. Suppose that in Mrs. Drew's fourth-grade class, in preparation for the state reading and language arts examinations, the students were extensively drilled on items that were suspiciously like those used on the state exam. We still get a score on a test, but is the test a valid indicator of the underlying construct of interest in this class? Or, has the construct changed from something that might properly be called "achievement in reading under ordinary conditions of instruction" to something that might better be called "achievement in reading under conditions of extended drill with items very similar to those used on the tests." If we can measure the original construct accurately, we may get information that could help inform the policies that would allow schools and students to achieve more. But if the students taking the test had extensive test preparation, what is it that we have learned about them? The construct that is of interest to us is reading in real-world contexts. But the ability to make inferences about ability from a test score is seriously compromised when extensive test preparation takes place. And if Mrs. Drew's entire school or district did this but other schools and districts did not, what can we say authoritatively about what the state scores mean in terms of the underlying construct of interest? Would it be fair to compare our measure of the construct in one district with a measure of the construct in another district?

The issue we deal with here is whether the constructs we measure under high-stakes testing are those that we think we are measuring. With low-stakes testing, the links between the test and the underlying construct we are trying to measure are probably not compromised, but under high-stakes testing distortions occur. Mrs. Drew, by her heavy use of a test preparation program, may have invalidated our interpretation of what the reading test actually measures.

This is a complex issue. Let us look at another example, then. Suppose that in another school with high-stakes testing, Mr. Valdez temporarily cuts the creative-writing and social studies courses out of the curriculum, reduces the music and physical-education program to twice a week, and abandons art altogether. Time spent on reading and mathematics is increased accordingly. Has construct validity been compromised due to the pressures of high-stakes testing and the need to do well? Are our indicators of important processes being distorted and corrupted? These are the serious questions we take up in this chapter.

The problem of distortion and corruption of our indicators, the undermining of validity, is no trivial problem. Establishing the validity of any test is important, but that process takes on even more importance when test scores are used to make important decisions about such things as grade retention and promotion, whether high school degrees are withheld or granted, or whether bonuses are given to teachers and administrators for high student scores. It is morally imperative that we be certain about what a test score means if life-altering decisions about teachers and students are going to be made on the basis of that score.

Criterion validity

A test's ability to predict certain kinds of achievement now, or in the future, is what we are concerned about when we ask if a test has criterion validity (or criterion-referenced evidence of validity). If we wanted to use a test to select students for admission to a school, a special curriculum, a course, or a job, we must make sure the test is valid for that purpose. In the United States, the well-known ACT and SAT tests, taken by huge numbers of high school seniors, are selection tests of just that type. Although they predict very little else in life, they actually do a reasonably good job of predicting college grades in the early semesters of college attendance. High school grades and rank in class, however, also have predictive power when college grades are the measure we want to predict. But many people do not consider grades and rank-in-class "objective" indicators because they are susceptible to all sorts of influences, such as difficulty of classes

Box 5.2 A Classic Example of How Test Preparation Distorts and Corrupts the Construct to Be Measured

From the files of George Madaus comes a classic case of test preparation. After World War II, the government of Ireland wanted to assess writing. So in 1946 they put a prompt for writing into a primary-grade national examination and looked at samples of the writing it elicited. The prompt, and an essay chosen as representative of good expository writing, were subsequently given to teachers:

1946 Prompt: The Bicycle Ride

Exemplary essay

> I awakened early, jumped out of bed and had a quick breakfast. My friend, Mary Quant, was coming to our house at nine o'clock as we were going for a long bicycle ride together.
>
> It was a lovely morning. White fleecy clouds floated in a clear blue sky and the sun was shining. As we cycled over Castlemore Bridge we could hear the babble of the clear stream beneath us. Away to our right we could see the brilliant flowers in Mrs. Casey's garden. Early summer roses grew all over the pergola which stood in the middle of the garden.

In 1947 they gave another prompt and learned that it elicited many essays that looked remarkably like the one chosen as exemplary the year before. One of many examples is given next:

1947 Prompt: A Day in the Bog

Sample response

> I awakened early and jumped out of bed. I wanted to be ready at nine o'clock when my friend, Sadie, was coming to our house. Daddy said he would take us with him to the bog if the day was good.
>
> It was a lovely day. White fleecy clouds floated in a clear blue sky. As we were going over Castlemore Bridge in the horse and cart, we could hear the babble of the clear stream beneath us. Away to our right we could see the brilliant flowers in Mrs. Casey's garden. Early summer roses grew all over the pergola which stood in the middle of the garden.

The Ministry of Education told teachers that they didn't mean students should copy the exemplary essay from the 1946 test. They said it was merely an illustration of what they took to be good writing. So in 1948 they provided a new prompt, and here is a typical essay from that year's cycle of testing:

Box 5.2 (*Continued*)

1948 Prompt: A Bus Tour

Sample response

> I awakened early and sprang out of bed. I wanted to be ready in good time for our bus tour from the school. My friend, Nora Green, was going to call me at half-past eight as the tour was starting at nine.
>
> It was a lovely morning. White fleece clouds floated in the clear blue sky and the sun was shining. As we drive over Castlemore Bridge we could hear the babble of the clear stream beneath us. From the bus window we could see Mrs. Casey's garden. Early summer roses grew all over the pergola which stood in the middle of the garden.

Moral: People will do whatever they must to make the indicators by which they are judged look the way they need them to look. Campbell's law was applicable in Ireland about 60 years ago, and it looks no different there than anywhere else. Too bad we don't learn lessons from old and solid findings.

Adapted from George F. Madaus and Vincent Greaney, "The Irish Experience in Competency Testing: Implications for American Education," *American Journal of Education* 93 (1985): 268–94.

and number and talent of classmates. Therefore, in admission decisions for college, they are not used as much, or weighted as much, as are the scores from the ACT and SAT exams. Nevertheless, as predictors of later performance in college, rank and grades are usually about as good as the tests, and in some cases they may even be better.[2]

Precisely what is predicted by the scores on the high school examination and the tests in grades 3–8 that are required by NCLB is not well known. But those scores are likely to have some validity in predicting a student's grades in classes in the next school year. Essentially, any properly constructed curriculum-based test in reading, mathematics, or science should predict the score on another properly constructed curriculum-based test of reading, mathematics, or science administered soon after the first test, say, the next semester or the next year. So a test that is technically well designed and meets the requirements of NCLB probably will identify students who will need help in the future. This is precisely the stated goal of NCLB: through testing, to identify students who need help early, and then not leave them behind! But about the same accuracy in the prediction of future achievement by students can be obtained from end-of-course exams, teachers' judgments of portfolios of student work, or even by simply asking teachers to give their personal rating of student achievement in a curriculum area.[3]

Teachers' judgments actually appear to be as good as high-stakes tests in predicting future achievement in the early grades, so there probably is no justification at all for testing young children under NCLB. Nevertheless, NCLB demands that high-stakes standards-based achievement tests be used to assess student achievement, even the achievement of our very youngest students, despite evidence of the predictive validity of teachers' judgments and the much lower cost of obtaining these judgments. It should also be noted that low-stakes standardized achievement tests have been available for half a century, and they give precisely the same information as the high-stakes standardized tests. They identify quite reliably who might need more help in a curriculum area. America's problem has never been in identifying these children; it's been in deciding whether to spend time and money on them, particularly those who are poor and of color.

Our concern with the criterion validity associated with high-stakes tests is that there exist few studies of what these tests predict. In essence, schools, teachers, parents, and students simply receive a score and inferences are made from that score, but we have no way of knowing if those inferences are predictive of future circumstances (e.g., dropping out of high school, being retained for a second year in a grade, being admitted to a particular class of colleges). We end up assuming that if these high-stakes achievement tests have content and construct validity, then a score on that test might be a trustworthy indicator for predicting a student's success in later work. But we don't know whether that is true or not. The prediction is a guess: it is not usually determined empirically, as it should be. It is like letting students into college, or keeping them out, on the basis of high and low scores on the ACT or SAT, without ever having checked whether those scores actually do predict college grades.

Even if the test is useful in determining a student's current achievement level on content about which we all agree, or even if the test has measured growth in achievement over time, we still have no valid knowledge about whether we can make the inference from the test score that a student is *proficient* or not in the domain of knowledge the test was designed to cover. States must pick a score on a test they have devised that convinces the federal monitors that a student is really proficient in reading, mathematics, and science. They are claiming that they are measuring the construct well and can determine how much of that construct the student possesses.

But the judgment that a student is at the proficient level in some domain, or below or above that level, based on a test score, will always be problematic since no one knows where to draw the line—the cut score—on an achievement test that separates the proficient from the less (and more) proficient. The setting of a cut score determining who is proficient and who is not proficient is always a political decision (see chapter 4), and therefore it is unverifiable through psychometrics.[4] In sum, even with judgments of high content validity, which should be easy to obtain, and even with judgments about construct validity suggesting that the test measures what it says it measures, a high-stakes standards-based test may still be problematic in terms of what it predicts and will always be indefensible when it comes to distinguishing the proficient from the nonproficient students on the construct of interest.

Consequential validity

The final kind of validity has to do with the consequences and decisions that are associated with test scores. Judgments about the consequential validity of a test rely more on personal values than do the other forms of validity. We judge how test results are used, asking who gets hurt, who gets helped, and is it worth it? As we hope we have made clear throughout this book, it is this type of validity we worry about most because considerable evidence is accumulating that test scores are hurtful and damaging.

In California, Massachusetts, Arizona, and other states, high school diplomas are denied thousands of students. Thousands of others leave school expecting not to pass the high school exit exams, and their numbers are disproportionately greater among black and Hispanic students. The use of high-stakes testing has important consequences for all these students and results in a disparate impact on the lives of minority students, in particular.

Given what we know about the lifelong earnings and the lifelong problems associated with not having a high school diploma, is our reliance on a single score, on a single test, to make a decision to withhold a diploma justifiable? Are we sure we want to live with the consequences of high percentages of minority students not finishing high school? Are there alternatives to this form of testing that have less merciless consequences?

Given that scores on these tests result in millions of students being left back in grade each year and that being over-age in grade is one of the best predictors of dropping out, do we want to live with the decisions that flow from these test scores? Given that the high-stakes test culture is hurting the morale of teachers and increasing teacher dropout and burnout due to tests,[5] is the continued use of high-stakes testing warranted?

Obviously, people will differ in their answers to these questions about the consequences of high-stakes testing. Some will ask whether high-stakes testing is improving test scores around the country, and if they answer yes to that question, the other consequences may not seem important at all. This appears to be the position of the U.S. Department of Education. Based on the slight rise in some of the NAEP test scores of 2004, Secretary of Education Margaret Spellings is on record as being pleased that NCLB is working so well.[6] What Secretary Spellings doesn't seem to realize is that the test scores for 2004 do not reflect the results of NCLB at all, since NCLB didn't become law until 2002, and most states hadn't put into effect their testing programs until well after that. Moreover, the rise in 2004 test scores that so impressed Secretary Spellings is really no different from the continuous rise in NAEP test scores that has been going on for about 35 years, *without* NCLB. Secretary Spellings also forgot to mention that 17-year-olds showed no gains whatsoever, in reading and mathematics, and even the reading results for 13-year-olds showed no gains. Furthermore, as we have made clear previously, there is little evidence of a relationship between the pressures for achievement that accompany NCLB and test scores on NAEP, indicating that the basic theory of action which undergirds NCLB is flawed. Moreover, it is not clear if the gains seen on three of the six NAEP tests can be clearly attributed to the use of high-stakes testing, since so much else is going on in education. Despite evidence to the contrary and common sense, Secretary Spelling sees clear signs of high-stakes testing under NCLB working well, and so she blithely ignores many of the negative consequences associated with high-stakes testing. Others among us, however, are convinced that NCLB is not working well, and so we worry a lot about the consequential validity of these high-stakes tests.

In sum, content validity ought to be achieved easily. Standards-based assessment ought to eventually result in a good match between tests and curriculum. This is the only form of validity about which we are sanguine. Construct validity is constantly being distorted and corrupted through high-stakes testing. If we end up unsure of the construct we are measuring, we will make inappropriate inferences concerning what a test score indicates about what a student knows and is able to do. Criterion validity is rarely investigated, but we can still expect that scores on one academic test will predict scores on other academic tests, so some criterion validity is assured if the criterion (say, math grades in high school) is very much like the predictor test (say, an eighth-grade math test). But will a high-stakes achievement test predict anything about a person's future achievement in life? Doubtful. Will the high-stakes test provide guidance for counselors about differential abilities in students? Not likely. So that no child will be left behind, will a high-stakes achievement test predict who needs help any better than would classroom grades, portfolios of student work, or teachers' judgments of competence? Probably not. Finally, we asked whether there are serious consequences associated with high-stakes testing that could be avoided by using other forms of assessment? We are sure that there are. In short, the validity of high-stakes testing is of great concern, undermining all the interpretations we might make from scores on these tests. In what follows, we highlight some of the common and concrete ways in which validity is compromised in high-stakes testing environments.

TEACHING TO THE TEST: ONE FORM OF DISTORTION AND ONE CAUSE OF TEST INVALIDITY

It is true that if we have a good test, then teaching to that test is appropriate.[7] Instruction and assessment would be aligned, as they should be. But there is a fine line between teaching to the test and teaching the test itself. That line is often difficult to see, and it is possible that some educators and test-preparation companies deliberately cross that line. This would corrupt the indicator, making it quite difficult to interpret any assessment so compromised.

What does it mean to "cross the line" in a way that threatens construct validity? One factor is time devoted to test preparation. Certainly, there are different forms of test preparation—some of which are perfectly acceptable, such as reviewing content that is likely to be tested. It is also acceptable, when children are young, to have them learn how to "bubble in" (fill in) the forms if that is the kind of answer sheet used. But other types of test preparation are much more questionable, such as when teachers spend excessive amounts of class time pushing rote memorization of likely content onto students.

We found numerous examples from schools across the country that had dedicated hours upon hours preparing students for the test—drilling, emphasizing rote memorization, teaching students how to take tests, reviewing over and over again the concepts that will be represented on the test, and giving multiple practice tests, all at the expense of other content, ideas, and curricula that may not be represented on the test. At some point a line is crossed, and it messes up the interpretation of what a test score means. Construct validity is compromised when that line is crossed. No longer are we measuring real-world math or reading skills. Instead, it becomes a test of how well students memorized math content or how adept students are at filling in test-booklet bubbles. In these instances, it isn't content mastery that matters but how well (or efficiently) students can memorize information that is rewarded.

New Hampshire is apparently on the lighter side of test-preparation time, where the average sixth- or tenth-grader spends up to 25 hours each year preparing for state exams. Third-graders spend about 18 hours in test preparation.[8] Twenty-five hours of preparation is the equivalent of about four days of instruction; 18 hours is the equivalent of about three days of instruction. Is this reasonable? We don't know. In another research study, in the state of Colorado more time seems to be spent in test preparation.[9] In this study, more than one-third of the teachers studied spent more than two weeks giving students old forms of standardized tests for practice. In Buffalo, New York, however, fourth-graders at D'Youville Porter Campus School 3 engage in work every morning that prepares them for the state assessment tests. According to the principal, "It's test after test after test. It's getting to the point where we're doing test preparation the whole year. We think we're testing kids to death."[10] And with the addition of all the new tests (NCLB requires students be tested in math and English in every grade from third through eighth), students will be taking a consequential assessment at a pace of about one a month.

Yet another state, North Carolina, seems to be winning the race toward having schooling be only about test preparation, with school days devoid of genuine instruction. Survey research found that 80 percent of elementary teachers in North Carolina reported that they spent more than 20 percent of their total teaching time practicing for high-stakes tests.[11] This is about the equivalent of 36 days of test preparation. But even more dismaying was that 28 percent of those teachers reported spending more than 60 percent of their time practicing for the state's tests. That would be over 100 of the typical 180 days of instruction spent in various forms of test preparation! When asked if this was more or less than in years prior to testing, 71 percent of the teachers said that they spent more time practicing for the high-stakes tests. In yet another survey of teachers and students,[12] 83 percent of teachers indicated concern that teaching to the test could become the norm, and 20 percent of responding students felt that teachers focused so much on test preparation that "real learning" was neglected.[13] These teachers and students may well be correct.

We have known for some time that as consequential tests approach, teachers increase their time in test preparation.[14] Some of that is sensible. But under the high-stakes testing requirements of NCLB, it appears that much of that increased time is inappropriate, both bad for teachers and children and destructive of the very indicator that is used to measure student achievement and the effects of schooling on its students. The pressure to engage in more and more test preparation often comes from school administrators: "One principal told his teachers not to introduce new material in the six weeks before the test; this time was to be spent on review, especially in formats used in the upcoming exam."[15] Similarly, it was found that 80 percent of the elementary teachers in Arizona were encouraged to raise scores on the standardized test used by the state, and 32 percent said that they were "required" to do test preparation with students. Twenty-eight percent of the Arizona teachers surveyed said they begin their test preparation at least two months before the test administration.[16] In Texas, the Royse City school district developed worksheets for teachers to use in test preparation. These worksheets articulated the specific objectives that needed to be taught throughout the year, ensuring that teachers focused on the content that would be on the test.[17] Is this crossing the line or just a sensible reminder for teachers about what is most important in the curriculum to teach?

In West Virginia, teachers acknowledge they basically know what the test will cover after about five years of distributing old test copies. But in case they don't, teachers there receive a set of helpful tips for preparing students for the test throughout the school year. The teachers are regularly told to (1) practice answering problems on a worksheet using a grid; (2) know what is tested on CTBS and teach these concepts early in the year and then review all year; (3) use test-preparation materials throughout the year, a little bit each day, and talk about why other choices are not right; and (4) practice testing comprehension using multiple-choice formats.[18]

Also in West Virginia, teachers in one county were given "Scoring High," a test-prep workbook to use to prepare students for the TerraNova/CTBS standardized tests in an attempt to specifically raise students' test scores. Teachers were given credit for their hard work in preparing students for the test. According to the county's director of counseling, William Mullett, "Finally, because of what other school systems were doing, we felt our students were being compared unfavorably. We leveled the playing field a little bit."[19] What we see here is the whole state undermining the construct validity of the test. If one district engages in extensive test preparation, then all the districts feel the need to do so. Each district worries that they will look bad and be shamed in the press or perhaps reconstituted under NCLB. So the rush is on to corrupt the indicator. High stakes will do that. But questions remain: Will students in West Virginia score higher on their state tests? Probably. Can we be confident that they acquired more academic knowledge and skill for use in their natural environment? Absolutely not! In all the states mentioned above, the construct we set out to measure has been distorted and corrupted. Some aspects of the validity of the tests in use are unknown.

The business side of teaching to the test

Many stories from around the nation make it clear that too much time is given over to test preparation, so much so that it has become a big business. Test-preparation companies provide tutoring for individual students and also offer large, formal curricula packages of test-preparation materials to schools and districts. These private enterprises are driven by profit, which means their test-preparation strategies need to "work." To work well, the test-preparation company needs an understanding of the test format and items for training students and teachers that are very close to the actual items and formats used on the tests themselves. Thus, there are incentives to cross the line and prepare students too directly for the test.

This seems to have happened in Tacoma in 1995, where CTBS scores were at the 42nd percentile and rose to the 63rd in a few months. Superintendent Rudy Crew was then hailed as a miracle worker, received a large bonus, and on the basis of this work was then promoted to the chancellorship of the New York City Public Schools. But to help get scores up, Dr. Crew had hired a "test prep" consulting firm, and the students were drilled on tests very much like those on the CTBS. Many practice tests with items suspiciously similar to the CTBS were used. The Tacoma miracle stopped (i.e., scores dropped) after Dr. Crew left Tacoma and the test-prep company stopped working there.[20]

Tutoring students who are designated as failing, in schools that are in their third year of failing to make adequate yearly progress (AYP) on state

Box 5.3 Commercial Test-Preparation Advertisement: For $29.95, Get Credit for Some Questions Without Really Even Knowing Anything About Them!

TAAS Secrets Study Guide

How to ace the TAAS test, using my easy step-by-step TAAS test prep study guide, without weeks and months of endless studying.

Dear Friend,

Are you interested in the only TAAS test study guide written by *actual* test experts, who painstakingly researched every topic and concept you need to know to ace your exam? Our original research into the TAAS reveals specific weaknesses never before discovered that you can exploit to increase your score more than you've ever imagined—and it's all available for less than the retail price of the rest of the filler-packed "guides" on the market. So, if you'd like to get the TAAS score you deserve, to quit worrying about whether you can score "good enough" to pass and to beat the graduation game so you can get your diploma, then this might be the most important letter you read this year. Now, I know you're probably skeptical. That's normal and healthy. Let me give you three good reasons we can back up what we claim:

Three Reasons to Believe What I Say

Reason one: In case you don't already know me, my name is Peter Morrison and I'm the head of a team of standardized test researchers who set out to find and exploit the weaknesses of the TAAS. I have very strict standards for who gets to work on the team—I demand the best for my customers, and only those who met my exacting standards made the cut. My company's name is Morrison Media LLC, a limited liability company operating under the laws of the state of Texas. Our main offices are in Beaumont, TX, with customer service and fulfillment facilities in Florida and Louisiana—our address is listed at the top of this page. We are the opposite of the fly-by-night outfits that are so common these days on the Internet. We maintain a full time research staff, all of whom are nationally recognized experts on standardized testing *and* (more importantly) have years of experience in cracking the code of the toughest exams.

(*continued*)

Box 5.3 (*Continued*)

Reason two: As the research team went to work, we were initially discouraged, since academic studies have revealed that test takers do not really benefit from traditional study guides and test-prep courses. But we knew there had to be a solution—if high performing students were not doing well on the TAAS despite near-perfect grades, there had to be a set of secret keys to the test that would open the door for these academically superior but TAAS-challenged students. A few days into the project, we started to have success to a degree that we never realistically expected. What we found was surprising, and in some cases so *ridiculously simple* that we wondered why others hadn't found them sooner. We put our findings together in a thorough, concise study guide that allows any student, at any skill level or TAAS score, to *improve his or her score dramatically* with a minimum of effort.

Reason three: I created this product because I was sick of the options available to test takers who really wanted to do well on the TAAS. Most of the guides on the market are nothing but 30 pages of instructions and 200 pages of useless unofficial practice tests. Even the better guides completely miss the boat—they try to *teach* the material, instead of *teaching the test.* Knowing geometry or vocabulary words isn't good enough for the TAAS—you have to know how to apply the knowledge—most test takers have already learned everything taught in these guides anyway. The reason some test takers do well on test day is that they have made the critical connection between the material they learned and how to use that material to succeed on the TAAS. Our guide is the only product on the market that addresses the difference between merely knowing the material and knowing how to use the material to *perform on test day.*

TAAS Secrets website, *http://www.taas-test.org.*

tests, is also big business. Tutoring companies earn anywhere from $1,300 to $1,800 per child, depending on the district. Innovative Ideas, a tutoring company housed in a three-bedroom, two-bath home in Memphis, Tennessee, earned nearly $790,000 from a local school district during the 2004–5 school year. Nationwide, the tutoring business has earned $2.3 billion since the passage of the NCLB legislation, which requires districts to offer tutoring.[21] By design, there is absolutely no oversight of these programs. The federal government has stated that it wants these providers to be free of oversight. Not surprisingly, instructors hired by these companies may have no credentials to be a teacher, let alone a tutor. Since there is money to be made, these teachers and the company executives often promote the company's success despite a lack of data supporting such advocacy. Some companies have walked into classrooms during instruction and barged in at pep rallies and on registration days to market themselves. Others boldly lie to parents, saying that their services are "guaranteed" and that by enrolling their child for up to 15 weeks, they will see a jump in their child's test performance.[22] Companies have used photos of students without parental permission to advertise their services, or they hire sports stars or host cheerleading camps to trigger student interest. What is important to remember is that test preparation and tutoring companies depend on student and school failure. They only make money if tests detect those failures. The indicators they want are those that will always find schools faulty. These businesses are big supporters of NCLB since over 90 percent of America's schools are likely to be identified as failing because of the impossibility of reaching the goals that have been legislated through NCLB. It is important to know who the supporters of NCLB are, and whether they have legitimate educational reasons for supporting the legislation or whether they have financial interests in giving their support to NCLB.

Teachers' and administrators' views on test preparation

Test preparation has its supporters. But for most teachers and administrators, the time allotted and the trivial nature of test-preparation programs is irksome. For example, in Texas, they have been teaching a single writing format as preparation for their state test called "the five-paragraph persuasive essay." In this approach, students are taught that each paragraph has exactly five sentences: a topic sentence, three supporting sentences, and a concluding sentence much like the introductory sentence. In honor of their last major state test, the Texas Assessment of Academic Skills

(TAAS), the teachers call this "TAAS writing" as opposed to "real writing." In their study of this issue, Linda McNeil and Angela Valenzuela write:

> Teachers of writing who work with their students on developing ideas, on finding their voice as writers and on organizing papers in ways appropriate to both the ideas and the papers' intended audience, find themselves in conflict with this prescriptive format. The format subordinates ideas to form, sets a single form out as "*the essay*" and produces, predictably, rote writing. Writing as it relates to thinking, to language development and fluency, to understanding one's audience, to enriching one's vocabulary and to developing ideas, has been replaced by TAAS writing to this format.[23]

Rubrics—clear rules and examples—are needed to score these essays. Although rubrics make sense intuitively, they raise validity issues. Rubrics standardize scoring, increasing the reliability that is so important for large-scale assessments. But the rubrics also standardize the writing that is to be scored. Standardized writing, however, is not necessarily good writing, because good writing features individual expression, which is not standardized. The standardization of any skill that is fundamentally an individual,

Box 5.4 Stifling Creativity in Writing

From the time they start taking the FCAT writing test in the fourth grade, Florida students are taught how to navigate the 45-minute exam. That's good for scores, critics say, but often terrible for the emerging writer. One student talks about how the test forces her to subdue her creativity. When she writes for pleasure, she strives for effect, atmosphere, and subtlety. But when she writes for the test, she takes no chances. On February 10 [2004], the next time the test will be given, she will do the best she can in five paragraphs, making three points and using the kinds of transitional words she has been told readers enjoy—"first," "next," "in conclusion." "It's like mechanics," the student says. "I do what they want, I spit it out, and then I move on."

Rebecca Catalanello, "Kicking the 'FCAT Essay' Habit," *St. Petersburg Times*, Feb. 1, 2004.

unique, or idiosyncratic skill complicates its assessment. This, of course, presents a validity problem because the assessment cannot then produce scores that support valid inferences about the writing achievement of our students in more natural environments. This is a basic construct validity problem. Under rubric writing and rubric scoring, our tests can end up measuring *not* the construct of *writing achievement* but the construct of *compliance to the rubric,* which is certainly not the same thing!

McNeil and Valenzuela provide another example of corrupting the indicator and the educators in the system by having teachers narrow the curriculum through drill activities, so that their students will perform well on Texas's high-stakes tests:

> High school teachers report that although practice tests and classroom drills have raised the rate of passing for the reading section of the TAAS at their school, many of their students are unable to use those same skills for actual reading. These students are passing the TAAS reading section by being able to select among answers given. But they are not able to read assignments, to make meaning of literature, to complete reading assignments outside of class, or to connect reading assignments to other parts of the course such as discussion and writing.
>
> Middle school teachers report that the TAAS emphasis on reading short passages, then selecting answers to questions based on those short passages, has made it very difficult for students to handle a sustained reading assignment. After children spend several years in classes where "*reading*" assignments were increasingly TAAS practice materials, the middle school teachers in more that one district reported that [students] were unable to read a novel even two years below grade level.[24]

On this issue, the voices of teachers and researchers have been well documented by Jones, Jones, and Hargrove in their excellent book, *The Unintended Consequences of High-Stakes Testing.*[25] They cite Alfie Kohn, who noted: "To be sure, many city schools that serve low-income children of color were *second* rate to begin with. Now, however, some of these schools in Chicago, Houston, Baltimore, and elsewhere, are arguably becoming *third* rate as the pressures of high stakes testing lead to a more systematic use of low-level, drill-and-skill teaching, often in the context of packaged programs purchased by school districts."[26]

Box 5.5 Teachers in Florida Discuss Teaching to the Test

Teacher A: "I can say one thing, if my kids learn one thing in third grade, it is this: how to pass a standardized test even if you are not familiar with the material. Now is that what our goal is? Perhaps we should revisit it."

Teacher B: "I have seen that schools are teaching to the test (how can you not?) and that is not a true reflection of student abilities. This is only a reflection of the abilities of each school to teach effective test-taking strategies, not academics."

Teacher C: "Schools aren't improving their academics as students score better on the FCAT. They are just taking more time to teach to the test and unfortunately, away from real learning. We aren't getting smarter students, we are getting smarter test takers. That is *not* what we are here for! . . . The schools who score well are focusing on teaching to the test at a very high cost to their students."

Brett Jones and Robert Egley, "Voices from the Frontlines: Teachers' Perceptions of High-Stakes Testing," *Education Policy Analysis Archives* 12, no. 39 (2004), *http://epaa.asu.edu/epaa/v12n39.*

A principal in another study reported: "The accountability system has an impact on everything we do. To focus on specific basic skills, you have to drill. We would like to get away from drill and pounding stuff into kid's heads; they don't remember it the next year. But if the accountability looks at scores to judge school effectiveness, you can't take your eyes off of basic skills."[27] Other researchers reported: "Everywhere we turned, we heard stories of teachers who were being told, in the name of 'raising standards,' that they could no longer teach reading using the best children's literature but instead must fill their classrooms and their days with worksheets, exercises, and drills."[28]

Teachers in Colorado have said similar things.[29] They reported using formats similar to the Colorado Student Assessment Program (CSAP) in regular instruction to help familiarize students to the official format of the CSAP; using commercially produced test-preparation materials similar to CSAP and test items released by the state to prepare students for the

CSAP; and spending time teaching test-taking strategies to prepare students for CSAP, with the teachers in low-performing schools spending about double the time that teachers in high-performing schools spend on test preparation. They were not at all happy about taking time away from what they knew to be a richer curriculum.

Harold Wenglinsky's research sounds a sadder note about the ubiquity of test-preparation programs.[30] Wenglinsky looked at 13,000 students who had taken the fourth-grade NAEP tests in 2000. He found that frequent testing actually reduced scores on NAEP and that emphasizing facts (over reasoning and communication) also reduced students' scores. Since both frequent testing and an emphasis of facts over reasoning are prevalent in most of the test-preparation programs we have examined, it is quite likely that many of the activities engaged in during test preparation are counterproductive and also compromise the construct validity of the tests to be taken.

NARROWING THE CURRICULUM: RESTRICTING ACCESS TO NONTESTED SUBJECTS

Related to the issue of teaching to the test directly is the issue of narrowing the curriculum so as to concentrate attention on just those subjects that are tested. The lack of respect for teachers' professional judgment about curriculum offerings as a function of high-stakes testing pressure is inappropriate and might be unhealthy for students. It also compromises the validity of the test since we cannot be sure what we are measuring if a good deal of traditional schooling is jettisoned so that the school subjects that are being assessed can be given more time. It is now quite clear that under the weight of NCLB, schools and districts reduce what they teach that is not on the test or remove from the curriculum subjects that are not likely to be contributors to test-score growth. Curriculum activities, like students, can be considered score suppressors or score increasers and are judged in a purely instrumental way. This plays out in odd and perhaps harsh ways. For example, for very young children the pressure to do more academics every day is increasing, while time spent in play and leisure is decreasing at a rapid pace. This means cuts to naps and recess for children in school.

Nap time is a daily ritual for the prekindergarten students at countless schools across the country. But in the increasingly urgent world of public education, is it a luxury that four-year-olds no longer can afford? "Nap time needs to go away," Prince George's County schools chief Andre J. Hornsby said during a 2004 meeting with Maryland legislators. "We need to get rid of all the baby school stuff they used to do."[31]

Recess is being questioned too. The *Waltham (MA) Daily News* reports that recess for elementary students has been cut one day a week to make time for high-stakes testing and to be sure they look good on NCLB requirements.[32] The report says that some nearby districts have completely done away with recess at the elementary level. The educators around St. Louis have cut back on recess and physical education too.[33] At one low-performing elementary school in Texas, where the pressure is on to raise test scores, teachers have also been taking away recess from students. Some teachers have decided to reduce their classes' recess to just 15 minutes *per week* in order to provide more instructional time for students. Other teachers, feeling pressure to do the same thing, are resentful:

> We only have recess one day a week for 15 minutes. You can't be caught out there. Oooo—I'm not sure what would happen. These people don't understand child development. I wonder if they ever went to college. Where are they getting their ideas from? They think we shouldn't have recess because we should focus on academics. This year I said, forget it, there's no way I can teach these kids if they don't have a break, so I've been taking them out.[34]

We applaud the fact that when the schools in the city of Tacoma, Washington, reiterated their ban on recess, the *Seattle Post-Intelligencer* editor was prompted to advise the school administrators to get a life![35]

Lunch is obviously wasted time, too, for those who succumb to testing pressure. A teacher at a district near Waltham, Massachusetts, expressed concern that lunch had been reduced at her elementary school to less than 15 minutes on many days so that more time could be put in on the rigorous curriculum areas. (Those are code words meaning the areas that are tested. It is as if music, art and social studies are not rigorous!) The school has abandoned traditional luncheon meals and started serving finger food—wraps and chicken nuggets—to get the students in and out of the cafeteria faster![36]

The Council on Basic Education is looking at some of the bigger issues of curriculum narrowing in the post-NCLB world, like the atrophy of the liberal arts in contemporary America.[37] Most of the areas they are concerned about (history, social studies, civics, geography, art and music, and foreign language) are not usually the focus of high-stakes testing. Therefore, under the pressure to succeed on the high-stakes tests, these courses are abandoned. The loss of such courses was found to be greatest in minority communities. It appears that we cheat our most vulnerable students of the curriculum that might most make them successful in the world—the liberal arts. The root of the term *liberal* in the "liberal arts" has nothing to do with the term *liberal* in the political realm. Instead, the essence of the liberal arts is *liberty*—with art, music, government, rhetoric, philosophy, and the like being the arts of free men and woman. Instead, we teach our poor and minority students what Benjamin Barber calls the servile arts,[38] business and law enforcement, catering and medical assistance, aerospace mechanics and computer technology. Wealthier students, if they are lucky, will get some of the liberal arts in their high schools and certainly will encounter them in their colleges. But poorer students may not be exposed to these ways of thinking in high school at all, and since their college attendance rates are low and apparently getting lower at the most prestigious schools, they may never get formal tutoring in the liberal arts. Not only will these individuals suffer, but, as Barber notes, we may be endangering our democracy as well.

The pressure of performing well on state standardized tests is squeezing out the arts everywhere, even in the schools of advantaged students. Massachusetts may well be a bellwether state. The public school systems there lost 178 teachers of the arts (visual arts, dance, music, and theater) over a two-year stretch, going from 3,996 in 2002–3 to 3,818 in 2004–5. Although much of the decline is attributed to shrinking budgets, many superintendents and school board members also note that the focus on language arts and math (both subjects that are tested statewide) may be

Box 5.6 A Sampling of Curriculum Cuts Associated with NCLB Legislation

Maryland, 2003: Anne Arundel County in Maryland loses 23 middle school art teachers.

Oregon, 2003: Rosenburg Public Schools in Oregon cancel seventh- and eighth-grade foreign-language classes.

Arizona, 2003: Arizona legislature cuts $7 million in arts funding to schools and other groups.

Wisconsin, 2003: Milwaukee has lost 9 percent of its art, music, and physical-education teachers.

Rhode Island, 2004: Providence eliminates elementary science and technology-enrichment classes.

Kansas, 2006: High school freshmen required to "double dose" their English classes to raise test scores, at the expense of electives.

California, 2006: Havenscourt Middle School requires its students to take two periods of all core subjects, drops funding for shop, art, music, and Spanish.

Claus Zastrow and Helen Janc, *The Condition of the Liberal Arts in America's Public Schools: A Report to the Carnegie Corporation of New York* (Washington, DC: Council for Basic Education, 2004); Heather Hollingsworth, "Students Double Up On Math and English," Associated Press, Aug. 4, 2006.

the reason for the concomitant increase in the number of English (145) and math (341) teachers. The Plymouth Public Schools, like so many others, are increasing time spent in English and math and have laid off three of their five middle school art teachers. Beginning in the fall of 2005, Stoneham has elementary art and music lessons in half-year stints rather than year round. Layoffs in Southbridge forced them to give elementary students art and music once every three weeks in the fall of 2005 rather than once a week. One teacher, Mary Forrest, had taught elementary art for 27 years but moved to a high school after layoffs made her the most senior person for the district's only visual-arts teaching job—a position that is only part-time.[39]

California has its problems with the arts too. It ranks 50th in the nation in the ratio of music teachers to students. There has been a 50 percent decline in the percentage of music students in California public schools over the past few years, from 19.5 percent in 1999–2000 to 9.3 percent in 2003–4. The greatest decline came in general music, which suffered an 85 percent decrease in student enrollment, with the number of music teachers declining by 26.7 percent during the same time period (1999–2000 through 2003–4). One San Jose district severely cut back its music program, going from nine classes and two teachers to five classes and one teacher.

In some communities, special homeowner assessments can help supplement music program needs; however with Governor Schwarzenegger eliminating any funding to the arts education program, many communities are forced to make cuts—and the arts tend to go first. Many teachers must raise funds to support their program. For example, one teacher in Coleman has "sold thousands of dollars worth of cookies and other things" but still has two bus bills from last year that haven't been paid. "I have an outstanding bill at the local music store that does my repairs. I'm asking my Booster Club parents to help pay for these things, but the district should pay for them, too."[40]

A 2006 report by the Center on Education Policy reveals that 71 percent of districts surveyed report reduced instructional time in at least one other subject to make more time for reading and mathematics, the subjects tested under NCLB.[41] In some districts, struggling students received double periods of reading or math or both. Of course, when this happens, it disproportionately affects poor and minority students. According to the CEP report, 97 percent of high-poverty districts (where more than 75 percent of students are eligible for free or reduced-price lunch) compared with 55–59 percent of lower-poverty districts had policies that restricted curriculum offerings.

The voices of teachers in response to this phenomenon are clear. It happens every time high-stakes testing is instituted. From Colorado we hear the following:

Teacher A: "We only teach to the test even at second grade, and have stopped teaching science and social studies. We don't have assemblies, take few field trips, or have musical productions at grade levels. We even hesitate to ever show a video. Our second graders have no recess except for 20 minutes at lunch."

Teacher B: "I eliminated a lot of my social studies and science. I eliminated Colorado history. What else? Electricity. Most of that because it's more stressed that the kids know the reading and the math, so, it was pretty much said, you know, you do what you gotta do."

Teacher C: "Those things [science and social studies] just fall to the back burner and quite frankly, I just marked report cards for the third grading period and I didn't do science at all for their third grading periods. Same for the social studies."

Teacher D: "We don't take as many field trips. We don't do community outreach like we used to like visiting the nursing home or cleaning up the park because we had adopted a park and that was our job, to keep it clean. Well, we don't have time for that anymore."

Teacher E: "I had to cut out some things in order to do the CSAP stuff. It's not the number of days. I think it would be more accurate to say the number of labs. I think what is more significant is that I have had to cut the number of hands-on investigations. I would say I have had to cut one quarter of the labs."

Teacher F: "Projects, [I] eliminated curriculum such as novels I would teach, we didn't have time to go to the library, we didn't have time to use the computer labs because they had to cut something. [I] cut things I thought we could live with out. [I] cut presentations, anything that takes very much time, I cut film. We have been cutting like crazy."[42]

The following Florida teachers know what test pressure really feels like.[43] They seem to have had their professional judgment about curriculum dismissed.

Teacher A: "The FCAT is teaching teachers to stay within the narrow confines of the FCAT. Too many times I've been told, when going beyond the confines (especially in math): 'Why are you teaching that? It isn't on the FCAT.'"

Teacher B: "Our total curriculum is focused on reading, writing, and math. There is no extra time for students to study the arts, have physical education, science, or social studies. Our curriculum is very unbalanced."

> *Teacher C:* "While it is a way of testing some components of standards-based performance, it leaves many gaps in the educational process. If we just 'teach to the test,' which many teachers in our district are pressured to do, then the students are left with *huge* educational gaps that have not been covered in their education. Students deserve a well-rounded education, not just bits and pieces that are presented on a state test."
>
> *Teacher D:* "Before FCAT I was a better teacher. I was exposing my children to a wide range of science and social studies experiences. I taught using themes that really immersed the children into learning about a topic using their reading, writing, math, and technology skills. Now I'm basically afraid to *not* teach to the test. I know that the way I was teaching was building a better foundation for my kids as well as a love of learning. Now each year I can't wait until March is over so I can spend the last two and a half months of school teaching the way I want to teach, the way I know students will be excited about."

This small selection of stories barely touches on the problem of a narrowed curriculum as a function of high-stakes testing. Not only are courses and areas being jettisoned; within courses that are related to the tests, a narrow vision of the curriculum is being fostered. The overall result of high-stakes testing, for many teachers and school districts, seems to be a restricted vision of what should be taught and how it should be taught. Less obvious but of equal concern is that a restricted vision of the kind of person who should be teaching also exists. Implied is that a good deal of teaching in high-stakes testing environments is of a technical rather than a professional nature. Technicians and professionals are prepared differently, are expected to work differently, and have different obligations to those they serve.

Evidence of the effects of narrowing the curriculum shows up also in analyses that look at the effects of high school exit exams on students' SAT performance. Marchant and Paulson examined SAT performance in states that required students to pass a high school exit exam against those states that did not have such a requirement. They found a significant difference in the SAT performance. Students in states without an exit exam statistically outperformed students in states with an exit exam. Marchant and Paulson hypothesize the following:

> High stakes testing . . . seems to encourage the use of instructional approaches and materials that resemble the tests used. Because the nature of items on the SAT, as a "reasoning" test, can look very different than those of a typical achievement test; focus and preparation for the [ordinary high-stakes] achievement test are unlikely to transfer. Rituals of giving multiple-choice quizzes and providing test preparation often take the place of "normal" instruction when high-stakes tests are a factor. Teachers exploring instructional practices informed by current views of learning and supported by cognitive psychology that seek deeper understanding and critical thinking may find those techniques, and even those goals, at odds with the drill and practice suggested by the broader, rather superficial coverage typical of schools with graduation exams. . . . Therefore, as more flexible, responsive, innovative student-based instructional approaches are abandoned in favor of achievement test preparation, the ability to reason verbally and mathematically, as reflected by SAT scores, may suffer.[44]

A report by the ACT suggests that high school graduates are not prepared for college-level reading and writing work.[45] According to the report, just 51 percent of test takers met the ACT "college-readiness benchmark in reading" (representing the skill level required for students to have a "high probability" of success in college courses). Students from minority groups or from poverty were much less likely to reach this benchmark. Only half of ACT-tested high school students who graduated in 2005 met the benchmark in reading.[46]

One explanation the authors give for their findings is that high school standards in reading are insufficient. Most relevant to this discussion is the finding that the type of text to which students are exposed matters. Students who master text complexity are more prepared for college-level work than students who do not. That is, "performance on complex texts is the clearest differentiator in reading between students who are likely to be ready for college and those who are not."[47] Thus, if the curriculum is not emphasizing critical thinking, forms of complex comprehension, then it appears that students are at risk for being less prepared for college. As we write, it is not clear yet from the data, but it is possible that high-stakes testing may be contributing to lower levels of preparedness for college in our high school graduates. This unintended consequence remains a distinct possibility.

Box 5.7 A Texas State Republican House Representative's Wife Weighs In

The worries of teaching to the test and curriculum regulating were articulated by Cheri Isett, wife of Texas state representative Carl Isett, who at the time was in the naval reserves and had been called up for active duty. Mrs. Isett gave a personal privilege speech to the Texas House of Representatives on May 12, 2006, after the House passed a bill that would cut $400 million promised to Texas schoolchildren and provide a $400 million windfall to big oil, insurance, and utility industries.

> I believe we would all agree that studying to a test and regurgitating is not a true education. We would all agree that the minds of Albert Einstein, Ben Franklin, Thomas Edison, Samuel Morse, Bill Gates, Steve Jobs, and Michael Dell would never have tolerated such infliction upon them. They would never have allowed their creativity and their courage to step into unknown territories to be held back by the boxes that we force our schoolchildren to conform into. These children . . . are aching to break free from the tyranny of standardized tests and curriculum "scope and sequence" and express those gifts and talents. But we have legislated them out. We have told the artist that he has to pull back and cut back on blossoming in his chosen art because he doesn't have time. He has to take another math and science class. We have told the very, very bright entrepreneur that his pursuits are worthless because he is not a good test taker and pulls our school ratings down. We have told our teachers that they are not good teachers and don't deserve merit for their efforts because the artists and entrepreneurs in their classes don't deliver the goods in test results.
>
> There is a whole world of knowledge and all of history to study. We could never impart all of it to every child. There's just too much of it. So who has the right to determine what body of knowledge has merit? Who was it anyway that said "every seventh-grader needs to know all parts of the cell and their function"? Why is that more important than, say, the intricacies of weather systems? And why are either of those more important than any other body of knowledge which delights the heart of a child? Who gives merit to one body of knowledge over another? And yet, through our essential skills and standardized tests, we praise one type of learner and condemn another. We tell our classroom teachers that it doesn't matter that you want to reach the heart of a child. We want you to mold his mind to conform to what we believe is a productive, college-prepped student.

Garnet Coleman, "HB1 Shortchanges Our Children's Schools: Gives Big Oil and Big Business a $400 Million Tax Holiday," *Texas State Representative Press Release,* May 12, 2006, *http://texasedequity.blogspot.com* and *http://www.quorumreport.com.*

CONCLUSION

We have shown how instructional practice becomes distorted when the pressure to score high on a test increases. Holding teachers and students accountable for what students know in math and reading has guaranteed that strong efforts and lots of resources will be devoted to doing well on those tests. Effort is not necessarily directed to learning at deeper levels nor at learning unrelated but interesting and useful content. Activities such as test preparation and curriculum narrowing are efforts designed simply to get scores up. When that is done, however, there is likely to be some undermining of the meaningfulness (or validity) of the resultant test score.

There is a little-noted consequence of pushing commercial publishers into doing tests cheaply, and it too affects validity. It is under the radar for news reporters and thus often escapes public notice. This problem is related to the "dumbing down" of the test over time. In this case, however, it is not politics that drives such decisions, as we argued above, it is costs—the costs of making and scoring items that can more closely relate to the constructs in which we have interest. Richard Rothstein describes this problem:

> Consider a typical elementary school reading standard, common in many states, that expects children to be able to identify both the main idea and the supporting details in a passage. There is nothing wrong with such a standard. If state tests actually assessed it, there would be nothing wrong with teachers "teaching to the test." But in actuality, students are more likely to find questions on state tests that simply require identification of details, not the main idea. For example, a passage about Christopher Columbus might ask pupils to identify his ships' names without asking if they understood that, by sailing west, he planned to confirm that the world was spherical. In math, a typical middle school geometry standard expects students to be able to measure various figures and shapes, like triangles, squares, prisms and cones. Again, that is an appropriate standard, and teachers should prepare students for a test that assessed it. But, in actuality, students are more likely to find questions on state tests that ask only for measurement of the simpler forms, like triangles and squares. It is not unusual to find states claiming that they have "aligned" such tests with their high standards when they have done nothing of the kind.[48]

In this narrowed vision of what students should know and be able to do as we go from standards to items, we see three things at play. First is the inherent difficulty of getting complex items to be sufficiently reliable for large-scale assessments. This is by no means a simple problem to solve. Second is the logistical problem of getting complex items created and scored in a timely manner. A testing program in which new and complex items are required annually is enormously difficult and expensive to manage. Finally, there is the problem of costs for scoring complex and authentic tasks. The latter two problems are managerial, to be solved by increasing both development time and money, should we ever have the will to do so. But that is not likely.

From our perspective, we are faced with the following problems:

- Tests that are not very strong in validity
- Test-preparation programs that undercut any sensible inferences we might make about what the tests measure
- Curriculum narrowing designed to cheat many students of a liberal education, particularly America's poor and minority children
- Public schools that have been opened up to profit-making by businesses that have a stake in school failure
- Tests that measure skills as cheaply as possible, because we choose not to invest public money in assessments that are more complex and therefore probably more worthwhile indicators of what we want students to know and be able to do
- And, worst of all, testing programs that alienate and anger most teachers and administrators, thus silencing their voices and denying their professionalism

We are convinced that the high-stakes testing programs associated with NCLB are hurting America. We cite incidents from so many different states to make the point that this is no local problem. Through test-preparation and curriculum narrowing, in particular, we see Campbell's law in operation throughout the nation. Activities are undertaken almost everywhere to manipulate important and closely monitored indicators. The pattern we uncovered turns out to be as predictable as Campbell's law suggested it would be. But we reiterate: neither standards nor assessment is the enemy of good schooling. The enemy of good schooling is high-stakes testing and the inevitable distortion and corruption that follows its introduction.

CHAPTER 6

HOW HIGH-STAKES TESTING UNDERMINES PUBLIC EDUCATION AND THE TEACHING PROFESSION

While Also Destroying Both Teacher and Student Morale

A Massachusetts teacher summed up nicely our concern in this chapter: "The MCAS is one of the reasons I'm leaving, because of the pressure it puts on the kids and everyone else. And, we don't even have the right materials to teach for it."[1] In the following pages, we discuss how high-stakes testing is attacking the professionalism of our teachers, those to whom we have entrusted both the socialization and education of the next generation. We hold the simple view that teachers are special people in a democracy, and as such, most of them have earned the right to our respect. But listening to teachers across the country makes us aware that their treatment under NCLB is simply as "pawns." They have had little or no input into the accountability systems by which they are judged. Their work is often under the control of others, mostly politicians, of which some have as their goal the privatization of the American public school system. This is not good.

You would think that accountability in a democracy would provide ample opportunity for the voices of teachers, students, parents, and administrators to be heard—that they would be allowed to give an account, a first-person account, of what is happening under high-stakes testing. We are sure that if this were the case, there would be more of a negative view of NCLB among our politicians than there is now. In our estimation, only the late senator Paul Wellstone, a former teacher, understood completely the dimensions of this problem. He was one of the few who spoke out and voted against the kinds of accountability systems that he knew to be both unfair and unworkable. In the appendix, we quote extensively from a speech he gave before his untimely death. In a way, this whole book is merely an expansion on all the points he made in that prescient speech.

Our experience with teachers across the country, like Senator Wellstone's, highlights the damaging effects of high-stakes testing. We see much more teacher anxiety and lowered teacher and student morale. We see the exodus of teachers and administrators from a profession that has been changed in some ways from being associated with the proud title of "educator" to that of "trainer," a title that evokes working with dogs and other animals. Teachers of some subjects are now script readers, curriculum and testing technicians, not professionals in the sense in which the term is usually used. In this chapter, we ponder the demise of the professional culture within which our teachers now serve and our students learn.

USING PRESSURE TO MOTIVATE PEOPLE

The threat and incentive system of high-stakes testing exerts a tremendous amount of pressure on teachers and their students. For the teacher who has, indeed, become complacent, this threat is enough to spur them into action. No one denies that high-stakes testing focuses attention on outcomes. But that attention is inappropriate if the outcome is seen as the most important aspect of an educational system. W. Edwards Deming, the father of Total Quality Management and arguably the most important thinker about manufacturing in modern times, put his emphasis on improving processes, *not* on having the outcome move in the desired way. Deming understood that indicators were not to be viewed as providing summative information, leading to the firing of workers or teachers. Indicators provided formative information, data to be used to improve a factory or a school.[2] Indicators were the starting point in helping to empower teams of people as they discussed how to improve the processes of manufacturing.

Applied to education, Deming would have argued for the use of formative assessments to spark discussions among school staff about how things might be done differently and better. He saw staff involvement as the best way to improve quality and was quite leery of attaching rewards and punishments to outcome measures, thinking of them, instead, as "perverse incentives." He argued that individual workers are usually doing their best and that what prevents them from doing better is the system in which they work. The solution, therefore, is not to set individuals in competition with one another but to organize their work so they can collaboratively improve the system. For the most part, however, the voices of teachers and administrators have been excluded from discussion of how to improve the American educational system. Instead, school improvement has been mandated by politicians who believe in high-stakes testing as a powerful instrument of school change. They ignore the fact that, just as Deming suspected and Campbell predicted, high-stakes testing invariably leads to a system of perverse incentives. High-stakes testing adds a layer of worry, anxiety, and stress to what teachers see as an undervalued, underpaid, and undersupported profession.

Two problems with pressure

There are two main problems with the pressures associated with high-stakes testing. First, pressure doesn't always succeed in changing behavior in the long run, though it may appear to work in the short run. Think of it this way: many parents use threats and incentives to control and shape their child's behavior. They may ask their child to eat dinner in order to get dessert or to clean her room if she wants her allowance continued. The problem with this simple psychology is that too often it doesn't work to effect change in intended ways. Most of us are not surprised when we learn that given the prospect of a tantalizing dessert or more money for iTunes downloads, children are tempted to feed the dog the rest of their dinner or to shove the mess of clothes in their room under the bed. In short, without commitment to the goals that are held by the parent, the child figures out ways to take a shortcut to the prize. Although reward and punishment might work to gain a child's compliance in the short run, these kinds of incentives and threats do not necessarily translate into something a child wants for herself. So why, we wonder, would any policymaker think that this same system of motivation might be any more effective for changing educational practice?

Margaret Spellings, however, the current secretary of education, espouses exactly these kinds of simple childrearing practices as a general theory of management. In her view, when districts don't make the progress they are expected to make, punishing them until they do is no different than how she parents her daughter: "It's like with Grace [her daughter]: You're not going to play soccer till you clean your damn room. With these chief education officers, I've let them go to the movies; now I better see a clean room."[3] She is on record as believing that "bribery is the cornerstone of good parenting. And good management." Perhaps, then, we should admire the stories we have collected indicating that some schools are now paying students to show up?[4] Perhaps that is just good management, but bribing students to learn undermines their natural curiosity and motivation to discover new truths. Moreover, a system built on bribery ignores a huge social-science literature on motivation.

Using incentives to shape a child's behavior is very common among parents who want their children to comply with the rules of the house. And, given the right incentive structure, it is usually very successful in influencing short-term compliance. Threaten teens that their phone will be taken away or entice them with an iPod, and more than likely they will do what is asked of them. The rewards/threats are simply too salient to ignore. However, as most parents understand, this kind of approach is less successful when it comes to helping children adopt their own set of values and behaviors. It is one thing to ask a child to clean because a parent said so, and another thing for a child to clean because they choose to have a clean room. Parents who want to socialize their child to adopt goals of cleanliness must work harder and must invest more time and energy toward understanding the needs, goals, and dispositions of their child so they can determine what is necessary to guide them toward an "attitude" of cleanliness. Thus, it is often much easier to employ threats because it doesn't take as much thoughtfulness, and the results are usually quick, though not necessarily enduring. This is exactly the type of incentive system associated with high-stakes testing.

A system of rewards, punishment, and pressures on self-esteem sounds like a logical way to motivate teachers and students, and some psychologists support this approach. But it doesn't work very well. Motivational researchers Richard Ryan and Kirk Brown present evidence strongly suggesting the opposite. They claim that it is the more autonomous motives, such as intrinsic motivation (e.g., I do it for *me*, not for *you*) or a well-internalized value system (e.g., I am guided by my own goals, not ones set by someone else), that result in higher quality of learning, persistence in the face of difficulty in learning, and greater enjoyment of the learning process. These are not the motivational systems elicited by high-stakes testing.

Test scores, researchers found, can have *informational* significance to teachers and students, *controlling* significance, or *amotivational* significance. Psychological theory and research is quite clear that tests that have informational significance, which do not try to control behavior but provide feedback about behavior, usually motivate people to do better. The intrinsic desire to do well and valuing the subject being learned result in motivation to teach or learn better. On the other hand, tests that have rewards and punishments associated with them are designed to control behavior, and they do usually produce temporary compliance. People do what they need to do to gain the extrinsic rewards and to avoid punishment. But tests that attempt to control behavior ultimately undermine self-motivation in the area being tested. These tests reduce investment and commitment to the goals of the activity. Amotivational tests are those that have harsh consequences or whose goals are too hard to reach, as is true for some special-education and ELL students. They lead to a withdrawal of effort, to not caring what happens. The end result is students dropping out and teachers leaving the profession.

The second problem with the pressure that accompanies high-stakes testing is that conditions for work are being permanently altered in unfortunate ways. In this new environment, teachers can be more easily dismissed from their work, but the reasons for their dismissal are often largely out of their control. Teachers are put in the precarious position of putting their livelihoods squarely on the shoulders of their students. That is, unlike many others whose work is evaluated based on their performance, teachers succeed or fail based on the performance of others! This erodes a sense of empowerment, of professionalism, and affects job satisfaction. This was put starkly to us in the comments of one South Carolina teacher: "It's just mind-boggling to know that for two weeks [the test period], I am putting what I do in the hands of a 12-year-old. I remind them that it's not just their name on the test. What they score is a reflection of me and the school."

Another teacher repeated this concern and expressed the personal responsibility that teachers almost always feel about their students: "[High-stakes testing] unnerves teachers somewhat because we know every child is not going to be proficient, but they can be the best they can be. Still, I feel solely responsible for their test results."

In Virginia, teachers are feeling increased pressure from administrators and the federal government to push students to do well on tests.[5] Teacher morale is reportedly low, turnover is high, and the consensus is that talented teachers have been leaving the profession due to the pressure of high-stakes tests. Teachers in high ethnic-minority-population schools may feel especially distressed because those schools tend to do poorly on such tests. Many teachers say they feel as if they must shoulder the burden of ensuring that their schools receive funding and that, when scores are not up to par, they are blamed. But the pressure is also felt in middle-class schools that usually score well on such exams, as described in box 6.1.

We have met many teachers who tell us they believe that every child can learn, but then they go on to say something that the designers of NCLB refuse to hear. Teachers also say that students "cannot all learn at the same speed, nor to the same levels of proficiency, if they have the same amounts of instructional time." An elementary teacher in Virginia expresses this sentiment quite well:

> I'm not against raising the standards of learning. The only thing that bothers me is that children are asked to perform up to SOL standards [the Virginia Standards of Learning] at a given grade and age. I firmly believe that curriculum standards or SOL's should not be age- and grade-dictated. Many students come to my second- and third-grade class and

> cannot read. Well, you can't very well learn the states and capitals if you can't read. Children will succeed and learn core knowledge if we let them work at their own pace to acquire knowledge. . . .
>
> My classroom contains children from different cultural backgrounds, socioeconomic levels, and academic abilities. I do follow the [county] Program of Study and try my best to meet each child's needs and abilities. [But] if Sally can't remember her street address, I do not want to move on to teach her the seven continents. I feel it is vital for children to master one task or skill before moving on to another, this way I can avoid confusion and build self-esteem. I hear of teachers simply "exposing" children to the many, many standards put upon us by the state. Instead of helping students master some of these standards, they are pushing to expose them to every item for fear of accountability. Are the SOL's going to sacrifice the quality of instruction our children are receiving? I believe that is a threat.[6]

It is one thing that teachers are being evaluated on the basis of student test scores but yet another to humiliate and devalue them by judging performance for which they are at most co-creators. They are clearly not solely responsible for that performance, but teachers and schools are judged as if they were. Do physicians get punished when their patients supersize their food portions and develop diabetes? Do dentists get punished if their patients will not brush after every meal? This peculiarity of the teaching profession adds to the anxiety teachers feel.

In Aurora, Illinois, the failing label at one school was especially humiliating in light of how hard the school had worked "to pull off a few test-score miracles this year with one of the suburb's most vulnerable student populations [in] a cash-strapped district where nearly every child is low-income and minority. . . . The failing label is crushing to staff morale and threatens to draw resources from the programs that have fueled [our school's] turnaround. And, the fact that [our failure label] was caused by a test that never was intended to measure academic achievement makes the label all the more painful."[7]

In Miami, Florida, one high school had received a label of "FF" for failing to make progress the previous two years in a row. The principal expected that label to be increased to "FFF," anticipating that the school

Box 6.1 From Dedicated and Trustworthy to Self-Serving in One Day of Testing

David Berliner's grandchild, K, was in a school serving middle-class children on test day in Arizona. K had a dedicated, competent, and trustworthy fourth-grade teacher who he liked a lot. The night before his second day of testing, during high-stakes testing week, K had an asthma attack. This was not unusual, and probably not caused by the first day of testing since K was a top student who actually enjoyed testing. He liked showing off his status as a high achiever in school. But he had had a really bad night.

In the morning K felt better and wanted to attend school to continue the test, although his parents wanted him to stay home. He convinced his parents to let him go to school and promised he would call them immediately if he had another attack. K's father took him in and explained to the teacher what had happened. The teacher was told that he and his wife would take turns staying close to the school, would always have K's "breathing machine" with them, and that each had cell phones whose numbers he gave to the teacher.

The test began shortly after that. In the middle of the test, K got another asthma attack. Dutifully, he went up to Mrs. P, his teacher, and asked her to call his parents. She said, "Oh K, can't you wait a little longer and finish the test? I'll call your parents as soon as you're done."

We are lucky that K did not die that morning. He obediently went back to his desk, and wheezing away, finished the test. The teacher and the school got what it wanted, a high score on the high-stakes achievement test, while literally putting the life of a child at risk. Before bed that night, K said to his mother, "I guess I can't trust Mrs. P anymore, can I?"

Mrs. P had gone from dedicated and trustworthy to self-serving in a matter of minutes. Although our family all blames Mrs. P for what she did, we also all wonder if it is in the nation's best interest to build accountability systems that make usually decent people act this way? Do we really want an accountability system that corrupts people so?

would not make progress again during the 2005–6 school year. Is this principal expressing low expectations, or does he have a better handle on reality than the state of Florida? The principal went on to explain the problems with labeling a school as a failure where two-thirds of the student body do not speak English because they just arrived from Haiti. Tragically, this exasperated principal is retiring because of the extensive humiliation associated with the public mischaracterization of students and teachers. He claims his teachers all work extremely hard and want desperately for their students to succeed. The state is expected to take over the school, but the principal isn't worried, just concerned with the injustice of it all:

> I'm not worried because I'm leaving this job. I'm tired of being humiliated. We work hard here—the faculty is dedicated and gives its all, and the kids are great. They try their best and we have very few behavior problems here. They just can't be expected to pass an exam in a language they don't understand. The worst thing about this is the state doesn't have any suggestions for what we should do differently. They're just applying the pressure, and I'm fed up with it.[8]

This is not an isolated case of one administrator feeling testing pressure. It is reported that in Denver, upper-level administrators were leaving in record numbers in part because of the pressures associated with high-stakes testing.[9]

We have borrowed some of the examples about morale and pressure that follow from the excellent book on high-stakes testing by Jones, Jones, and Hargrove.[10] They report that in one survey, almost 90 percent of the teachers agreed that they were under "undue pressure" to improve students' test scores.[11] In two other independent surveys, three-quarters of the teachers or two-thirds of the educators reported that their jobs were more stressful since the implementation of high-stakes testing.[12] These educators reported that they experienced such emotions as anger, tension, frustration, anxiety, and depression from the imposition of high-stakes tests. Most teachers characterize the regime of high stakes with similar sentiments:

Box 6.2 The Joy of Teaching Has Disappeared

In California, one teacher, Marie Avera, came to the realization that the pressures of testing were forcing her to alter her method of instruction. An article in the *California Educator* notes, "Stressed out about raising test scores, the Vallejo City teacher was trying to drill a math concept into her students' brains when it became obvious that one child just didn't understand. 'I said, somewhat sharply, "Don't you get it?" He just looked at me with his big brown eyes. I felt terrible.' At that point, she told her students to close their books. 'It's time for us to go out and play.' And I thought to myself, 'What are we doing to our children?'"

CTA president Barbara E. Kerr says the biggest challenge facing schools is that the joy of teaching and learning is hard to find in today's classrooms. "Testing mania has gotten way out of hand, and the Elementary and Secondary Education Act further exacerbates the problem," says Kerr, who taught first grade and kindergarten in Riverside for more than two decades. Everywhere she goes, teachers share the same concerns. In growing numbers of schools, scripted learning programs take up most of the school day, and the rest of the day is lost to pretesting and testing.

As for the joy: "It's as if someone is trying to throw a wet blanket over it every time you try and grab it. You see the glint in the eye of a kid after a great lesson, and you feel like you changed a life. No one can take that away from you. But we aren't given the chance to revel in that; we aren't encouraged to find more of those moments, because we are under pressures that have nothing to do with what is best for children."

Sherry Posnick-Goodwin, "Bring Back the Joy of Teaching and Learning," *California Educator* 8, no. 4 (2003).

"A few years ago, I really loved teaching, but this pressure is just so intense . . . I'm not sure how long I can take it."[13]

"Before [the state program], you know, I could just go with kids if something came up which hooked them. But now if we just start off in a different direction, I get worried we won't get back to what's required, and I have to kind of rein them in. I know they get frustrated, and I sure do. I think, well, is this what I got into teaching for?"[14]

"These tests, and all of this pressure to make kids do well on the tests . . . it's an insult. It's saying we aren't a profession and we can't be

> trusted to do our jobs, so high-pressure tactics are necessary to make us behave. They're treating us like stupid children; they're turning us into bad teachers, taking away every bit of pride."[15]
>
> "I have seen some of the most bubbly teachers in this school . . . in this system and probably in the state, lose their enthusiasm, that zest they had for teaching [as a result of the testing]. [I have] seen a lot of good teachers leave already, and I'm afraid the numbers are going to become more massive. I think that's when they are going to open their eyes when they see teachers walking out by the droves."[16]

We hear voices that are quite similar to those collected from Florida teachers under the FCAT. Here, for example, are Colorado teachers' reactions to CSAP, the Colorado Student Assessment Program, another high-stakes test:

> "We are under so much pressure to get good results there is little time for anything else. CSAP definitely decreases morale."
>
> "I had to cease a lot of projects and other activities and programs in my room to make time for the teaching of test-taking strategies. I felt demoralized and unappreciated by all of the negative press in the newspapers and have doubted myself as an educator for the first time. I'm not sure I would go into this profession if I had to choose all over again. I feel pulled from many directions—to make education more personal and then, from the CSAP—to standardize their learning—forcing them into a box whether they are ready developmentally or not."
>
> "A number of my friends are retiring because they don't want to be associated with a partially proficient school. And from their gut level, they are giving their all but getting a slap in the face. They know their kids are making advancements."
>
> "I find that it is a demoralizing, stressful situation. Teachers are being judged year to year on completely different students. The pressure put on teachers has increased to the point where teachers will be leaving the profession."
>
> "We can't even get teachers to come into schools like the one I am in because they are afraid that they will be called failing. Why should a young teacher come here when they can go to a wealthy school district? . . . The stigma that the grading has put on all schools in minority neighborhoods is just absolutely incredible. The talk that the good teachers don't come

> here, it basically frightens away anybody with any ability who doesn't know the community. Why should they come somewhere when they are going to be called a failure? I can't blame those teachers."[17]

Pressures such as these, naturally enough, have tragic consequences:

> Last year Betty Robinson, a married mother of two, and principal of the Simonton school, attended a meeting where Gwinnett County school officials discussed school performance, which is based almost entirely on standardized test scores. Each school is expected to show 5 percent improvement over the previous year. Last year, Simonton, which has a substantial new immigrant population, improved by 4.9 percent.[18]
>
> Simonton had been one of four Gwinnett schools included on a list of 436 Georgia schools that were failing new standards under President Bush's "No Child Left Behind" education plan. Under that program, if Simonton does not improve enough, students could transfer to other public schools and Simonton would have to pay the busing costs.
>
> Early the next morning, before her students were to take yet another important test, Robinson locked her office door and shot herself in the head.

There is little more to say. Pressure cookers, with just the right amount of heat, can speed up the meal and increase the efficiency of cooking. Too much heat, however, always results in pressure cookers exploding. As we continue to tell the stories of the effects of high-stakes testing on our schools and those who work there, we need to be asking whether those environments are overheating.

Stress and anxiety among our students

Teachers, of course, are not the only victims of high-stakes testing. Students also feel increased anxiety and stress as result of the pressures to perform on tests. The pressure is all around them, as symbolized by the posters on walls everywhere they look at one Texas high school.

The long-term effect of such stress is still unknown; however, anecdotal evidence paints a largely frightening picture of what happens to our

Box 6.3 Students Stressed Out? No Problem! "Test Monster" to the Rescue

Since the passage of NCLB, requests for the Test Anxiety Inventory created by Charles D. Spielberger have increased, suggesting that more students are becoming stressed out in the face of high-stakes testing. Students' test-related anxiety is so great in New York that teachers and administrators engage their students in destressing activities. According to one *New York Times* article, testing is so stressful for students—a potential cause of lowered test scores—that educators must help their students feel less anxiety. In one school, social workers introduced the "test monster"—a drawing of a monster handed out to students to then write on or deface as they see fit—an outlet for frustration and anxiety. Other methods include lectures about test taking and time management, teaching of yoga, and isometrics in a gym class to help with relaxation. At the end of the destressing activity, "test monsters" end up crumpled up and locked away in a box.

David Herzenhorn, "Toughening Up for Tests," *New York Times*, Jan. 10, 2006.

students every spring come testing time. In 2001, as the standards for passing New York's Regents examination were raised, school psychologists in the state worried about the stress the tests were causing students. According to an assemblywoman from Long Island who had been a social worker for 17 years, "The kids are under such stress with the raising of the standards that it hasn't been recognized that that's what's causing their problems in school. We have kids who can't learn because they are so stressed out." One school psychologist noticed that "children in fourth grade [are] panic-stricken because they're going to take this big test. They know it's high-stakes testing—parents are telling them and teachers are telling them." He also noted, "It's like the SATs, but in spades. Children's mental health is [affecting] learning."[19]

We found hundreds of reports of individual cases of student stress. For example, in Georgia, one student worries that if he doesn't pass the state test, he'll get held back, and thinking about it makes his "head hurt."[20] That's

Box 6.4 Poor Students in an Almost Entirely Hispanic School in Texas, Trying to Make Sense of the Pressures and Test Preparation Associated with High-Stakes Tests

- "We learned that this test is so important, important enough to stop learning. We started reading a novel in October and had to stop reading it because we had to learn TAKS. We are just now picking up where we left off after all this time. That was five months ago? That was a long time ago, yet we are supposed to remember where we left off and cram all of it into the rest of the semester?"
- "I learned that I could get in trouble. I was written up and sent to the office because I didn't want to do a TAKS assignment. I was told in the office that I had to do it because it was important that I pass this test. I am tired of doing TAKS, TAKS, TAKS. I am not learning anything."
- "TAKS is just preparing us to take a test. School should be for educating and to educate means to teach us, not to teach us to take a test."
- "We learn in isolation. We learn one skill one day or in a week and then we never see it again until test time."
- "In other schools, students are learning and teachers are teaching. . . . Over here, some teachers have given up on some students. We should be learning like them. It's not fair that we have nothing to do but TAKS. Yeah, we're smart too and we can learn other things, you know?"

Sandra L. Foster, "How Latino Students Negotiate the Demands of High Stakes Testing: A Case Study of One School in Texas" (PhD diss., Arizona State University, 2006).

a gentle kind of stress, but stress nevertheless. Other students worry that they'll forget everything they've learned on test day, and one student worries he doesn't have the stamina to make it through such a long testing period. After it was ruled in New York City that any third-grader who failed the state exam in 2004 would not be promoted, teachers, parents, and third-graders reported sleepless nights and butterflies in their stomachs. One mother complained that her daughter, a third-grader at Public School 203 in Queens, "cried at night and turned into 'a frazzle.'" As a result, the young girl "dropped off the softball team" because "something had to give."[21]

Of course, the stress and morale of students for whom the test is especially challenging is often more severe. These are often those for whom English is a second language, those who come from poor homes, and special-education students. For them, the consequences of repeated test failure are especially demotivating and demoralizing. In such cases, students end up voting with their feet and drop out of school altogether (see chapter 4). Unfortunately, this level of stress is forced upon even our youngest students (see box 6.5).

Another side effect of the pressure on students is passive resistance to the test-preparation programs that heighten tests' pressure or complete apathy toward participating in the programs. What follows is a transcript from a school that thinks it is preparing students for the state's high-stakes

Box 6.5 Pressure in Head Start: Is It Really Necessary?

In Midland, Texas, four-year-olds in the Head Start program individually took their first standardized test, which consisted of a set of questions posed by a teacher about letter recognition, vocabulary, and math while she showed the child pictures of objects and events. The test was being applied to half-a-million Head Start children throughout the nation as part of the No Child Left Behind program. In Midland, Nate Kidder was typical of the four-year-olds being quizzed. At one point the teacher showed Nate a page with four black-and-white drawings and asked him to point to the one that matched the word *vase*. The boy chewed on his lip, obviously nervous, and pointed to the picture of a canister, not a vase. Another drawing showed a tree stump and grass sticking out of the water; children were expected to identify the picture as a swamp. After the session, the teacher explained that many children didn't have vases in their homes, and "We don't have swamps in Midland." She worried that standardized testing would damage the confidence of children like Nate, who, she said, was bright but afraid of making mistakes. "If you ask him to do something [like the test questions], his smile freezes, and you see him worry, 'Am I going to get this right?'"

Sara Rimer, "Now, Standardized Achievement Tests in Head Start," *New York Times*, Oct. 29, 2003, cited in R. Murray Thomas and R. Murray, *High-Stakes Testing: Coping with Collateral Damage* (Mahwah, NJ: Erlbaum, 2005), 252.

test. An English class at Parker High School (pseudonym), Texas, with 16 Latino juniors as students (S), is taught by a young Anglo teacher (T), who has handed out an essay similar to those that are to be written on the test:

> T: Okay, this is last-minute work for TAKS. You can pass the test. You don't want to take it again, right?
> S: (*no response*)
> T: You don't want to have to all practice again, right?
> S: (*no response*)
> T: Please say yes.
> S: (*no response*)
> T: You are brilliant. . . . The test is not hard. Take your time; in fact take all the time you need.
> S: (*no response*)
> T: Remember, be here for the test and give it all you got—take your time and do your best.
> S: (*no response*)
> T: You're awesome. If someone tells you differently, don't listen to them. Don't be afraid to use those dictionaries. If you don't know a word, look it up. If you want to use another word, look it up.
> S: (*no response*)
> T: Okay, there will be three types of open-ended questions and three types of literary selections. What does "literary" mean?
> S: (*no response*)
> T: Is it fiction, nonfiction, or biography?
> S: (*no response*)
> T: Are you going to talk to me or you don't know?
> S: (*no response*)
> T: It's fiction you all (*in an angry voice*). (*Pause*) First thing you do is answer the question. It must be insightful and thoughtful. Do not restate the question. You have five lines to fill in. Then you have to support a response. If you summarize in an open-ended question you get a zero. But if you use support for the passage, you get points. Look at this essay. Do you see how this student used textual support?
> S: (*no response*)
> T: Come on! (*in an angry voice and shaking her head signaling "no"*). Oh, before I forget, it is important that you must stay inside the box and you must use all five lines.
> S: (*no response*)
> T: See how this student answered the question with insightful evidence?
> S: (*no response*)

And so it goes. Another exciting day at school marked only by passive resistance to what is accurately perceived to be an inferior education by Parker's students.[22]

Pep rallies and ice cream parties for coping with stress

What is so alarming about the stress we impose on our students is that, despite our awareness of it, we do it anyway (see box 6.6). Politicians apparently want this kind of pressure applied, since it constitutes their theory of action, with pressure viewed as a way to motivate students. But as teachers and parents know, the increased pressure to perform well on a single test on a particular day often raises students' anxiety and stress levels beyond what is reasonable. Therefore, teachers and administrators will try to calm their students, engaging in all sorts of creative efforts aimed at reducing their students' level of stress.

Box 6.6 Aiding and Abetting Throwing Up

An elementary principal we know in the suburbs of Boston received her box of test materials from an armored truck guard a few days before the state high-stakes test was to be given. She opened the large carton containing the tests and answer sheets and found also her instructions, a large ziplock bag, and latex gloves.

Her instructions directed her, on test day, to put on the latex gloves and insert the test booklets that children had vomited on into the ziplock bag, and to return those tests along with the others to the Department of Education. So the good people of the Commonwealth of Massachusetts fully understand that these tests are stressful to children, and they expect a goodly number of children to throw up as a function of their assessment program. Besides high-stakes testing, do we have other programs that are sure to make some of our children sick? Why do we allow ourselves to design testing programs that have these effects? And who is the poor person who has to open these ziplock bags, perhaps months later, and check them in to maintain security? Do we pay that person enough?

One tactic to quiet or at least to channel stress, and to assure participation, is to hold pretesting pep rallies aimed at getting students excited about the test. For example, in preparation for the upcoming test, districts in Pennsylvania held educational pep rallies and ran homeroom TV quizzes. Pep slogans were used throughout Christopher Columbus Elementary School in Chester to energize students and, according to the principal, to hype "them up more about the test and the competitive nature of doing better than before." We worry that such hype is more harmful than helpful, but the principal and teachers at this school have their jobs on the line, and we do not.

At the same time they are exhorting and cheering students on with clichés and inspirational slogans, teachers have to reassure students who dread the tests and are prone to freeze up. According to Haverford School District assistant superintendent Kathleen Taylor, "It's all based on that one test, and, boy, the pressure is unbelievable. . . . It's something that is felt by the kids, felt by the teachers and administration, all of us. When you have third- and fifth-graders really worried, that's not fair."[23] In Elmont, New York, the principal holds pep rallies every spring to ready students for the test. They come together and sing songs that will "inspire" them before and during the test. Some of these songs included "I'm a Believer," "I've Been Working on My Writing," and "At Dutch Broadway We're Prepared." For one sixth-grader, these pep rallies helped ease her fears about passing the test. She was especially relieved when, at the pep rally, the principal took off his coat to reveal a four on his shirt (the highest test grade he wanted students to aim for). "It was fun and it made me feel like I didn't have to worry about it. It made me feel like it wasn't a test anymore."[24]

Clearly, many of the administrators and teachers, along with many parents, believe that the circuslike atmosphere created by such pep rallies helps to alleviate the weight and seriousness of upcoming tests for many of their students. But when adults must act like circus clowns to help students cope with a test that has very serious consequences for educators and students alike, we suspect something has gone awry. We worry about the message a pep rally sends to students. We wonder if we are somehow telling our students that we believe they need to be entertained in order to cope with academic challenges. Rallies also seem to be presenting a

Box 6.7 Tostadas, Cheerleaders, and Magic: A Pep Rally in Texas

A vast number of gold and maroon ribbons frame the door to the cafeteria, as if for a prom or a graduation ceremony. Teachers at the door are giving the parents who enter tickets for the drawing of prizes that will end the meeting. Every wall is decorated with numerous signs exhorting the students to "EAT the TAKS" or "Take us to Exemplary" (the rating the school is trying to achieve). The band in full regalia is ready to play as the smell of tostadas, rice, and beans wafts through the room. After meeting and greeting parents and students, the principal takes the podium and faces the 250 people that came out. He solemnly requests (but virtually begs) them to take the test seriously, to help their children get ready for the tests, reminding them that the reputation of the school and the community rest on the children's performance. Dinner is served, and the science teacher comes out and does some science "magic" tricks to the delight of the audience. A student does some too. Then, at every table, a student lights a tissue paper while the principal reminds them all not to let their dreams go up in smoke. This is followed by the cheerleaders who do a routine, waving and chanting: "Let's beat the TAKS!" "Push your skills!" "We are the almighty panthers and we will prevail." "Beat the TAKS, *hooray!*" This is followed by somersaults, flips and jumps.

The principal once more talks about the seriousness of the moment. He compares the new TAKS test to a marathon, in which students need endurance. He informs parents and students that "this is the test of your lives!" Some student leaders then exhort their classmates, and the junior class president asks students to stand and repeat after her: "I pledge my knowledge, my commitment, my whole heart, and myself to passing the test and taking Parker High School to the top and leading us to exemplary." Two English teachers who do a (really bad) hip-hop routine about how it is "up to the students / to get a degree / to lead the school / to exemplary." The raffle was then held, and cheers for the students and their parents ended the evening.

Sandra L. Foster, "How Latino Students Negotiate the Demands of High-Stakes Testing: A Case Study of One School in Texas" (PhD diss., Arizona State University, 2006).

mixed message, as if we are saying that the test is serious but not serious enough for you to "worry" about. Is this the message we want to send? As we read about these pep rallies, we could not help but think that this is a very odd practice, indeed!

Incentives, some of which look like bribes, for getting test scores up

Schools have often used incentives to increase student attendance, since attendance brings schools and districts more revenue from the state. But increasingly, since NCLB, schools have gotten very creative and unapologetic in their use of incentives to get students to attend test-preparation classes and to work harder to achieve higher test scores.[25] In one school, a shopping spree was offered as an incentive for students to attend test-preparation classes. Another school in Chicago offered rent payments and grocery vouchers to students with perfect attendance.[26] In ordinary language use, most people would call this bribery.

Offering cash and prizes to students for engaging in activities they should ordinarily be engaging in is a lamentable policy for guiding our youth toward adulthood. There is a persuasive literature demonstrating that extrinsic motivators are much less effective than intrinsic ones.[27] Such research provides scientific support for the position reached through consideration of the moral dimensions of this issue.

What is even more disturbing is that we have created a system that forces educators to use incentives, bribes, and threats to get some of our students to engage in behavior we know could end up hurting their self-esteem, possibly even resulting in their not being promoted to another grade or preventing them from graduating high school. We have created a system that pushes educators to cajole and entice some less able students, some special-education students, and some English-language learners to prepare for and take the high-stakes tests. Yet these same educators largely acknowledge that the tests have severe limitations as indicators of what it means to be a successful student or a successful human being. Teachers know the test isn't worth that much. Students know it isn't worth that

Box 6.8 "Incentivizing" and Enticing Students to Learn

The *Orlando Sentinel* notes that many enticements are tied to preparation for the Florida Comprehensive Assessment Test, which children across Florida took in the spring of 2006. In Orlando, Ivey Lane's new principal, Ruth Baskerville, sparked a buzz among the students with the FCAT Mall. Baskerville lobbied local businesses and the community for donations, and her office now overflows with toys, candy, clothes, furniture, DVD players, even a refrigerator. Students who attended any of the FCAT tutoring sessions earned play money. When testing is finished, they can use their money to shop the mall, which is set up in the school cafeteria.

Principal Marvin Gordon at Dolores S. Parrott Middle School in Brooksville gives intensive-reading teachers $100 to buy gift cards for low-level readers who make progress. Higher-level readers, too, can earn $25 Wal-Mart gift cards for their progress. At the end of the year, anyone with good attendance, behavior, or grades can qualify to win bikes, trophies, or CD players. "The state gives us as educators incentives to do a good job," he said, "so why shouldn't schools reward the students?"

Erika Hobbs, "Schools Entice Kids with Cash, iPods, Cars and More: Facing Pressure to Boost Student Performance, Many Educators Say They'll Do Whatever It Takes," *Orlando Sentinel*, Mar. 1, 2006.

much. Yet educators are forced to try to sell it as best as they can because if the students do not show up for the test, the school will be labeled failing, even if the students could pass the test were they to take it. At its worst, educators are asked to lie to their students, and students are asked to believe the lies. What are the costs of such mixed messages to students? What are the costs to professional integrity?

Erosion of the teaching pool and concerns about the future of the profession

It seems relatively clear that teacher morale is eroding under the weight of high-stakes testing. As a function of worrying about how well their students will perform on their states' high-stakes tests, most individual teachers have no trouble expressing their feelings about job-related pressure and anxiety to anyone who will listen. These pressures push good teachers, as well as poor ones, out of the profession.

Many teachers think about leaving their profession—or have already—because of excessive testing pressures and overwhelming responsibilities, which are exacerbated by dwindling resources and support. A poll sponsored by the *St. Petersburg Times*, for example, suggests that not only is morale decreasing as a function of the exaggerated importance of the Florida Comprehensive Assessment Test (FCAT), but among veteran teachers, 41 percent state they wish they had chosen a different career path. Fifty-two percent of both veteran and new teachers report they had considered leaving the profession in the past year.[28] In Maryland, one editorial writer laments that many of the best teachers are leaving the profession because of the stress. "We are losing some of our best teachers and principals because they become frustrated with low scores and the intense pressure to move those scores up. Even our best teachers cannot make a child learn when he or she is not developmentally ready."[29] According to one recently retired teacher in North Carolina, it is undeniable that the pressures of the job are forcing good teachers to leave or retire early (see box 6.9).

A survey of teacher attitudes taken in North Carolina revealed that almost 70 percent of its teachers believe the statewide testing program would not improve education at their schools, and many reported "that their colleagues have developed negative attitudes toward low-achieving students." According to an associate professor of education, "We knew that a lot of teachers seemed to have a lot of concerns about the . . . accountability program, but we were surprised at the depth of the degree to which they felt negatively." She goes on, "They have indicated that their job is much more stressful. . . . And in a time when they are projecting severe teacher losses in North Carolina and we already have problems recruiting and keeping good teachers, rather than running them off, I feel like we ought to be supporting them."[30]

One principal in Kentucky said he watched his colleagues "disappear from the ranks. No one wants to blame it on [high-stakes testing programs], but from my perspective as a practicing principal, many of them

Box 6.9 One Teacher's View on the Flight of Teachers from the Profession in North Carolina

"As a recently retired teacher, I read with interest your article on the Professional Practices Commission's study of teacher turnover. Teachers do not flee their classrooms because they lack expertise but because they feel unbearable frustration and stress. Under great pressure to raise test scores, teachers feel more accountable for student progress, while effective classroom management has become less and less achievable. Teachers must deal daily with increasing numbers of troubled, disruptive students who suffer the same ills which torment current society: poverty, abuse, values that glorify violence, drug and alcohol use, and criminal acts that go largely unpunished. These young people indeed need help, but no teacher, however well trained, can provide that help while simultaneously instructing 25 to 30 other would-be learners. Obviously, learning diminishes as disruption accelerates."

"Schools Will Fail If Alternatives Not Provided," letter to the editor, *Greensboro (NC) News and Record*, Oct. 13, 1995, A14.

made it clear they weren't going to put up with unreasonable demands."[31] In Colorado, the 2003–4 year saw a record number of new superintendents hired across the state. The pressures put on schools and districts to perform well on the annual CSAP exam was cited as one reason for the increasing attrition rate among the retired, fired, or otherwise departing superintendents.[32] As with student data, we do not have a good way to track teachers who enter and leave the profession at a national level. Still, the data we have uncovered suggest that teachers are more likely to leave than stay under the weight of high-stakes testing pressures.

The pressures of high-stakes testing on the school, along with the normal concern of teachers about whether their students will pass or fail, is certainly a contributing factor toward teachers' attitudes about their job. However, we suspect that another problem facing teachers and leading to low morale is the effect of high-stakes testing on the profession at large. Many teachers now must present lessons from scripts, and they cannot often teach their favorite literature or spend time communicating their enthusiasm for certain curriculum topics, nor can they follow up on important current events because they are on tight schedules to cover only the content tested. Some teachers experience this de-skilling of their profession more than others. Those teachers fortunate enough to be in schools with students who test well are not under the same pressures as those in schools where the children are not making Adequate Yearly Progress. However, since over 90 percent of all schools in the nation are likely not to have 100 percent of their students proficient by the year 2014, over time, we suspect that even those teachers who now have latitude to make professional decisions will also be affected. As the high-stakes testing programs continue, the role of "teacher" as a professional with decisionmaking responsibility seems likely to be sufficiently downgraded to such an extent that they will end up resembling technicians and trainers. As that happens, we expect that most of the more thoughtful and exciting teachers will have left the field, and talented college graduates considering a job in teaching will avoid it altogether. What will this do to our youth and our nation?

CONCLUSION

High-stakes testing environments sap the strength and vitality out of most, though not all, teachers and administrators. We are quite aware that many administrators believe NCLB, with its use of high-stakes testing, gives them an edge in dealing with teachers who do not perform well. But this suggests that those administrators have been weak. Most of the best administrators we know manage to get the staff they want and to dismiss the teachers they do not want, especially in the many states that have weak or nonexistent unions. The best administrators also do not grant new and weak teachers tenure. It is true, however, that many of the weakest teachers are pushed out of the schools of the strongest administrators and end up in the schools of the weakest administrators, and those are often the schools with the least advantaged students. This annual "March of the Lemons," as it has been called in one district, must stop. Each state and district needs to find ways to involve unions and professional association in the retraining or removal of poor teachers. What we do not need is a high-stakes testing program that can be used as a weapon of mass destruction against our public schools, merely to provide weak administrators with a mechanism to shape the teaching behavior of a few poor teachers. It is the equivalent of using a cannon when a laser beam is needed.

This is probably a good time for teachers' unions and professional associations to help take away this reason for defending high-stakes testing. Those groups need to cooperate in the building of systems that do, in fact, lead to the removal of weak teachers, for among the over three million teachers this nation has, there are some that need help or new careers. If this cooperation were to occur, a major point in the defense of high-stakes accountability systems will have been taken away.

The issue of culpability and responsibility for low student test scores by teachers and administrators also needs to be rethought. Holding educators totally responsible for student and school improvement is a source of great stress because it is a great injustice to do so. We live in a society that has well over ten million children without health care. This ensures that vision problems, otitis media, asthma, and other childhood diseases will go unchecked, and these conditions affect test scores. At least one million children have some form of lead poisoning, and these are mostly the poorest children in America. Poor children also have lower birth weights and therefore have the highest number of birth defects that affect cognition. Our nation's poor grow up in neighborhoods segregated by income, so high-achieving peers and adults are absent as role models.[33] The neighborhood schools of the poor are strongly segregated, with fewer resources than white suburban schools, constituting a system of apartheid not unlike South Africa's in an earlier time.[34] In high school, millions of the nation's youth, both poor and middle class, work 20 hours a week or more. Only those in a society who want to evade the communal responsibility for our youth would hold teachers the sole agents responsible for test scores that are lower than desired.

As it stands now, the current system of rewards, punishment, and responsibility induces a great deal of stress, turning too many teachers and administrators against their profession. Teachers, in particular, are disenfranchised from their profession when they are told what to teach, how to teach, and are judged solely on the academic outcomes of their students. NCLB and the high-stakes testing that accompanies it impoverish their lives. For many teachers, it has taken away the joy of teaching. And if schools are not places where teachers and administrators want to be, how can they ever be good places for children to be?

We see evidence that students are feeling the weight of high-stakes testing pressure, over and above the stress that tests have always produced. This is especially the case for our most vulnerable, least advantaged populations of students, who typically have a harder time performing on such tests and for whom there is much more to lose. Senator Wellstone's prescient speech (see appendix), given many months before NCLB was discussed in Congress, made much of the unfairness of holding our poorest children responsible for our nation's failure to serve all of its children well.

When we "incentivize" or bribe our students to come to school, and when we hold cheerleading sessions for students prior to the "big test," we must wonder what messages we are sending to our youth. It seems relatively clear to us that we are sending numerous conflicting messages about what it means to be a student. We cannot easily communicate the importance of learning for its own sake when we make learning into a commodity with a value or communicate that learning only has instrumental value. We risk socializing the next generation of youth so that they never find enjoyment in a school task unless there is some external reward for their efforts and achievements. Similarly, we teach them to expect punishment for their failures to make the amount of progress dictated by someone else. It is hard to build responsibility in our youth, or require it of our teachers, if we choose to control the behavior of both through high-stakes testing. And when students end up believing both that their teachers are helpless to change things and that they come pretty close to lying to them about why they should do certain things, we have undermined a profession that could serve our nation better.

APPENDIX

A Harsh Agenda for America's Children: Edited Remarks by the Late Senator Paul D. Wellstone*

Education is, among other things, a process of shaping the moral imagination, character, skills, and intellect of our children, of inviting them into the great conversation of our moral, cultural, and intellectual life, and of giving them the resources to prepare to fully participate in the life of the nation and of the world. But today in education there is a threat afoot: the threat of high-stakes testing being grossly abused in the name of greater accountability, and almost always to the serious detriment of our children.

I want to speak out boldly against this trend toward high-stakes testing. It is a harsh agenda that holds children responsible for our own failure to invest in their future and in their achievement. . . . I would like to open my remarks with some excerpts from an article in the *Baton Rouge Advocate* earlier this year. As many of you know, Louisiana is in the process of implementing high-stakes tests for promotion. This article addresses how schools and students near Baton Rouge are dealing with the preparation and stress of the pending LEAP test. The test, which lasts five days, will determine, among other things, whether students will be promoted and whether schools will be sanctioned for poor performance.

The article describes one teacher who said, "I'm thinking about letting us have a scream day sometime in March, when we just go outside and scream," and it continues, "her principal . . . is keenly aware of the stress on both students and teachers. He told teachers during a meeting . . . that he expects some students to throw up during the test. He's arranged to have all of the school's janitors on duty to clean up any messes."

*Paul D. Wellstone, "High Stakes Tests: A Harsh Agenda for America's Children," Columbia University, Mar. 31, 2000, Alternative Education Resource Organization website, *http://www.educationrevolution.org/paulwellstone.html.*

It is no wonder that students are stressed. According to the article, "For the past eight weeks, Northwestern's school billboard has been updated daily with the number of school days left until the test." When I read this story, I wonder why we cannot let children be children? Why do we impose this misplaced pressure on children as young as eight years old? . . . In too many places, testing, which is a critical part of systemic educational accountability, has ceased its purpose of measuring educational and school improvement and has become synonymous with it.

Making students accountable for test scores works well on a bumper sticker, and it allows many politicians to look good by saying that they will not tolerate failure. But it represents a hollow promise. Far from improving education, high-stakes testing marks a major retreat from fairness, from accuracy, from quality, and from equity.

Using a single standardized test as the sole determinant for graduation, promotion, tracking, and ability grouping is not fair and has not fostered greater equality or opportunity for students. . . . It is grossly unfair to not graduate, or to hold back a student based on a standardized test if that student has not had the opportunity to learn the material covered on the test. When we impose high-stakes tests on an educational system where there are, as Jonathan Kozol says, savage inequalities, and then we do nothing to address the underlying causes of those inequalities, we set up children to fail.

It is simply negligent to force children to pass a test and expect that the poorest children, who face every disadvantage, will be able to do as well as those who have every advantage. When we do this, we hold children responsible for our own inaction and unwillingness to live up to our own promises and our own obligations. We confuse their failure with our own. This is a harsh agenda indeed, for America's children.

If one does not believe that failure on tests has to do with this crushing lack of opportunity, look at who is failing. In Minnesota, in the first round of testing, 79 percent of low-income students failed the reading portion of the high school exit exam and 74 percent failed the math part. These numbers have improved with repeated rounds of testing, but it is clear who is losing out in public education—those with the least opportunity. This pattern extends nationwide.

In Massachusetts, African American and Latino students are failing tests at twice the rate of whites. In Texas, the gap between blacks and Latinos and whites is three times. It is unconscionable.

But affording children an equal opportunity to learn is not enough. Even if all children had the opportunity to learn the material covered by the test, we still cannot close our eyes to the hard evidence that a single standardized test is not valid or reliable as the sole determinant in high-stakes decisions about students. The 1999 National Research Council report, "High Stakes," concludes that "no single test score can be considered a definitive measure of a student's knowledge," and that "an educational decision that will have a major impact on a test taker should not be made solely or automatically on the basis of a single test score."

The *Standards for Educational and Psychological Testing,* which has served as the standard for test developers and users for decades, asserts that: "In educational settings, a decision or a characterization that will have a major impact on a student should not be made on the basis of a single test score" (1999 ed.). . . . Even test publishers, including Harcourt Brace, CTB McGraw-Hill, Riverside, and ETS consistently warn against this practice.

Politicians and policymakers who continue to push for high-stakes tests and educators who continue to use them in the face of this knowledge have closed their eyes to clearly set professional and scientific standards. They demand responsibility and high standards of students and schools while they let themselves get away with defying the most basic standards of the education profession. It would be irresponsible if a parent or a teacher used a manufactured product on children in a way that the manufacturer says is unsafe. Why do we then honor and declare "accountable" policymakers and politicians who use tests on children in a way that the test manufacturers have said is effectively unsafe?

The effects of high-stakes testing go beyond their impact on individual students to greatly impact the educational process in general. They have had a deadening effect on learning. Again, research proves this point. Studies indicate that public testing encourages teachers and administrators to focus instruction on test content, test format, and test preparation. Teachers tend to overemphasize the basic skills, and underemphasize problem-solving and complex thinking skills that are not well assessed on standardized tests.

Further, they neglect content areas that are not covered such as science, social studies, and the arts.

For example, in Chicago, the Consortium on Chicago School Research concluded that "Chicago's regular year and summer school curricula were so closely geared to the Iowa test that it was impossible to distinguish real subject matter mastery from mastery of skills and knowledge useful for passing this particular test." These findings are backed up by a recent poll in Texas which showed that only 27 percent of teachers in Texas felt that increased test scores reflected increased learning and higher quality teaching. Eighty-five percent of teachers said that they neglected subjects not covered by the TAAS exam.

Stories are emerging from around the country about schools where teachers and students are under such pressure to perform that schools actually use limited funds to pay private companies to coach students and teachers in test-taking strategies. According to the *San Jose Mercury News,* schools in East Palo Alto, which is one of the poorest districts in California, paid Stanley Kaplan $10,000 each to consult with them on test-taking strategies.

The richness and exploration we want our own children to experience is being sucked out of our schools. I was moved by an op-ed I read recently in the *New York Times*, written by a fifth-grade teacher who obviously had a great passion for his work. He said, "But as I teach from day to day . . . I no longer see the students in the way I once did—certainly not in the same exuberant light as when I first started teaching five years ago. Where once they were 'challenging' or 'marginal' students, I am now beginning to see 'liabilities.' Where once there was a student of 'limited promise,' there is now an inescapable deficit that all available efforts will only nominally affect." Children are measured by their score, not their potential, not their diverse talents, not the depth of their knowledge and not their character.

We must never stop demanding that children do their best. We must never stop holding schools accountable. Measures of student performance can include standardized tests, but only when coupled with other measures of achievement, more substantive education reforms, and a much fuller, sustained investment in schools.

CHAPTER 7

WE CONCLUDE THAT HIGH-STAKES TESTING PROVIDES PERFECT CONDITIONS FOR CAMPBELL'S LAW TO OPERATE,
Ignores Standards for Professional Conduct and Appropriate Test Use, and Is Unnecessary Because Alternative Systems of Accountability Exist

We are going to do something unheard of in the history of academic research. In this concluding chapter, we are *not* going to call for more research. There is absolutely no need for new research on high-stakes testing! Sufficient evidence to declare that high-stakes testing does not work already exists. In this book, we have used Campbell's law to explain why high-stakes testing can never be made to work effectively and have gathered a wide-ranging body of evidence to demonstrate the law in action. We provided research that shows the harmful effects of high-stakes testing. We provided expert opinion from scholars in the assessment and psychometric community, all saying the same thing—namely, that the demands being made of the tests by politicians exceed the capability of the psychometric community to oblige them. We provided testimony from teachers, administrators, students, and parents concerning their unhappiness with many aspects of high-stakes systems. We have seen also that big business has found ways to make big profits from public funds that ought to be used, instead, for instructional purposes and not for increasing shareholder value. So it seems unnecessary to call for any more research. We think that any fair-minded person, were they impaneled in a jury, could see that high-stakes testing does not work. Based on our findings, we are compelled to ask for a moratorium on programs of high-stakes testing.

THE VIOLATION OF PROFESSIONAL STANDARDS WHEN RELYING ON HIGH-STAKES TESTING

We both belong to the American Educational Research Association (AERA). It is the largest educational research organization in the world. Its members include those who never saw a test they liked as well as those who make a living designing and selling tests. After hammering out a consensus among all these highly opinionated people, the AERA has stated that *all* high-stakes achievement testing programs in education should meet *all* of the following conditions, Otherwise, the system of assessment would be in violation of our professional norms for behavior.[1] As you read these professional norms for responsible testing programs, you will see that every state in America is in violation of our professional association's norms because no state satisfies *all* of the conditions recommended by AERA.

We hope you will wonder why it is unacceptable for hospitals to be in violation of the conditions of sterilization in their operating rooms even though violation of the professional standards of testing are permitted. Why are restaurants cited for violations of rules for sanitary food preparation but states that violate standards of testing held harmless? Why are military personnel held to a code of conduct—and face jail terms for breaking those codes—while states that break codes regarding the proper uses of tests are lauded? Our society asks and expects that professions police themselves. Yet even though educational researchers are quite clear about what is responsible testing and what is not, the federal government and the majority of the states say, essentially, "The hell with your professional standards!" This is not right.

Condition 1. The AERA states what we have noted many times throughout this book—namely, that "decisions that affect individual students' life chances or educational opportunities should not be made on the basis of test scores alone. Other relevant information should be taken into account to enhance the overall validity of such decisions. . . . More importantly, when there is credible evidence that a test score may not adequately reflect a student's true proficiency [say for English-language learners], alternative acceptable means should be provided by which to demonstrate attainment of the tested standards." Simply put, don't make decisions based on one measure of human ability, a rule that is even more important to consider when a person is not like the group you ordinarily assess. The state of Wyoming, among others, uses a body-of-evidence notion of assessment. The high-stakes test required by NCLB plays a role, but it *never* is the determiner of whether a child is retained in grade or given a high school degree. The state uses all the evidence it has a about a student from teachers, guidance counselors, coaches, parents, and others before it makes a final decision about a child's future. That seems to us to be much more responsible and fair than the systems in some other states.

The state of Arizona uses an augmentation system—which means educators have some flexibility to "augment" students' test scores on the basis of their course grades, in order to raise a failing score to passing on the high-stakes test. At first blush, it sounds a bit like the body-of-evidence system and has the tenor of compassion, but it has two requirements we do not like. First, in contrast to a body-of-evidence system, Arizona chooses to look *only* at students' grades, accepting no other evidence of competency in a given subject area. For some low-ability and English-language learners, this may not always be appropriate. But more important is that the augmentation system for demonstrating competency to graduate high school kicks in only after the student fails the high-stakes test four or five times! So first we humiliate students and then we say, "Okay, we'll let you graduate anyway." Furthermore, we see in this system an incentive for teachers and schools who are trying to avoid the harsh penalties of NCLB to increase students' grades in courses. In this way, the numbers of students who pass the state test will be increased. In such cases, the course grades and the test, as indicators of a student's competency, have both been corrupted.

Condition 2. The AERA states that "when content standards and associated tests are introduced as a reform to change and thereby improve current practice, opportunities to access appropriate materials and retraining consistent with the intended changes should be provided before schools, teachers, or students are sanctioned for failing to meet the new standards." Simply put, if you expect higher standards to be met in algebra, you need to ensure that every child had quality instruction in algebra, was exposed to all the content on the test, and also that every teacher of algebra was well trained in the subject.

Professional standards for assessment cannot be met if we have children being taught algebra by their coaches and history teachers, as is common in the schools that serve the poor.[2] It is both immoral and unprofessional to hold students responsible for our own failures to provide high-quality instructors for our children. In a debate in which one of us (David Berliner) said exactly that, he was accused of "showing the soft bigotry of holding low expectations for our poor and minority children." He wasn't fast enough on his feet that day to think of the proper response to that charge, which is "that this is preferable to putting hard bigotry into law by holding poor and minority children responsible for meeting state standards for which we have not prepared them." The current system makes sure that poor and minority children are most likely to get the newest and least well-trained teachers as well as those teachers who are working out of their field. Under high-stakes testing, these are the children who will most often fail a grade and fail to graduate high school. So, it is hard bigotry made into law that prepares too many poor and minority children to be the washers of cars and the mowers of lawns.

As we write in 2006, under NCLB all states are to have solved the problem of unqualified teachers. It is not clear that a single state has met that benchmark, although a few claim to have done so by using definitions of quality that are as suspicious as their definitions of academic proficiency. And the federal government seems unwilling to hold states fully accountable, since they know that the present salary structures in education will not attract into our schools all the math and science teachers that are needed, nor will it attract high-quality teachers of any kind to schools with difficult-to-teach students.[3] Still, every state is going ahead with its high-stakes testing program, without exemptions for schools that cannot provide their children with high-quality teachers as required by the law! It's a perfect catch-22.

Condition 3. You must pay attention to validity. Tests valid for one use may not be valid for another. Each separate use of a high-stakes test, for individual student evaluation or for the evaluation of an entire school, "requires a separate evaluation of the strengths and limitations of both the testing program and the test itself." Content, construct, criterion, and consequential validity are all important. Thus, if, over time, satisfactory responses to validity questions are not provided, a test is in violation of professional standards. Virtually all U.S. high-stakes tests are now or will eventually be noncompliant with this professional obligation. The AERA in particular worries that where "credible scientific evidence suggests that a given type of testing program is likely to have negative side effects, test developers and users should make a serious effort to explain these possible effects to policymakers." We have provided evidence in this book that many and serious negative effects exist with high-stakes testing, but we do not know how to get policymakers to listen.

Condition 4. There must be alignment between the test and the curriculum. This is not the simple content validity question we discussed in chapter 5. This is a requirement that the content of the test and the *cognitive processes engaged in while taking the test* should adequately represent what was desired when the curriculum was drawn up. The AERA goes on to note that "high-stakes tests should not be limited to that portion of the relevant curriculum that is easiest to measure." What worries AERA is students' engagement with simple multiple-choice problems that are cheap to score but which fail to capture what was in the standard. Suppose the curriculum standard to be mastered is concerned with learning problem-solving in geometry through computation of area and volume, which is not an unreasonable requirement for students. A multiple-choice test item could be written with an image of a rectangle or a cylinder, along with its dimensions. The ability to determine the area of a rectangle or a cylinder could then be assessed with four or five choices provided for each question. Students could be trained for hours on the various ways to do this, and scores on tests with such items can rise dramatically.

But notice that problem-solving was *never* assessed. What was assessed was the ability to apply formulas to a narrow range of pictorial representations. Therefore, the cognitive processes actually in use were not the ones that were desired when the standard was designed. Never was the amount of fencing needed for an irregular-shaped piece of land estimated and the logic of that answer checked. That would have tapped problem-solving. Never was the amount of dirt that a bucket of a certain size could hold estimated, so that the number of buckets needed to move a certain volume of dirt, in a certain amount of time, could be determined, as it must be in real-world circumstances. The AERA knows full well that the test makers would rather assess the easiest to score items and will try not to have tests with too many, or any, open-ended items, where students make their cognitive processes visible and therefore subject to evaluation. State budgets are limited, and cheap items are recommended over expensive ones, although we often lose thereby the kinds of things we wanted to measure. It's a construct problem, certainly, concerned as it is with whether you are measuring exactly what you had hoped to measure. Perhaps it might even be expressed as a law: Cheap items usually drive out rich cognitions!

Condition 5. The AERA says that "because high-stakes testing inevitably creates incentives for inappropriate methods of test preparation, multiple test forms should be used or new test forms should be introduced on a regular basis, to avoid a narrowing of the curriculum toward just the content sampled on a particular form." Notice the first part of this condition for success. It says high-stakes testing *inevitably creates incentives for inappropriate test preparation.* This is AERA's statement of Campbell's law: If high stakes are contingent on an indicator, the indicator will be corrupted. Multiple forms and new tests do not often solve the problem. Besides, to make many equivalent forms of a test, or to regularly design a new but psychometrically equivalent test, is both hard to do and very expensive. It is probably better to use an alternative to high-stakes testing than to try to meet this condition. If a pig is ugly, ain't no use cloning him, since that would just give us a whole bunch more ugly pigs!

Condition 6. This condition for high-stakes testing focuses attention on the language differences among examinees. "If a student lacks mastery of the language in which a test is given," according to the AERA, "then that test becomes, in part, a test of language proficiency. Unless a primary purpose of a test is to evaluate language proficiency, it should not be used with students who cannot understand the instructions or the language of the test itself. If English-language learners are tested in English, their performance should be interpreted in the light of their language proficiency. Special accommodations for English-language learners may be necessary to obtain valid scores." This is quite clearly a condition of fair testing that is violated in many states, once again compromising the professional standards of the educational research community.

Condition 7. This condition demanded by AERA to ensure fairness in high-stakes testing is about the procedures used in determining how "proficient" and other levels of performance are defined. The arbitrariness of the cut-score process is well known among AERA members. They understand that that the setting of cut scores is a political, not a scientific procedure, and so it needs to be explained in detail. Thus, we commend Wyoming for the process it used recently to determine cut scores for the new tests it designed to meet NCLB requirements. The cut-score process was not done in a back room, out of the light of day, as is often the case when cut scores are determined. Instead, Wyoming's process was done in the open, at a public meeting, involving the teachers of the state as well as members of the business, higher education, civic, and political communities.[4]

Condition 8. Another condition demanded is that remediation be provided for those who fail the tests. But here AERA demands not just test preparation but genuine instruction in the subject that the student has failed. Most states fail this condition, however, since they see student failure on a high-stakes test as the trigger for a program of intensive test preparation rather than an indication that further education in a subject is needed. We cheat our students and our nation when we confuse scores on a test with education in a curriculum area deemed important for life as a citizen.

Condition 9. This condition is concerned with explicit rules about who gets excluded from testing and why. This requirement exists to ensure transparency in the ways that states have assigned students to categories that are not tested. On one NAEP assessment, for example, North Carolina was found to have excluded over 200 percent more children from testing than other states, and, to no one's surprise, North Carolina's NAEP scores went up.[5] Although federal guidelines are now more explicit than in the past, schools will still find ways to bend rules to make themselves look better. So explicitness and transparency in determining who is in the testing pool and who is not is important information. In fact, without such information, comparisons between schools and districts are impossible.

Condition 10. Although AERA has listed a few more conditions for defensible use of high-stakes testing, we want to comment on only one more. This is a very complex one that almost all state tests are in violation of. It has to do with a little-remembered fact—namely, that you need a sufficient number of items to make judgments about a student's competency with regard to a particular standard. The Commission on Instructionally Supportive Assessment, chaired by the eminent W. James Popham and supported by five major professional associations in addition to AERA, made this point a cornerstone of their concerns about making testing useful to teachers.[6] The commission first noted that the typical state has many standards for each grade and subject. Sometimes these standards seem to teachers to be overwhelming and impossible to cover. But then the test companies design items to meet the standards being taught. Because tests cannot be too lengthy, the number of items on each test is constrained. Thus, we get tests that have an item reflecting this standard and an item reflecting that standard, which means that the test will never provide information about how a student is doing in mastering individual standards. Yet that is precisely the information that teachers need to design instruction!

It's not bad to know how a student is doing, overall, in meeting the third-grade mathematics standards or the fifth-grade reading standards, but that provides no information to teachers for directing instruction toward the standards that a student has not mastered. Currently, almost all states use tests that are instructionally worthless in a standards-based environment. Teachers need standard-by-standard information to target their instruction for individual students and for classes of students. But if there are only one or two items per standard on the test, the information they get is unreliable and the judgments they make about what students know, or do not know, are bound to be faulty. The solution is for each state to cut down on the number of standards they want mastered in each grade, and then for test designers to write, say, six to eight items per standard (field trials and psychometrics will determine the number needed). In this way, a teacher will learn if a student has probably mastered a standard, probably not mastered the standard, or if that decision is still indeterminate.

This is exactly what Wyoming is doing. Though not yet fully implemented, they are following the commission's recommendations to prioritize standards so that testing will cover a small number of very important standards. Then, an appropriate number of items per standard will be used to reliably determine student achievement, *standard by standard.* This also allows Wyoming to design the most humane high-stakes testing system we know of, since it allows students to bank their scores on standards that they have already proved they mastered. Subsequent student testing can be only over the standards for which they did not show proficiency. This is really a way to target instruction to precisely those curriculum areas in which students need help.

In making a number of other recommendations, the commission is quite blunt in characterizing most state high-stakes testing programs as failures, and they call the states that run such inadequate programs irresponsible. We echo their call for more instructionally sensitive tests for the improvement of learning. European educators make an important distinction that may help us see the error of our ways and which also meshes nicely with the commission's approach. Europeans talk about the vast difference between assessment *of* learning rather than assessment *for* learning. This is one of a number of alternatives to high-stakes testing that we discuss next.

ALTERNATIVES TO HIGH-STAKES TESTING

Because education is seen as a public good, states and/or school districts choose citizens to develop a curriculum for its youth. Politicians representing those citizens allocate the money needed to have that curriculum taught. Then educators translate the desires of the citizens and its politicians into classroom activities where the outcomes that are sought after are diligently pursued: responsible citizenship, getting along with others, mathematics abilities, safe automobile driving, reading skills, involvement in sports, knowledge of history, good health, writing skill, appreciation of the arts, and so forth.

It is a legitimate request for the citizenry who have designed and paid for the schools to want external measures of how those schools, teachers, and students are doing. So an assessment of progress in achieving the most important of the many desirable outcomes they have requested should be their prerogative. That is why we have stated a number of times that we are not anti-assessment. Our antipathy is reserved for the high-stakes assessments associated with NCLB. Those assessments are not only unsuccessful in improving education across the nation, as they were promised to do, but they also weaken our schools. In this section, we discuss other forms of assessment that we think could be part of a mixed system. The system we envision is one in which external but low-stakes tests have an important role to play alongside formative assessments, the development of an inspectorate, end-of-course examinations, and performance assessments of various kinds. We end this section with a warning about the use of value-added (growth) models of assessment.

Formative assessments: Assessment for *learning, not assessment* of *learning*

Most tests in the United States are assessments *of* learning. The tests are designed to tell us *what* and *how much* students know at any one point in time. They are snapshots in time, a determination of what education yields. High-stakes tests, however, use the results of these tests of learning to flog students who haven't met some predetermined, arbitrarily set standard, and under NCLB the results of student assessments can be used to humiliate and shame teachers and administrators. By contrast, assessment *for* learning is assessment used to *improve* teaching and learning—where test results and other classroom activities (classroom discussion, projects, homework) are specifically designed as feedback to teachers and students regarding what they know, what they don't know, and where they might go next.

The European Association for Research on Learning and Instruction (EARLI) compares these two approaches (table 7.1). We draw readers' attention to the terms "summative" and "formative" in this table—concepts

Table 7.1 The Differences Between Assessments of and for Learning

SUMMATIVE	FORMATIVE
Assessment *of* learning is:	Assessment *for* learning is:
One-dimensional	Multidimensional
Apart from the curriculum but drives the teaching (teaching for the test)	Integrated into the curriculum
Inauthentic	Authentic
Context independent	Context embedded
Inflexible	Flexible

Source: Menucha Birenbaum et al., "A Learning Integrated Assessment System," *Position Paper Series* (Leuven, Belgium: European Association for Research on Learning and Instruction, 2006), 4, *http://www.earli.org/position-papers.*

that are the cornerstone of the following recommendations we make in our effort to shift U.S. testing policy from an assessment *of* to an assessment *for* learning.

One idea associated with assessment for learning is to make assessment transparent to the learner. It is not some monster external test to get ready for and be nervous about. Rather, the goal of assessment for learning is to have assessment embedded in the ordinary life of the class for a more natural kind of feedback to the student and the teacher. Because they are embedded into the curriculum, formative assessments have authenticity: they become a natural part of learning a subject matter. Furthermore, formative assessments are ongoing and therefore quite flexible because they entail a range of activities selected at the teacher's discretion—that is, teacher questions, puzzles and problems to solve, learning games, and the like all can become assessment opportunities. Since high-stakes decisions are not made from the data obtained, these assessments can be quite informal.

A summative assessment, however, is a test that is given for the purposes of making an evaluative judgment about what a test taker knows. High-stakes tests are perfect examples of summative assessments since results are used to make judgments about whether a student can graduate from high school, whether a school should be closed or not, or to make other consequential decisions. An analysis of students' answers on the test may be used to help make instructional decisions, but that is not the primary goal of these high-stakes tests. Their primary goal is to make summary judgments. High-stakes standardized tests are not the only tests that do that. Teacher-made tests also are summative when they occur at the end of a curriculum unit or whenever they are used to make decisions about the grade a student should receive. In all cases, a summative assessment is a snapshot of one's knowledge at a point in time that is used to make a judgment or render a decision, as judges in trials do when issuing summary judgments.

Teachers' summative judgments are often based on teacher-made test and quiz results, homework, classroom questioning, and observations of students in discussions. These kinds of traditional summative evaluations are well accepted because they are linked to the day-to-day curriculum of the classroom and the many observations that teachers make of their students in different settings. We trust the teacher, as we do the judge at a trial, to have weighed the evidence fairly before issuing his or her judgment. But making summative judgments on the basis of high-stakes tests is more problematic for all the reasons described throughout this book. High-stakes testing associated with NCLB is very distant from the day-to-day curriculum, thus restricting the information we get from them. Of course, they offer no immediately useful instructional information since these tests are almost always given at the end of a school year. Most important, the data from which we make our decisions are as likely to be corrupted in some way as not.

With high-stakes tests, we also never get a chance to inquire of the students we are teaching whether their correct answers were just lucky guesses or based on thorough understanding of the material. We also never learn if our students knew more about the items that they got wrong on the test. No probes during assessment were possible. Why is this important? Because the answers we get on tests don't tell the whole story about what students do and do not know. For example, 38 children who took the Third International Mathematics and Science Study (TIMSS) exams were taken aside and interviewed about their answers to that well-made standardized test.[7] In the interviews, it was revealed that for 58 percent of the items students had a good deal of additional information than what they could provide on the test. Many of those who got items wrong would have gotten them right if they had been probed by a teacher or allowed to ask questions during the test. On 29 percent of the items that students got right, they showed an inadequate understanding of the concepts tested. Only on 13 percent of the items were the investigators satisfied that the item actually represented what students did or did not know.

Summative tests are static snapshots of knowledge. They never allow for this kind of probing and discussion of items. But probing students' knowledge is a part of formative assessment, similar to what is called dynamic assessment.[8] Dynamic, formative assessments also allow for teaching *during* the testing. In that way, a teacher learns how much scaffolding a student needs for learning, what the width of the zone of proximal development is, and how instruction might be better tailored to a particular student.[9] If we believe such information unnecessary for the improvement of instruction, then static, summative tests of learning will suffice. Otherwise, formative testing is useful for its informational value.

Paul Black, the distinguished British scientist who carefully studied the effects of these two forms of assessment, once described the difference between them this way: When the chef tastes the soup it is formative assessment; when the customer tastes the soup it is a summative assessment. Chefs or teachers sample the soup-to-be-served or the knowledge being learned, adjusting their ingredients or behavior as they sample until they feel all is right in the kettle or in the classroom.

The whole purpose of formative assessment is to stretch learners' experiences by repeatedly "checking in" to assess where students are in relation to curriculum goals. In this way, formative assessments are intimately linked to instruction because the information they provide allows teachers to formulate, adapt, and amend instructions based on where students are at any given point in time. Paul Black and colleagues from England define it this way:

> Assessment for learning is any assessment for which the first priority in its design and practice is to serve the purpose of promoting pupils' learning.

> It thus differs from assessment designed primarily to serve the purposes of accountability, or of ranking, or of certifying competence. An assessment activity can help learning if it provides information to be used as feedback, by teachers, and by their pupils in assessing themselves and each other, to modify the teaching and learning activities in which they are engaged. Such assessment becomes "formative assessment" when the evidence is actually used to adapt the teaching work to meet learning needs.[10]

Black and Wiliam convincingly argue that, in the end, standards for learning can only be raised by teachers and students in classrooms. We agree. Standards don't get raised by politicians or through humiliation and deprofessionalization! Black and Wiliam found that teachers who engage in the practice of formative assessment raise their students' achievement levels on traditional tests from 0.4 to 0.7 of a standard deviation, an effect that is quite large.[11] Most teachers, they say, have not learned how to do formative assessment properly, and so they have gone on to demonstrate how teachers can improve their formative assessment skills through professional development. More important for the current U.S. situation is that the use of formative assessments help low achievers more than high achievers. Formative assessment for the low achievers focuses on what is wrong with their work *and how to put it right.*

Our emphasis on the importance of formative assessments, however, does not render summative assessments obsolete. Rather, in this approach, it is recommended that a synchrony be found between them. With formative assessments helping to get a more accurate picture of what students know and can do, we gain another means to help parents and other citizens learn how students are doing in our schools and what teachers are doing to help them grow. From formative assessments teachers can provide richer descriptions of their students' performance and therefore improve our accountability system. Formative assessments, mixed with external, summative, no-stakes testing, could provide what the nation wants in an accountability system without having Campbell's law come into play and the system corrupted, which always happens with high-stakes testing.

An inspectorate

Australia, England, Holland, Germany, Sweden, and a few other countries have a school inspectorate devoted to visiting schools and providing feedback on their performance.[12] This accountability system focuses primarily on the processes of schooling—rather than using just the product of schooling—as a way to provide school personnel with information related to school improvement. The concerns of the inspectorate are much closer to what W. Edwards Deming suggested for the improvement of quality in manufacturing.[13] Inspectors of schools try to ensure that what goes on in school teaching and learning is reasonable, appropriate, sensible, efficient, and conforms to best practices, given the circumstances. High-stakes testing, in contrast, is more like yield studies in the field of agriculture. Both testing and yield studies are outcome- or product-oriented. But farmers learned a long time ago that they needed to focus their attention on watering, soil chemistry, fertilizers, weeding, insecticides, seed genetics, and so forth. That is, they learned to attend not just to yield but to the processes of farming as well. With this analogy in mind, education may be spending too much of its resources on yield studies and too little of its resources on examining its processes.

An accountability system based on yield, however, is usually cheap. To study processes is usually much more expensive. To evaluate whether a school is performing satisfactorily means, first and foremost, having inspectors watch teachers teach. Inspectors have to sample a sufficient amount of the curriculum to make judgments about its depth and breadth, its conformity to national or state curriculum standards, and the competency of teachers to implement that curriculum in an exemplary manner. An inspector also checks if uncertified teachers and teachers teaching out of their field are employed at the school. Inspectors inquire about the school's efforts in the area of community involvement, and they often hold focus groups to determine community satisfaction. Inspectors visit with students to evaluate if their motivational needs are being met. Inspectors also judge the staff-development plans the school has made, its preparedness for its demographic future, administrative leadership, and so forth.

The inspectors also consider student mobility rates and the rates of poverty and English-language learners for the school, because there is no way to interpret yield, or outcomes, without having these data available. Under NCLB, variables like mobility, poverty, crime rates in the neighborhood, percent unemployment, percent single-parent households, and so forth are considered to be excuses that schools use to hide their laziness and inefficiency. In an inspectorate, they are descriptive variables that are known to affect what happens inside of school.[14] Poverty rates, for example, affect rates of lead poisoning, which always damages brain functioning. Poverty influences the rates of students needing special education because poverty is strongly correlated with low birth weights and, therefore, cognitive ability. Otitis media, which in young children can hamper oral language acquisition, is a problem for the poor. Asthma, which influences attendance, affects poor children more than rich ones and is less often treated medically among the poor since they do not have health insurance. These and many other social and economic factors affect how schooling is carried out yet are totally ignored in the yield studies—the outcome-oriented, high-stakes approach of NCLB. It is as if using bushels per acre were always a proper measure of the success of a farmer, without ever considering climate and weather, insects, soil conditions, the equipment available to the farmer, and so forth. High levels of bushels per acre tell us what is possible under optimal conditions and provide a goal to which we can aspire. It is not a standard that can be reached by every farm and farmer. Schools work the same way. Rather than using social conditions as an excuse for poor student performance on outcome measures, an inspection informs us of the conditions of schooling that affect those outcomes *and how they need to be changed!*

For example, instead of more test preparation, a prescription that might follow from a high-stakes test failure, an inspection could call for more school counselors to help students with their school adjustment, study habits, and preparation for college or work. Or there may be a call for more social workers because the home and neighborhood life of many children is interfering with their school work.[15] Perhaps the call is for improved home–school programs, a finding less likely to occur when a school's accountability system is limited to its high-stakes test results.

Instead of a district being forced to provide tutoring or transportation out of a failing school, as required under NCLB, the recommendation from an inspector may be that the same amounts of money be spent on language classes for the parents of the students at the school. Feedback is of higher priority in these inspections than humiliation and punishment, though a strong negative report will carry those messages too. It is not a toothless and strictly symbolic operation. An inspector can make life difficult for a school staff that is not performing well. But the inspectorate is an accountability system that appears more humane than the one we are currently using.

In the United Kingdom, every school is inspected and judged against specific standards every six years. Inspectors in the UK look closely at student work, talk with students and faculty, follow faculty and students into extracurricular activities, and talk with staff and parents. Headmasters and staff get a preliminary report before it is made public, so no one is surprised and information that is misstated or wrong can be changed. The local educational system is expected to respond to the defects noted in the report. In addition to the national inspections, some local districts also have their own inspectorate. The British believe that inspection provides both the means of ensuring increased accountability and a mechanism for promoting good education. This sounds like something the United States ought to try.

What is needed, of course, is an independent inspectorate. Australia has one like that. Their inspectors are seasoned and distinguished educators who receive additional training and work for an agency completely separate from the government and the schools. They are short-term contract employees, working for a week or ten days at a stretch. Their services are so highly valued, and the prestige of being a school inspector is so great, that many well-trained professionals are willing to perform these duties for very modest remuneration. What we must avoid, were we to try an inspectorate in the United States, is an old-boy/old-girl network that merely consists in patting schools on the back. Professional and independent inspectors, like those demanded by Admiral Rickover to ensure quality for the nuclear submarine fleet, are a model for how this can be done.

Of course, inspectorates have their flaws and thus their critics. Reports don't always get made public. Evaluation criteria may differ from inspector to inspector, as in any system that relies on human judgment. Money must be found for the inspectors, and that may include finding substitutes to cover the inspectors' own classes in another school district. But every evaluation system has costs and weaknesses. We do not think that an inspectorate will cost as much or do as much harm as the high-stakes system we have now. Combined with formative assessments and mixed in with low-stakes (no consequences) standardized tests of achievement, an inspectorate could provide educators and the general public another approach to accountability and school improvement. We urge unions of teachers, and associations of administrators, to design some pilot programs to see if we are right. We think the data provided from each inspection, and the results of change over time, might quench the political and parental desire for school accountability and school change. If that is so, we would also be substituting a more humane system for one that is harsh and does not work.

End-of-course examinations

Yet another alternative to high-stakes testing is to build a low-stakes accountability system that involves teachers at the local level, say a district or county, in making the tests themselves. There are bound to be concerns about reliability and validity when this is done. But reliability can be assessed easily enough by amateurs, and, as we have seen, validity is even hard to establish for the current high-stakes tests designed by experienced and well-paid psychometricians working at big corporations. What a locally designed test is almost sure to have is content validity and something we might call curricular validity—it would be a test of the "stuff" that is actually taught!

Let's try a thought experiment. Imagine a test with consequences for students and teachers but without the involvement of McGraw-Hill, Riverside, Pearson, or other standardized test makers. Think instead of local teachers meeting and working on understanding the subject-matter standards, sharing designs and teaching tips for the classroom teaching of the standards, sharing course syllabi, and making decisions about text selections. Most important, think of the teachers designing some common, locally produced tests for the identical courses that are taught throughout the region. In this little thought experiment, imagine also that teachers are paid for these activities, for picking the cut scores to determine student proficiency, and for scoring the tests. The last activity, scoring the test, is very important. If open-ended questions, essays, writing samples, and other forms of extended response items are used—and most teachers want to use such items—then having teachers scoring them in groups is a great way to stimulate discussion of curriculum content and student capabilities.

End-of-course exams that are constructed by teachers and other educational professionals who are embedded in the community at large provide an enormous opportunity for teacher professional development. That is what makes the development of these kinds of end-of-course exams that we're proposing unique. It is a system of assessment *and* professional development, because there is ownership of the curriculum and the assessment system by local teachers and teachers must collaborate in ways that will foster growth in content and pedagogical knowledge. In some states (California, Georgia, Hawaii, Maryland, New York, North Carolina, Tennessee, and Virginia), steps have already been taken to implement these types of end-of-course evaluation systems. These tests seem best suited for middle school and beyond, where courses are usually distinct (science, mathematics, earth science, etc.). Sometimes these tests serve as the exit tests for graduation of high school, in lieu of broad-spectrum state high school exit exams. Many judge tests designed by local shareholders to be successful even when used as high-stakes tests.[16] Certainly, if high-stakes testing is necessary, then it is preferable that they at least serve the dual purpose of encompassing the needs and goals of those who help create them. Of course, our preference would be exams of this type that are low-stakes and offer few (if any) consequences that would threaten the livelihoods of our teachers and students.

The well-known New York State Regents Examinations are an example of this kind of common, end-of-course examination. All biology, history, or algebra tests are the same throughout the state and taken at the end of a course in those and many other areas. Historically, these tests were made by teachers and scored by teachers and as such provided in-service pedagogical training and greater content knowledge as teachers discussed the tests' design and engaged in scoring. Maryland now has in place a system of secondary assessments that are given as end-of-course exams to test student's knowledge of state standards.[17] The tests are given in English, government, algebra/data analysis, and biology. Other states are also creating these end-of-course, common, external-to-the-classroom tests, which we think are more sensible than the broad-spectrum high school exit exam.

We started this section, however, by saying teachers have to be involved to have ownership. Yet contracts with test publishers to design the tests, and then having the tests scored by test publishers, greatly hinders the possibility that teachers will feel any ownership of the curriculum and the assessments. Bringing in the professional test makers also takes a good deal of money out of the educational system and puts it into corporate hands. The same money might be used to have teachers make lower-stakes tests and score them in groups. Lower-stakes tests need not be held to the same rigorous standards of reliability and validity as a test where the stakes are high, where important decisions follow from test scores. With minimum help from local measurement people, the design of reliable and valid tests should not be an obstacle.

Two impediments to using the system we propose, however, are the distrust of teachers that permeates the political world and the lobbying of corporations who want to sell their services. Instead, we would like to see an assessment system that has teachers built into its design rather than seeing teachers as passive implementers of tests designed by others. We want to abolish high-stakes testing that pushes our teachers to work harder out of fear or to chase bonuses. Instead, we offer an alternative. We offer a model of assessment that is equal parts test construction *and* staff development. It is a model that generates motivation by appealing to professionalism, an intrinsic motive, not fear or incentives, which are extrinsic motivators. As almost every motivational theorist will agree, intrinsic motivation is more likely to lead to sustained work and less likely to be undermined.[18] That strikes us as closer to what we desire, since the improvement of schools that are not now succeeding is sure to take a long period of time and a lot of hard work.

We think the system we describe here—a low-stakes, end-of course assessment of learning designed to help teachers grow professionally and elicit intrinsic motivation to succeed among them—would have pleased John Dewey. Dewey believed that until the public school system could be organized in such a way that every teacher had some way to register judgment upon matters of educational importance, with the assurance that those judgments would somehow affect the school system, the schools must be regarded as undemocratic. What does democracy mean, Dewey asked in 1903, other than that the individual should have a share in determining the conditions and the aims of his or her own work? While Dewey was against tests that compared students to one another, he might well accept the end-of-course test we propose here as a way to democratize the profession at a time when it is becoming merely the operational arm of a distant government bureaucracy.

Performance tests, including project and portfolio defenses, before judges

We offer another assessment device whose flaws are well known but whose strengths are many. These are performance tests.[19] We include in performance tests not just the notion of a piano recital or a parallel bar routine, which might be appropriate end-of-course exams in a music or gymnastics course, but also projects that are defended before judges and portfolios of work submitted for evaluation by judges. The common element we stress here is that judges look at student work and communicate their evaluations about the quality of that work directly with the students. Not only do these kinds of tests have a different quality about them, but they involve members of the community in judging how schools are educating their children. So testing of this type often has a remarkably salutary effect on citizens' concerns about how youth are being educated.

This is a very democratic form of accountability, since the public is invited in to see what has been learned. The yield of schooling becomes transparent, and the community is invited to judge its significance. Moreover, because teachers are displaying their students' work to the outside community, they invariably work hard on preparing them to do well. This is motivation for teachers and students that is healthy, not fear induced, though the kinds of anxiety associated with the performance of a musical review or holiday pageant are surely present. For these kinds of tests, teachers are more like coaches, since the judges are others. This allows for a nice distinction, then, between the roles of teacher and judge. One role requires a mentor, coach, friend, advisor; the other role could turn out to be an executioner! Thus, students have greater chances to bond with their teachers in a positive way whenever it is possible to separate the roles of teacher and summative evaluator.

Psychometricians do not like these tests at all. Appropriately, they worry about idiosyncratic performances. A performance test or defense of one's project or portfolio before judges is a one-time event, and thus it is like a one-item test. It is more like the Olympics. It is a single event that might not be characteristic of the person's typical performance on other days. If the judges are not looking to give a single gold medal, however, but trying instead to determine if the person mastered a sufficient body of knowledge to be considered competent, that moderates concerns about the atypicality of a single performance.

A more difficult criticism to counter is the costs for administering a performance test. These costs include both time and money, with time being the much bigger concern. Performance testing takes a good deal of time to organize and implement. Unlike traditional, standardized achievement tests of low or high stakes, students don't all get an identical test simultaneously and don't all finish in exactly 60 minutes. Every child is judged separately, and so this kind of testing cannot be done every year. But at the end of primary school, middle school, and high school, these kinds of tests can be used in lieu of the more traditional paper-and-pencil high-stakes exit tests for judging students, their teachers, and their schools. They can also be used in mixed systems of assessment.

The time required of this form of testing might well be worth spending. We certainly have accepted this form of testing in many other fields, such as sports and music. Architects regularly defend their work publicly when they bid and are judged. Artists bring portfolios of their work to galleries for judgment. Projects are brought to committees in the workplace or to town councils to be assessed. Doctoral degrees, as well as many master's degrees and senior theses, have oral defenses attached to them. These are one-time, highly idiosyncratic, high-stakes performance assessments. For a few hundred years, student work in higher education has been examined by judges, and honors or degrees have been awarded based on the evaluations of the judges. It is curious that such a well-entrenched model of evaluation doesn't ordinarily apply to the pre-collegiate years. Certainly, performance tests, including defenses of student work, have deficiencies, as does every other form of assessment. But they are also remarkably powerful motivational devices for students and the teachers who help their students get ready to perform.

The famous Central Park East School is a New York public school in a poor neighborhood. Under the leadership of its founder, the remarkable Deborah Meier, that school has used performance tests successfully for years.[20] Juniors and seniors in the school work for two years on 14 different portfolios to demonstrate in a variety of very creative and original ways what they have learned. They must prove to a committee that they deserve their diploma. Meier has another school in the Boston area that works in a similar way, and others have adopted the model, particularly those in the Coalition of Essential Schools, under the leadership of Nancy and Ted Sizer.[21] The International Baccalaureate (IB) programs, a worldwide and highly regarded set of independent schools, have their middle schools set up in this way. And their high-prestige high school degrees make use of a mixed model, with some performances judged locally and some external assessments that are designed at IB headquarters.

The most engaging way to see the potential in these kinds of exams is to describe them carefully, as Richard Rothstein did in a *New York Times* column:

> Vincent Brevetti, principal of one portfolio school, Humanities Preparatory Academy in Manhattan, says its system works and wants the high-stakes Regents examination waived for his school and his students. When students plunge into a topic, he says, they develop advanced skills by evaluating conflicts in evidence and methods. Breadth of knowledge can be sacrificed for that, he says.

> Humanities Prep admits transfers like 17-year-old Asma Fouathia, at risk of dropping out elsewhere, as well as ninth graders who reflect a city-wide range of reading skill. Mr. Brevetti thinks Asma, an Algerian immigrant, ranks about in the middle of 12th graders in ability.
>
> In January, Asma appeared before evaluation panels at the school. To one panel, she defended a paper on whether sanctions or South Africans themselves had made apartheid fall. To another, she presented her calculations of a pinball trajectory.
>
> In social studies, she got three out of four points (two is passing) from a panel of two teachers and an outsider, Joseph Cassidy, principal of Clinton Junior High. The panelists had read Asma's paper concluding that sanctions had ended apartheid, and then questioned her for half an hour.
>
> Mr. Cassidy asked how Bantu children felt about school. (Asma said that she couldn't speak for the children but that their Afrikaner-run classes had skipped many topics.) Another panelist told Asma to define sanctions (she did) and asked whether they were now used in foreign policy (she didn't know). Mr. Cassidy challenged the full-page length of a paragraph in her paper (Asma realized that new ideas needed new paragraphs, but hadn't applied the rule here).
>
> The panelists then met privately to assign points on standardized forms. Asma was penalized because a Nelson Mandela quotation had been poorly utilized, but gained for overall subject knowledge. Asma also got three points from her math panel, whose outside evaluator was Justin Leites, a United Nations official who had taught logic at Yale. Mr. Leites praised Asma's algebra, geometry, trigonometry and physics skills. But he reduced her score because she failed to identify friction as the reason real pinballs don't follow her mathematical model.
>
> Such learning has a price. Months of apartheid research may not leave time to cover all the important dates from global history. But while knowing chronology is important, students may better remember facts learned in an inquiry.
>
> Mr. Brevetti says students not only love to do projects but also are under pressure to do them well. Alternative-school leaders [also] claim success in sending potential dropouts like Asma Fouathia to college, without need for remediation.[22]

It is easy to see the attractiveness of these kinds of performance assessments, portfolio defenses, and project defenses if they are done well.

What we particularly like is that they typically involve community members as external evaluators, making this a good way for the community to understand what is going on in their schools. Their involvement also lends an air of seriousness and authenticity to the assessments. The excerpt above also reveals how time-consuming such assessments are, so they obviously cannot be done frequently in our mass education system. But they could be used at important transition points in a student's career. And they could be used with low-stakes, broad-spectrum assessment devices to ensure that breadth of coverage was not being sacrificed in a performance-oriented assessment system. These tests offer exciting ways to involve youth and mature citizens in discussions about the school curriculum and its worth. That cannot be all bad.

Value-added assessment: Progress and dangers

As we write, we note that more and more educators and politicians are pushing for a form of evaluation of our schools called value-added assessment. These are ways to look at growth in achievement of students and schools over time and perhaps—if the statistics ever are refined enough—to pinpoint the effects of particular teachers on students' growth. Certainly, growth over time is a better way to conceptualize how schools affect students, rather than expecting schools to have every student proficient by 2014. And it is better than demanding that every school make large yearly gains on their way toward the 2014 debacle, which was always a nonsensical goal. So although we think value-added models of growth still need to be refined and tried out, they do appear as if they could assess students, teachers, and schools much better than does the current assessment system. But there is a danger that is not now a part of the conversation about value-added models of evaluation.

If achievement-growth reports become high stakes, as now occurs with the static measures of achievement used throughout the nation, then value-added models of assessment will suffer the problems we describe in this book. Campbell's law will still be operating. The type of measurement system used does not affect the operation of Campbell's law. It is the kinds of stakes attached to indicators that set the conditions for the corruption and distortion of indicators and educators. So value-added models of growth may well be a solution to one of the problems associated with NCLB. The stakes associated with the test scores on any indicator that is used is yet another problem, and that problem is not solved by changing from a static measure of achievement to one that looks at value added over time.

We see no letup in the demands for punitive measures for students, teachers, administrators, and schools who do not meet certain goals. This is an era of mistrust of schools, a good deal of which is based on disingenuous politicians, advocates of privatization, religious separatists, and overly negative and misleading news reports. That distrust leads to increased control over the schools, with incentives and sanctions used to influence curriculum, pedagogy, and the outcomes of education. As we have illustrated throughout this book, the imposition of those controls are destroying America's greatest invention, its public schools.

CONCLUSION

Because of Campbell's law, the high-stakes tests associated with NCLB are corrupted and distorted, as is the work of the educators who labor in this system. Thus, NCLB—which is almost entirely dependent on high-stakes testing—appears to be unworkable. Although a state's own tests may show gains in student achievement, audit tests (assessments based on something other than the states' own tests) do not show such growth. And even when growth in achievement within a particular state is found, it is hard to link it causally to NCLB in general—and high-stakes testing specifically—because of the many other activities occurring simultaneously in education in each state:

- We believe that NCLB needs to be extensively rethought, or done away with, and that a new model of school improvement should be tried.
- We cannot defend a law that is built around impossible-to-meet performance standards for schools.

- We cannot defend a law that condones the callous and unfair treatment of our special-education students and those for whom English is a second language.
- We cannot defend a law that uses a single test to make important decisions about the lives of students and teachers and the fate of their schools.
- We cannot defend a law that forces educators to violate their own professional standards.
- We cannot defend a law that ends up traumatizing so many teachers and students because of the stakes it has attached to a test score.
- We cannot defend a law that equates testing with teaching.
- We cannot defend a law that takes so narrow a view of achievement when the public has said it seeks so many other outcomes from our educational system as well.
- We cannot defend a law that completely ignores the out-of-school conditions that affect what happens in school, such as poverty, segregation, unemployment rates, lack of medical care, and so forth.
- We cannot defend a law that recognizes that teacher and school quality differs enormously for children of different social classes and yet has done nothing to address that issue.
- We cannot defend a law that recommends scripted lessons for teachers to deliver.
- We cannot defend a law that demands that large expenditures of public funds be spent with private, for-profit corporations.
- We cannot defend a law that undercuts local and state authority for the operation of public schools.

In this book, we have tried to focus most on the harm done by the high-stakes tests associated with NCLB. Howard Gardner has eloquently expressed our views about the broader educational issues raised by the use of high-stakes testing.[23] He asked those who supported high-stakes testing to think of what it means to be educated in a discipline in which one learns to think like a scientist, a mathematician, an artist, or a historian. He asked them to think of what it meant in the disciplines to pursue the meaning of truth and its equally important opposite, what is false or what is indeterminate. He asked them to think of what it means to understand beauty, and its equally important opposites, ugliness or kitsch. He challenged them to think of what it means to deal with what is good and what is evil in this world. After we think about Gardner's questions, we must ask ourselves if the assessment tools used in high-stakes testing are designed to measure these things, or are they likely to miss them completely?

The scores we get from high-stakes tests cannot be trusted—they are corrupted and distorted. Even worse, the high-stakes testing programs corrupt and distort the people in the educational system, and that cannot be good for a profession as vital to our nation as is teaching. In addition, these tests cannot adequately measure the important things we really want to measure. This leads to the obvious conclusion that a moratorium on their use is needed immediately. We need to stop the wreckage of our public educational system through the use of high-stakes testing as soon as possible.

NOTES

FOREWORD

1. Deborah Meier and George H. Wood, eds., *Many Children Left Behind* (Boston: Beacon Press, 2004).
2. Nel Noddings, *When School Reform Goes Wrong* (New York: Teachers College Press, 2007).
3. Nel Noddings, *The Challenge to Care in Schools*, 2nd ed. (New York: Teachers College Press, 2005).
4. Nel Noddings, *Happiness and Education* (New York: Cambridge University Press, 2003).
5. Nel Noddings, *Critical Lessons: What Our Schools Should Teach* (New York: Cambridge University Press, 2006).

PREFACE

1. Audrey L. Amrein and David C. Berliner, *The Impact of High-Stakes Tests on Student Academic Performance: An Analysis of NAEP Results in States with High-Stakes Tests and ACT, SAT, and AP Test Results in States with High School Graduation Exams* (Tempe: Education Policy Studies Laboratory, Arizona State University, 2002), *http://www.asu.edu/educ/epsl/EPRU/documents/EPSL-0211-126-EPRU.pdf*; Audrey L. Amrein and David C. Berliner, "High-Stakes Testing, Uncertainty, and Student Learning," *Education Policy Analysis Archives* 10, no. 18 (2002), *http://epaa.asu.edu/epaa/v10n18.*
2. Sharon L. Nichols, Gene V Glass, and David C. Berliner, "High-Stakes Testing and Student Achievement: Does Accountability Pressure Increase Student Learning?" *Education Policy Analysis Archives* 14, no. 1 (2006), *http://epaa.asu.edu/epaa/v14n1/*; Sharon L. Nichols and David C. Berliner, *The Inevitable Corruption of Indicators and Educators Through High-Stakes Testing* (EPSL-0503-101-EPRU), *http://www.greatlakescenter.org/pdf/EPSL-0503-101-EPRU.pdf.*

1. A SHORT HISTORY OF HIGH-STAKES TESTING

1. National Commission on Terrorist Attacks Upon the United States, *The 9-11 Commission Report: Final Report of the National Commission on Terrorist Attacks Upon the United States* (Washington, DC: U.S. Government Printing Office, 2004), *http://www.gpoaccess.gov/911/index.html.*

2. M. Gail Jones, Brett Jones, and Tracy Hargrove, *The Unintended Consequences of High-Stakes Testing* (Lanham, MD: Rowman & Littlefield, 2003); Alfie Kohn, *The Case Against Standardized Testing: Raising the Scores, Ruining the Schools* (Portsmouth, NH: Heinemann, 2000); Gary Orfield and Mindy L. Kornhaber, eds., *Raising Standards or Raising Barriers? Inequality and High-Stakes Testing in Public Education* (New York: Century Foundation Press, 2001); Peter Sacks, *Standardized Minds: The High Price of America's Testing Culture and What We Can Do to Change It* (New York: Perseus Publishing, 2001); James Ryan, "The Perverse Incentives of the No Child Left Behind Act," *New York University Law Review* 79 (2004): 932–89.
3. For example, see Gerard Giordano, *How Testing Came to Dominate American Schools: The History of Educational Assessment* (New York: Peter Lang, 2005).
4. For a review of accountability from a political perspective, see Joan L. Herman and Edward H. Haertel, eds., *Uses and Misuses of Data for Educational Accountability and Improvement: The 104th Yearbook of the National Society for the Study of Education*, part 2 (Malden, MA: Blackwell, 2005).
5. Lorraine McDonnell, "Assessment and Accountability from the Policymaker's Perspective," in Herman and Haertel, *Uses and Misuses of Data* (2005).
6. National Commission for Excellence in Education, *A Nation at Risk: The Imperatives for Educational Reform* (Washington, DC: U.S. Department of Education, National Commission for Excellence in Education, 1983).
7. David C. Berliner and Bruce J. Biddle, *The Manufactured Crisis: Myths, Fraud, and the Attack on America's Public Schools* (Reading, MA: Addison-Wesley, 1995); David Tyack and Larry Cuban, *Tinkering Toward Utopia: A Century of Public School Reform* (Cambridge, MA: Harvard University Press, 1996).
8. See Herman and Haertel, *Uses and Misuses of Data* (2005).
9. New York State Department of Education, quoted in P. Favato, S. Mathison, and C. Calalano, "A Murmur of Dissent: A Story of Resistance to High-Stakes Testing in New York State," paper presented at the meetings of the American Educational Research Association, Chicago, IL, 2003.
10. Unknown, quoted in Gillian Sutherland, *Policy-Making in Elementary Education, 1870–97* (New York: Oxford University Press, 1973).
11. Bess Keller, "Denver Teachers Approve Pay-for-Performance Plan," *Education Week*, Sept. 23, 2004, *http://www.edweek.org/ew/ewstory.cfm?slug=28denver_web.h23*; "Houston Ties Teachers' Pay to Test Scores," *New York Times*, Jan. 13, 2006; Christina DeNardo, "FCAT Moves Toward Factor in Teacher Pay, State Pushes for Performance Link," *Palm Beach Post*, July 4, 2005; Norman Draper, "State Will Test Teacher Merit Pay; Pawlenty Says Goal Is to Reward Performance," *Minneapolis Star Tribune*, Sept. 14, 2004; Mike Glover, "Republicans Propose $150 Million Teacher Pay Plan," Associated Press (Des Moines, IA), Feb. 21, 2006.
12. U.S. Congress, *No Child Left Behind Act of 2001 [H.R. 1, Public Law 107–110]* (Washington, DC: GPO, 2002), *http://www.ed.gov/policy/elsec/leg/esea02/107-110.pdf.*
13. For a recent comprehensive description of what is working and what is not working under NCLB, readers should refer to Center on Education Policy, *From the Capital to the Classroom: Year Four of the No Child Left Behind Act* (Washington, DC: Center on Education Policy, 2006).
14. We acknowledge that there are inherent challenges in assessing the efficacy of

high-stakes testing under No Child Left Behind. For example, see Bruce Fuller et al., *Is the No Child Left Behind Working? The Reliability of How States Track Achievement* (Berkeley: University of California at Berkeley Policy Analysis for California Education, 2006). But studies suggest that high-stakes testing does not increase what students learn. See Nichols, Glass, and Berliner, "High-Stakes Testing and Student Achievement." See also Henry Braun, "Reconsidering the Impact of High-Stakes Testing," *Educational Policy Analysis Archives* 12, no. 1 (2005): 1–40, *http://epaa.asu.edu/epaa/v12n1*.

15. Monty Neill, Lisa Guisbond, and Bob Schaeffer, with James Madden and Life Legeros, *Failing Our Children: How No Child Left Behind Undermines Quality and Equity in Education and an Accountability Model That Supports School Improvement* (Cambridge, MA: FairTest, 2004); Orfield and Kornhaber, *Raising Standards or Raising Barriers?* (2001); Gary Orfield et al., *Losing Our Future: How Minority Youth Are Being Left Behind by the Graduation Rate Crisis* (Cambridge, MA: Civil Rights Project at Harvard University, 2004); Jaekyung Lee, *Tracking Achievement Gaps and Assessing the Impact of NCLB on the Gaps: An In-Depth Look into National and State Reading and Math Outcome Trends* (Cambridge, MA: Civil Rights Project at Harvard University, 2006).
16. Orfield, *Losing Our Future* (2004); Jay P. Heubert and Robert M. Hauser, eds., *High Stakes: Testing for Tracking, Promotion, and Graduation* (Washington, DC: National Academy Press, 1999).
17. For example, see Gail Sunderman, *The Unraveling of No Child Left Behind: How Negotiated Changes Transform the Law* (Cambridge, MA: Civil Rights Project at Harvard University, 2006); Lee, *Tracking Achievement Gaps* (2006); Center on Education Policy, *From the Capital to the Classroom* (2006). Many politicians are against NCLB, as evidenced by the number of states who are considering opting out of the policy altogether. For example, see Sam Dillon, "Utah Vote Rejects Parts of Education Law," *New York Times*, Apr. 20, 2005; for a review of recent state-level legislative activity, see the Civil Society Institute, "NCLB Left Behind: Understanding the Growing Grassroots Rebellion Against a Controversial Law," Aug. 2005, *http://www.nclbgrassroots.org/landscape.php#*.
18. Edward H. Haertel and Joan L. Herman, "A Historical Perspective on Validity Arguments for Accountability Testing," in *Uses and Misuses of Data* (2005), 1–34.
19. Scott G. Paris, "Trojan Horse in the Schoolyard," *Issues in Education* 6, nos. 1–2 (2000); Scott G. Paris, Jodie L. Roth, and Julianne C. Turner, "Developing Disillusionment: Students' Perceptions of Academic Achievement Tests," *Issues in Education* 6, nos. 1–2 (2000).
20. Claus Zastrow and Helen Janc, *Academic Atrophy: The Condition of the Liberal Arts in America's Public Schools* (Washington, DC: Council for Basic Education, 2004).
21. For example, see Achieve, Inc., "NAEP vs. State Proficiency 2005," *http://www.achieve.org/node/482*. See also Kevin Carey, "Hot Air: How States Inflate Their Educational Progress Under NCLB," *Education Sector Online*, May 2006, *http://www.educationsector.org/usr_doc/Hot_Air_NCLB.pdf*.
22. Lee, *Tracking Achievement Gaps* (2006).
23. Nichols, Glass, and Berliner, "High-Stakes Testing and Student Achievement" (2006).
24. David C. Berliner, "Our Impoverished View of Educational Research," *Teachers College Record* 108, no. 6 (2006): 949–95.

25. Pennsylvania System of School Assessment, "Grade Eight Mathematics Performance Level Descriptors," Pennsylvania Department of Education, *http://www.pde.state.pa.us/a_and_t/cwp/view.asp?a=108&Q=114348& PM=1.*
26. Brenda Sugrue et al., *Mapping Test Items to the 1992 NAEP Mathematics Achievement Level Descriptions: Mathematics Educators' Interpretations and Their Relationship to Student Performance* (Los Angeles: National Center for Research on Evaluation, Standards, and Student Testing at the University of California Los Angeles, 1995).
27. Thomas L. Friedman, *The World Is Flat: A Brief History of the Twenty-first Century* (New York: Farrar, Straus & Giroux, 2006).
28. Dennis W. Redovich, *The Big Con in Education: Why Must "All" High School Graduates Be Prepared for College?* (New York: Universe, 2005).
29. Molly Hennessy-Fiske, "That Raise Might Take Four Years to Earn as Well: Those with Bachelor's Degrees are Finding Their Incomes Stagnate Despite a Growing Economy," *Los Angeles Times*, July 24, 2006, *http://www.latimes.com/news/nationworld/nation/la-na-wages24jul24,0,7409371.story?track=tottext.*
30. Lawrence Mishel and Joydeep Roy, *Rethinking Graduation Rates and Trends* (Washington, DC: Economic Policy Institute, 2006).
31. Gene V Glass, "Fertilizers, Pills, and Robots: The Fate of Public Education in America," lecture presented at the annual meetings of the American Educational Research Association, San Francisco, CA, Apr. 8, 2006.
32. "Scarsdale Parents Call Test Boycott a Success," *New York Times*, May 4, 2001, B1; Michael Powell, "In New York, Putting Down Their Pencils: Parent Rebellion Against Standardized Testing Strikes at Heart of Bush Plan," *Washington Post*, May 18, 2001, A1.
33. The tendency of media to overreport and exaggerate the bad news is well known. Readers are referred to Sharon Nichols and Tom Good, *American Teenagers—Myths and Realities: Media Images, Schooling, and the Social Costs of Careless Indifference* (Mahwah, NJ: Erlbaum, 2004), for a discussion on how the media exaggerates, distorts, and overrepresents the bad news about American youth's behavior. See also Michael Males, *Kids and Guns: How Politicians, Experts, and the Press Fabricate Fear of Youth* (Philadelphia: Common Courage Press, 2000), *http://www.commoncouragepress.com/*; and Michael Males, *The Scapegoat Generation: America's War on Adolescents* (Philadelphia: Common Courage Press, 1996). See also David C. Berliner and Bruce J. Biddle, "The Lamentable Alliance Between the Media and School Critics," in *Imaging Education: The Media and Schools in America*, ed. Gene Maeroff (New York: Teachers College Press, 1998).
34. David C. Berliner, "Our Impoverished View of Educational Research"; Bruce J. Biddle, ed., *Social Class, Poverty, and Education* (New York: Routledge Farmer, 2001).
35. Lisa Guisbond et al., *The Campaign for the Education of the Whole Child* (Boston: Alliance for the Education of the Whole Child, 2006).
36. Donald Campbell, "Assessing the Impact of Planned Social Change," in *Social Research and Public Policies: The Dartmouth/OECD Conference*, ed. Gene Lyons (Hanover, NH: Public Affairs Center, Dartmouth College, 1975).
37. George Madaus and Marguerite Clarke, "The Adverse Impact of High-Stakes Testing on Minority Students: Evidence from One Hundred Years of Test Data," in Orfield and Kornhaber, *Raising Standards or Raising Barriers?* (2001).

38. Werner Heisenberg, quoted in David Cassidy, "Quantum Mechanics 1920–1927: Implications of Uncertainty," American Institute of Physics, *http://www.aip.org/history/heisenberg/p08.htm*.
39. James Imamura, "Heisenberg Uncertainty Principle," University of Oregon Faculty website, *http://zebu.uoregon.edu/~imamura/208/jan27/hup.html*.
40. George Baker, Robert Gibbons, and Kevin J. Murphy, "Subjective Performance Measures in Optimal Incentive Contracts," *Quarterly Journal of Economics* 109 (1994): 1125–56.
41. For example, the *Journal of the National Cancer Institute* reported that too many men were having unnecessary prostate surgery: "Study Says Many Don't Need Prostate Surgery," *Milwaukee Journal Sentinel*, July 8, 2002; first published as "Overdiagnosis Due to Prostate-Specific Antigen Screening: Lessons from U.S. Prostate Cancer Incidence Trends," *Journal of the National Cancer Institute* 94, no. 13 (2002): 981–90. In the case of pharmaceuticals, this is especially true when it comes to ADHD and depression. For example, see Joseph Glenmullen, *Prozac Backlash: Overcoming the Dangers of Prozac, Zoloft, Paxil and Other Antidepressants with Safe, Effective Alternatives* (New York: Simon & Schuster, 2001).
42. George W. Bush, "State of the Union Address" (White House, Washington, DC, Jan. 31, 2006), transcript online at *http://www.whitehouse.gov/stateoftheunion/2006*.
43. Roddy Stinson, "The Biggest News That You Didn't Read or Hear Last Week," *San Antonio Express-News*, Sept. 25, 2005, 3A.
44. For examples, see Gerald Bracey, *High Stakes Testing* (Tempe: Educational Policy Studies Laboratory, Arizona State University, 2000), *http://www.asu.edu/educ/epsl/EPRU/documents/cerai-00-32.htm*; Center for the Study of Testing, Evaluation and Educational Policy (*http://www.csteep.bc.edu/*) and the National Board on Educational Testing and Public Policy (*http://www.bc.edu/research/nbetpp/*); Marguerite Clarke, Walt Haney, and George Madaus, *High Stakes Testing and High School Completion* (Boston: National Board on Educational Testing and Public Policy, Lynch School of Education, Boston College, 2000); Neill, Guisbond, and Schaeffer, *Failing Our Children* (2004); Jay P. Heubert and Robert M. Hauser, eds., *High Stakes: Testing for Tracking, Promotion, and Graduation* (Washington, DC: National Academy Press, 1999); Lyle V. Jones, *National Tests and Education Reform: Are They Compatible?* (Princeton, NJ: Angoff Lecture Series, Educational Testing Service, 1997), *http://www.ets.org/research/pic/jones.html*; Kohn, *The Case Against Standardized Testing* (2000); Susan Ohanian, *What Happened to Recess and Why Are Our Children Struggling in Kindergarten?* (New York: McGraw-Hill, 2002); Orfield and Kornhaber, *Raising Standards or Raising Barriers* (2001).

2. THE PREVALENCE AND FORMS OF CHEATING

1. David Callahan, *The Cheating Culture: Why More Americans Are Doing Wrong to Get Ahead* (New York: Harcourt, 2004).
2. Lawrence Kohlberg, *The Philosophy of Moral Development: Moral Stages and the Idea of Justice* (San Francisco: Harper & Row, 1981); Lawrence Kohlberg, *The Psychology of Moral Development: Essays on Moral Development* (San Francisco: Harper & Row, 1984).

3. Aimee Edmonson, "Exams Test Educator Integrity—Emphasis on Scores Can Lead to Cheating, Teacher Survey Finds," *Commercial Appeal*, Sept. 21, 2003.
4. Joseph Pedulla et al., *Perceived Effects of State-Mandated Testing Programs on Teaching and Learning: Findings from a National Survey of Teachers* (Boston: National Board on Educational Testing and Public Policy, Lynch School of Education, Boston College, 2003).
5. Brian A. Jacob and Steven D. Levitt, "Rotten Apples: An Investigation of the Prevalence and Predictors of Teacher Cheating [#9413]" (Cambridge, MA: National Bureau of Economic Research, 2002), *http://www.nber.org/papers/w9413/*; Brian A. Jacob and Steven D. Levitt, "Catching Cheating Teachers: The Results of an Unusual Experiment in Implementing Theory [#94149]" (Cambridge, MA: National Bureau of Economic Research, 2002), *http://www.nber.org/papers/w9414*.
6. Steve Leblanc, "Worcester School Principal Resigns in Wake of MCAS Cheating Probe," *Herald Tribune*, Apr. 9, 2004.
7. "Two Clark County Teachers Investigated for Leaking Math Exam," *Reno Gazette-Journal*, Jan. 8, 2004.
8. "Nevada Teacher Loses His License for Helping Students Cheat," Associated Press, May 9, 2004.
9. "Principal Takes Blame for Cheating Scandal on State Test," Associated Press State and Local Wire, June 6, 2000; "Probe Reveals Evidence of Cheating on State Test," Associated Press State and Local Wire, June 2, 2000; Linda B. Blackford and Lee Mueller, "Bell May Hire Controversial Educator: Former Principal Expected to Be Named County Superintendent," *Lexington Herald-Leader*, Mar. 22, 2004, A1; Sarah Carr, "MPS Looks into Claims Staff Helped on Tests, Tipster Alleges Students at Palmer Saw Answers," *Milwaukee Journal Sentinel*, Jan. 31, 2004, 1A.
10. Mary Vallis, "The 'Principle' Told Us To: Critics Blame Boston Cheating Scandal on Pressure to Score High in Standardized Tests," *National Post* (Don Mills, ON), June 24, 2004.
11. Callahan, *The Cheating Culture* (2004).
12. "Principal Resigns over Allegations of Cheating," Associated Press and Local Wire, June 6, 2000.
13. Blackford and Mueller, "Bell May Hire Controversial Educator" (2004).
14. Eleanor Chute, "Pupils Prompt Cheating Probe: Popular Fourth Grade Teacher Suspended over Math Testing," *Pittsburgh Post-Gazette*, May 25, 2003.
15. "Teachers Helped Pupils Cheat at East Palo Alto Public School," *San Mateo County Times*, June 15, 2002.
16. Anne Ryman, "District Audits Schools After Test Deceit," *Arizona Republic*, Oct. 8, 2003.
17. Carl Campanile, "Teachers Cheat: Inflating Regents Scores to Pass Kids," *New York Post*, Jan. 26, 2004.
18. We found stories like this in Utah: Katherine Kapos, "State Tries to Head Off Cheating: More Tests Mean More Pressure on Schools, More Temptation to Cheat," *Salt Lake Tribune*, Feb. 8, 2000. In Ohio, teachers are prepped to look for cheating: Ruth E. Sternberg, "Schools Tackle Test Security," *Columbus Dispatch*, Oct. 27, 2003.
19. Sharon L. Nichols and Thomas L. Good, *America's Teenagers—Myths and Realities: Media Images, Schooling, and the Social Costs of Careless Indifference* (Mahwah, NJ: Erlbaum, 2004).

20. Gregory Cizek, quoted in Justin Blum, "Test Score Drop Raises Doubt: Questions of Cheating Loom over SE School," *Washington Post*, Feb. 1, 2004, C1.
21. Jay Reeves, "Claims of Cheating at Alert School Prompt Furor, Firing," Associated Press State and Local Wire, Aug. 25, 1998.
22. Melanie Burney, Frank Kummer, and Dwight Ott, "Principal Fired, Says He'll Sue," *Philadelphia Inquirer*, May 2, 2006.
23. Martha Raffaele, "Lawsuit Alleges Teacher Was Fired for Reporting Test Cheating," Associated Press, Sept. 18, 2003.
24. Jay Mathews and Amy Argetsinger, "Cheating Rise with Test Mandates," *Albany (NY) Times Union*, June 4, 2000.
25. Erin Schmidt, "Foothills Teacher Resigns over Cheating Incident," *Explorer News Archives*, May 18, 2005, *http://www.explorernews.com/articles/2005/05/18/education/education01.txt*.
26. Robert L. Linn, "Assessments and Accountability," *Educational Researcher* 29, no. 2 (2004): 4–14, *http://www.aera.net/pubs/er/arts/29-02/linn01.htm*.
27. Robert L. Brennan, "Revolutions and Evolutions in Current Educational Testing [Occasional Research Paper #7]" (Des Moines: FINE Foundation and the Iowa Academy of Education, 2004), *http://www.finefoundation.org/IAE/iae-op-brennan-1.pdf*.
28. Steven Raudenbush, *Schooling, Statistics and Poverty: Can We Measure School Improvement?* (Princeton, NJ: Policy Information Center, Educational Testing Service, 2004), *http://www.ets.org/research/pic/angoff9.pdf*.
29. Gerald Bracey, *High Stakes Testing* (Tempe: Educational Policy Studies Laboratory, College of Education, Arizona State University, 2004), *http://www.asu.edu/educ/epsl/EPRU/documents/cerai-00-32.htm*; Brennan, "Revolutions and Evolutions" (2004); CSTEEP, Lynch School of Education, Boston College, *http://www.bc.edu/research/csteep/*; Marguerite Clarke, Walt Haney, and George Madaus, *High Stakes Testing and High School Completion* (Boston: National Board on Educational Testing and Public Policy, Lynch School of Education, Boston College, 2000); Monty Neill, Lisa Guisbond, and Bob Schaeffer, with James Madden and Life Legeros, *Failing Our Children: How No Child Left Behind Undermines Quality and Equity in Education and An Accountability Model that Supports School Improvement* (Cambridge, MA: FairTest, 2004), *http://www.fairtest.org/Failing%20Our%20Children/Summary%20Report%20%20final%20color.pdf*; Linn, "Assessments and Accountability" (2004); Jay P. Heubert and Robert M. Hauser, eds., *High Stakes: Testing for Tracking, Promotion, and Graduation* (Washington, DC: National Academy Press, 1999); Lyle V. Jones, *National Tests and Education Reform: Are They Compatible?* (Princeton, NJ: Angoff Lecture Series, Educational Testing Service, 1997), *http://www.ets.org/research/pic/jones.html*; Alfie Kohn, *The Case Against Standardized Testing: Raising the Scores, Ruining the Schools* (Portsmouth, NH: Heinemann, 2000); Susan Ohanian, *What Happened to Recess and Why Are Our Children Struggling in Kindergarten?* (New York: McGraw-Hill, 2002); Gary Orfield and Mindy L. Kornhaber, eds., *Raising Standards or Raising Barriers? Inequality and High-Stakes Testing in Public Education* (New York: Century Foundation Press, 2001); Raudenbush, *Schooling, Statistics and Poverty* (2004).
30. Michael Winerip, "How a Good School Can Fail on Paper," *New York Times*, Oct. 8, 2003.

31. "Teachers Call for Exam Boycott," *CBC News*, May 8, 2006, *http://www.cbc.ca/bc/story/bc_bctf-exam20060508.html.*
32. Simone Blais, "Teachers' Union Calls for Test Boycott," *Now News*, May 10, 2006, *http://www.thenownews.com/issues06/052106/news/052106nn1.html.*
33. Steve Lipsher and Karen Rouse, "Teacher Refuses to Translate CSAP Test, Cites Bias," *Denver Post*, Mar. 17, 2006, B3.
34. John Wood, "Reader's Forum: Here Are the Reasons Why I Didn't Graduate from Federal Hocking Last Weekend," *Athens News*, June 2, 2005, *http://www.athensnews.com/issue/article.php3?story_id=20780.*
35. Jenny LaCoste-Caputo, "Taking TAKS to Task," *San Antonio Express-News*, Mar. 18, 2006.

Notes to Box 2.1, page 38

1. Rosalind Rossi, "Grade School Under Investigation as Teachers Allege Test Cheating," *Chicago Sun Times*, May 5, 1996; Michael Weiss, "Clayton School Officials Deny Pressure to Succeed," *Atlanta Journal and Constitution*, Nov. 9, 1995; Steve Leblanc, "Worcester School Principal Resigns in Wake of MCAS Cheating Probe," *Herald Tribune*, Apr. 9, 2004; in this story from Delaware, principals and teachers thought they were passing out practice exam questions but had accidentally handed out exact exam questions: Joe Carmean, "Seaford Test Follow-Up," *Daily Times*, June 3, 2004.
2. Liz Seymour and William Branigin, "Theft Forces School to Give State Test Again," *Washington Post*, June 2, 2001, B2; Bruce Buchanan, "Teachers May Earn Bonuses Despite Scandal," *Greensboro (NC) News and Record*, Feb. 21, 2003; Darryl Campagna and Charity Vogel, "Teachers Under Pressure: New Goals May Tempt More Faculty to Cheat," *Buffalo News*, Aug. 29, 1999, 1A; in South Carolina, two teachers—husband and wife—shared a state exam writing prompt and gave it to their students, "Leaked Info from PACT Scores Cost State Money, Time," Associated Press, July 26, 2002, and "Two Clark County Teachers Investigated for Leaking Math Exam," *Reno Gazette-Journal*, Jan. 30, 2004; one teacher handed out a practice exam that was too close to the real test, "Nevada Teacher Loses his License for Helping Students Cheat," Associated Press, May 9 2004; Noemi Herrera, "Resignation Follows Test Irregularities," *Kansas City Star*, Apr. 17, 2004; in North Carolina, three teachers and one central-office testing coordinator resigned after allegations they shared test questions with students, "Former Guilford Testing Coordinator Fired," Associated Press, Mar. 8, 2003.
3. Michael Weiss, "Clayton School Officials Deny Pressure to Succeed," *Atlanta Journal and Constitution*, Nov. 9, 1995; "Teacher Fired After Admitting She Peeked at MAP Test," Associated Press, July 9, 2002; "Student Testing Irregularities Increase in Nevada," *Las Vegas Sun*, Jan. 18, 2004; "St. Charles Parish Students Allegedly Given Answers to Tests," Associated Press State & Local Wire, Apr. 28, 2004; Gina Smith, "Teacher Sentenced in First PACT Cheating Case: Columbia Woman Pleads Guilty, Chooses $800 Fine," *South Columbia (SC) State*, June 23, 2004; Andrea Schollkopf, "Test Breaches Linked to Teacher Training," *Albuquerque Journal*, June 12, 2002;

Matthew Bowers, "VA Group Reviews Range of SOLS Concerns," *Virginian Pilot*, Aug. 8, 2001.

4. Brigid Schulte, "School Allegedly Cheated on Tests," *Washington Post*, June 1, 2000; "Principal Resigns Over Allegations of Cheating," Associated Press State & Local Wire, June 1, 2000; "Principal Takes Blame for Cheating," Associated Press State & Local Wire, June 6, 2000; Rosalind Rossi and Nate N. Grossman, "Pressure Blamed in Test Scandal," *Chicago Sun Times*, Oct. 3, 2002; "AP Exclusive: Records Show Teachers Cheating on Test to Boost Scores," Associated Press, Oct. 28, 2003; Clive McFarlane, "MCAS Allegations Shock Parent; Chandler School High Scores Probed," *Worcester Telegram & Gazette*, Dec. 15, 2003; Martha Raffele, "Lawsuit Alleges Teacher Was Fired for Reporting Test Cheating," Associated Press, Sept. 18, 2003; "Teachers Helped Pupils Cheat at East Palo Alto Public School," *San Mateo County Times*, June 15, 2002; Ann Durbin and Ashley Lowery, "Cheating Claims Alter MEAP Plans," *South Bend Tribune*, Feb. 3, 2002; "Education Department Investigates Allegations of Cheating on AIMS," Associated Press, July 15, 2004; Jay Mathews and Ylan Mui, "MD Faults U.S. Law for Poor Scores," *Washington Post*, Oct. 10, 2003; Robert King, "Test Helper Won't Face any Charges," *St. Petersburg Times*, May 9, 2002; "Teacher Accused of Helping to Cheat on FACT," *The Bradenton*, Mar. 8, 2004; Carolyn Kleiner, "Test Case: Now the Principals Cheating," *U.S. News and World Report*, June 12, 2000; Gary Wisby, "Aide Fired in Test Cheating Scandal," *Chicago Sun Times*, Jan. 23, 2003.
5. Linda B. Blackford and Lee Mueller, "Bell May Hire Controversial Educator: Former Principal Expected to Be Named School Superintendent," *Lexington (KY) Herald Leader*, Mar. 22, 2004; Eleanor Chute, "Pupils Prompt Cheating Probe; Popular Fourth-Grade Teacher Suspended Over Math Testing," *Pittsburgh Post-Gazette*, May 25, 2003; "School Officials Suspended After Cheating Allegations," Associated Press, May 27, 2003; Randal C. Archibold, "Teacher Tells How Cheating Worked," *New York Times*, Dec. 8, 1999; Angela V. Rush, "Teachers Disciplined in Cheating," *Fresno Bee*, July 26, 2000.
6. Brigid Schulte, "School Allegedly Cheated on Test," *Washington Post*, June 1, 2000; Mary Vallis, "The 'Princible' Told Us To: Critics Blame Boston Cheating Scandal on Pressure to Score High on Standardized Test," *National Post* (Don Mills, ON), June 24, 2004.
7. "Principal Takes Blame for Cheating," Associated Press State & Local Wire, June 6, 2000; Jay Mathews, "Cheating Cases Rises with Test Mandates," *Albany (NY) Times Union*, June 4, 2000; Jodi Wilgoren, "Possible Cheating Scandal Is Investigated in Michigan," *New York Times*, June 9, 2001; Erika Hayaski, "One Poor Test Result: Cheating Teachers," *Los Angeles Times*, May 21, 2004.
8. Alison Gendar, "State Test on Hold Until HS Erases Cheat Label," *New York Daily News*, Nov. 13, 2002; Jeffery Meitrodt, "LA Voids Scores in 19 Schools: Erasures Blamed," *New Orleans Times-Picayune*, Sept. 17, 1997; Pauline Arrilaga, "Tampering Allegations Raise New Questions About the Role of TASS," Associated Press, Apr. 13, 1999; Jennifer T. Cook, "Teacher Cheating in Record Numbers," *Deseret Morning News*, Aug. 10, 2002.
9. Roddy Stinson, "TAAS Cheaters Meet National Standard," *San Antonio Express-News*, Sept. 17, 1998.
10. Carl Campanile, "Teachers Cheat," *New York Post*, Jan. 26, 2004.

3. EXCLUDING STUDENTS FROM EDUCATION

1. Jonathan Kozol, *The Shame of the Nation* (New York: Crown, 2005).
2. Alfie Kohn, *The Case Against Standardized Testing: Raising the Scores, Ruining the Schools* (Portsmouth, NH: Heinemann, 2000).
3. Francine Knowles, "Youth Unemployment Jumps in Chicago, Nation: Study," *Chicago Sun Times*, Apr. 8, 2004.
4. Bob Herbert, "Results of Pushing Out and Dropping Out," *New York Times*, Oct. 20, 2003.
5. Audrey L. Amrein and David C. Berliner, "High-Stakes Testing, Uncertainty, and Student Learning," *Education Policy Analysis Archives* 10, no. 18 (2002b), *http://epaa.asu.edu/epaa/v10n18/*; Gary Orfield and Mindy L. Kornhaber, eds., *Raising Standards or Raising Barriers? Inequality and High-Stakes Testing in Public Education* (New York: Century Foundation Press, 2001); Gary Orfield et al., *Losing Our Future: How Minority Youth Are Being Left Behind by the Graduation Rate Crisis* (Cambridge, MA: Civil Rights Project at Harvard University, 2004); Angela Valenzuela, ed., *Leaving Children Behind: How "Texas-Style" Accountability Fails Latino Youth* (Albany: State University of New York Press, 2005); Sean F. Reardon and Claudia Galindo, "Do High-Stakes Tests Affect Students' Decisions to Drop Out of School? Evidence from NELS," paper presented at the annual meetings of the American Educational Research Association, New Orleans, Apr. 2002.
6. "The Social Costs of Inadequate Education," symposium sponsored by the Laurie M. Tisch Foundation, Columbia University, New York, Oct. 24, 2005, *http://www.tc.columbia.edu/news/article.htm?id=5320* and *http://www.tc.columbia.edu/centers/EquitySymposium/symposium/resource.asp*.
7. Tamar Lewin, "City to Track Why Students Leave School," *New York Times*, Sept. 15, 2003.
8. David M. Herszenhom, "Brooklyn High School Is Accused Anew of Forcing Students Out," *New York Times*, Oct. 12, 2005.
9. Orfield, *Losing Our Future* (2004); see also "High-Stakes Testing Wobbly: Integrity Not a Reason to Give Up," *Birmingham News* (editorial), June 16, 2000.
10. Steve Orel, "Left Behind in Birmingham: 522 Pushed-Out Students," in *Silent No More: Voices of Courage in American Schools*, ed. ReLeah Cossett Lent and Gloria Pipkin (Portsmouth, NJ: Heinemann, 2003).
11. Karen W. Arenson, "More Youths Opt for G.E.D., Skirting High School Hurdle," *New York Times*, A14, May 15, 2004.
12. "Critics Say ABC's of Accountability Lead to Increased Suspensions," Associated Press, July 13, 2000.
13. Lisa Snell, "How Schools Cheat," *Reason Online*, June 2005, *http://www.reason.com/0506/fe.ls.how.shtml*.
14. Quote from page 5 of the report. Taken from Snell, "How Schools Cheat," (2005).
15. Orfield, *Losing Our Future* (2004).
16. Orfield, *Losing Our Future*, 59–60. Readers can also refer to the Advocates for Children of New York, *http://www.advocatesforchildren.org*.
17. Michael W. Apple, *Educating the "Right" Way: Markets, Standards, God, and Inequality* (London: Routledge, 2001), 71.

18. Center on Education Policy, *Rule Changes Could Help More Schools Meet Test Score Targets for the No Child Left Behind Act* (Washington, DC: Center on Education Policy, Oct. 22, 2004), *http://www.cep-dc.org/nclb/StateAccountabilityPlanAmendments ReportOct2004.pdf.* See *http://www.ed.gov/nclb/freedom/local/specedfactsheet.pdf.* See also *https://www.nea.org/esea/nclbdisabilitiesflex.html.*
19. Rebecca Catalanello, "Experts: Retaining Disabled Students Can Breed Failure," *St. Petersburg Times*, May 9, 2004.
20. These include AL, AK, FL, GA, IN, LA, MA, MN, MS, NV, NJ, MN, NY, NC, OH, SC, TN, TX, VA, AZ, CA, ID, and UT. States that are phasing in a high-school exit exam include MD (2009), OK (2012), and WA (2008). See Patricia Sullivan et al., *States Try Harder, but Gaps Persist: High School Exit Exams 2005* (Washington, DC: Center on Education Policy, 2005).
21. Nanette Asimov, "Disabled Students Call Test Unfair," *San Francisco Chronicle*, Mar. 3, 2003.
22. K. C. Myers, "Dream Denied: Tracey Newhart's Future Is Once Again in Limbo Because She Didn't Pass the MCAS," *Cape Cod Times*, Jan. 14, 2004.
23. Maureen Magee and Helen Gao, "Bill May Aid Special-Ed Students: Measure Allows Diploma Without the Exit Exam," *San Diego Union-Tribune*, Jan. 20, 2006, B1.
24. Chris Moral, Sherry Saavedra, and Maureen Magee, "High School Exit Exam Thrown Out," *San Diego Union-Tribune*, May 13, 2006.
25. Ruma Banerji Kumar, "Set Up for Failure? State Tests Pose Daunting Challenge for Special Education," *Commercial Appeal*, Oct. 6, 2003.
26. Jenny LaCoste-Caputo, "Most Fragile Can Break School's Academic Ranking," *San Antonio Express-News*, Oct. 3, 2004.
27. Wayne E. Wright, *Evolution of Federal Policy and Implications of No Child Left Behind for Language Minority Students* (Tempe: Educational Policy Studies Laboratory, Arizona State University, 2005), *http://www.asu.edu/educ/epsl/EPRU/documents/EPSL-0501-101-LPRU.pdf.*
28. Wright, *Evolution of Federal Policy* (2005).
29. Stanley Rabinowitz and Edynn Sato, *Technical Adequacy of Assessments for Alternate Student Populations: A Technical Review of High-Stakes Assessment for English Language Learners* (San Francisco: WestEd, 2005); Jamal Adebi, "Standardized Achievement Tests and English Language Learners: Psychometric Issues," *Educational Assessment* 8, no. 3 (2002): 231–57; Thomas Ricento, "The Courts, the Legislator and Society: The Shaping of Federal Language Policy in the United States," in *Language Legislation and Linguistic Rights*, ed. Douglas Kibee (Philadelphia: John Benjamins, 1996).
30. Lucy Hood, "Lessons of Change: The Newest Immigrants Challenge the U.S. Education System," *San Antonio Express-News*, Aug. 17, 2003, 1A.
31. These other passing rate data are available from a report by Keith Gayler et al., *State High School Exit Exams: A Maturing Reform* (Washington, DC: Center on Education Policy, 2004), *http://www.cep-dc.org/highschoolexit/ExitExamAug2004/ExitExam2004.pdf.*
32. Kevin Rothstein, "Minority Dropouts Sky-High in Mass," *Boston Herald*, Feb. 26, 2004; see also Orfield, *Losing Our Future* (2004).
33. Katie Pesznecker, "Minorities Struggle More with Exit Exam," *Anchorage Daily News*, May 10, 2004.

34. Lucy Hood, "Lessons of Change: The Newest Immigrants Challenge the U.S. Education System," *San Antonio Express-News*, Aug. 17, 2003, 1A.
35. Wayne Wright and Chang Pu, *Academic Achievement of English Language Learners in Post Proposition 203 Arizona* (Tempe: Language Policy Research Unit, Educational Policy Studies Laboratory, Arizona State University, 2005), *http://edpolicylab.org*.
36. Rebecca Catalanello, "FCAT's English Trips Non-Native Speakers," *St. Petersburg Times*, Apr. 24, 2004.
37. Wahinkpe Topa, "Wahinkpe Topa Says 'No More!' to Laws That Hurt Our Children," *Indian Country Today*, Mar. 8, 2004, *http://www.indiancountry.com/content.cfm?id=1078763884*.
38. Scott Travis, "Delray Teen with Stress Disorder Loses Bid to Avoid Taking FCAT," *Orlando Sun-Sentinel*, Mar. 15, 2004.
39. Rob Nelson, "Testing the Limits: New Federal Policy Will See Special Education Students Taking the LEAP Test, but Critics Decry the Move as Unfair," *New Orleans Times-Picayune*, Mar. 17, 2004.
40. Joel Rubin, "Are Schools Cheating Poor Learners? Officials Say Federal Rules Compel Them to Focus on Pupils More Likely to Raise Test Scores," *Los Angeles Times*, Nov. 28, 2004, B1.
41. Quote based on the work of British researchers Gillborn and Youdell: David Gillborn and Deborah Youdell, *Rationing Education: Policy, Practice, Reform, and Equity* (Buckingham, England: Open University Press, 2000), quoted in Jennifer Booher-Jennings, "Below the Bubble: 'Educational Triage' and the Texas Accountability System," *American Educational Research Journal* 42, no. 2 (2005).
42. Booher-Jennings, "Below the Bubble: 'Educational Triage' and the Texas Accountability System."
43. Jennifer Booher-Jennings, "Rationing Education in an Era of Accountability," *Phi Delta Kappan* 87, no. 10 (June 2006): 756–61.

4. STATES CHEAT TOO!

1. Lawrence Mishel and Joydeep Roy, *Rethinking Graduation Rates and Trends* (Washington, DC: Economic Policy Institute, 2006).
2. For more specific criteria, readers are referred to U.S. Department of Education, *National Institute of Statistical Sciences/Education Statistics Services Institute Task Force on Graduation, Completion, and Dropout Indicators* (Washington, DC: U.S. Department of Education, Institute of Education Sciences, 2005), *http://nces.ed.gov/pubs2005/2005105.pdf*.
3. Diane Jean Schemo, "Questions on Data Cloud Luster of Houston Schools," *New York Times*, July 11, 2003.
4. See Diane Jean Schemo, "For Houston Schools, College Claims Exceed Reality," *New York Times*, Aug. 28, 2003.
5. Jeff Archer, "Houston Case Offers Lessons on Dropouts," *Education Week* 23, no. 4 (2003): 14–17.
6. John Hildebrand, "Freeport's Dropout Problem: State Audit Rate Higher Than District Said," *Newsday*, Dec. 19, 2003, A26.

7. Jill Tucker, "State Issues Annual Data on Dropouts," *Tri-Valley Herald*, Apr. 27, 2003.
8. Drawn from Gary Orfield et al., *Losing Our Future: How Minority Youth Are Being Left Behind by the Graduation Rate Crisis* (Cambridge, MA: Civil Rights Project at Harvard University, 2004), 42.
9. Massachusetts Department of Education, *Progress Report on Students Attaining the Competency Determination Statewide and by School and District: Classes of 2004 and 2005* (Malden, MA: Massachusetts Department of Education, 2004), *http://www.doe.mass.edu/mcas/2004/results/0604cdprogrpt.pdf.*
10. Walt Haney, George Madaus, and Anne Wheelock, *DOE Report Inflates MCAS Pass Rates* (Boston: National Board on Educational Testing and Public Policy, Boston College, 2003), *http://www.bc.edu/research/nbetpp/pdf/doe_press.pdf.*
11. David P. Driscoll, "Statement on the Approval of House Amendment 507," Massachusetts Department of Education, May 7, 2003, *http://www.doe.mass.edu/news/news.asp?id=1503.*
12. Walt Haney, George Madaus, and Anne Wheelock, *MCAS Pass Rate for Special Ed Students Inflated by Massachusetts Department of Education: Discounting Thousands of Students from the Count Artificially Boosts Rates and Discourages Schools from Holding on to All Students* (Boston: National Board on Educational Testing and Public Policy, Boston College, 2003), *http://www.massparents.org/news/2003/sped_pass_rate.htm.*
13. This comparison is based on the Cumulative Promotion Index (CPI) crafted by Christopher Swanson of the Urban Institute. This index is considered one of the more robust among statisticians and is used by other organizations including The Civil Rights Project at Harvard University (see Johanna Wald and Daniel Losen, *Confronting the Graduation Rate Crisis in the South* [Boston: Civil Rights Project at Harvard University, 2005]) and selected research and readings on dropouts at the Education Commission of the States website, *http://www.ecs.org.* Importantly, these are not the only calculations. Another approach has been argued by John Robert Warren, "State-Level High School Completion Rates: Concepts, Measures, and Trends," *Education Policy Analysis Archives* 13, no. 51 (2005), *http://epaa.asu.edu/epaa/v13n51/.*
14. Daria Hall, *Getting Honest About Grad Rates: How States Play the Numbers and Students Lose* (Washington, DC: Education Trust, 2005), *http://www2.edtrust.org/NR/rdonlyres/C5A6974D-6C04-4FB1-A9FC-05938CB0744D/0/GettingHonest.pdf.*
15. For details on how the CPI is calculated, see Christopher B. Swanson, *Who Graduates? Who Doesn't? A Statistical Portrait of Public High School Graduation, Class of 2001* (Washington, DC: Urban Institute Education Policy Center, 2004), *http://www.urban.org/uploadedpdf/410934_whograduates. pdf.*
16. Lawrence Mishel and Joydeep Roy, *Rethinking Graduation Rates and Trends* (Washington, DC: Economic Policy Institute, 2006).
17. For a summary of the issues in the debate, readers are referred to Gerald Bracey, "Dropping in on Dropouts," *Phi Delta Kappan International* 87 (2006), *http://www.pdkintl.org/kappan/k_v87/k0606bra.htm.*
18. Quote taken from Daria Hall, *Getting Honest About Grad Rates*, 2.
19. The graduation-rate study is also cosponsored by the Urban Institute (*http://www.urban.org/*), Advocates for Children of New York (*http://www.advocatesforchildren.org/*), and The Civil Rights Project at Harvard University (*http://www.civilrightsproject.harvard.edu/*).

20. Taken from Orfield, *Losing Our Future*, 4.
21. John Robert Warren, Krista N. Jenkins, and Rachel B. Kulick, "High School Exit Examinations and State-level Completion and GED Rates, 1975 through 2002," *Educational Evaluation and Policy Analysis* 28, no. 20 (2006): 131–52.
22. For a full explanation of the APR and its development, see Sharon L. Nichols, Gene V Glass, and David C. Berliner, "High-Stakes Testing and Student Achievement: Does Accountability Pressure Increase Student Learning?" *Education Policy Analysis Archives* 14, no. 1 (2006), *http://epaa.asu.edu/epaa/v14n1/*.
23. The APR rank orders 25 out of the 50 states—chosen because of their full or almost full participation in NAEP since 1990. NAEP began disaggregating student achievement by state in 1990. Eighteen states participated in this assessment schedule since its inception and therefore have available a complete set of NAEP data on fourth- and eighth-grade students in math and reading: Alabama, Arizona, Arkansas, California, Connecticut, Georgia, Hawaii, Kentucky, Louisiana, Maryland, New Mexico, New York, North Carolina, Rhode Island, Texas, Virginia, West Virginia, and Wyoming. Seven states are missing one assessment—the eighth-grade math test from 1990. These are South Carolina, Massachusetts, Maine, Mississippi, Missouri, Tennessee, and Utah.
24. We recognize that progression rates are not the best estimate of school completion and that they do not account for migratory patterns and students who transition in and out of school.
25. Education Sector is an independent education think tank. According to their website (*http://www.educationsector.org/whoweare/*), "We are nonprofit and nonpartisan, both a dependable source of sound thinking on policy and an honest broker of evidence in key education debates. We produce original research and policy analysis and promote outstanding work by the nation's most respected education analysts."
26. Kevin Carey, "Hot Air: How States Inflate Their Educational Progress Under NCLB," *Education Sector Online*, 2006, *http://www.educationsector.org/usr_doc/Hot_Air_NCLB.pdf*.
27. Achieve.org, "NAEP vs. State Proficiency 2005," *http://www.achieve.org/node/482*.
28. Kevin Carey, "Hot Air: How States Inflate Their Educational Progress Under NCLB," *Education Sector Online*, 3.
29. See Gene Glass, "Standards and Criteria Redux (2003 Revision)," Arizona State University, *http://glass.ed.asu.edu/gene/papers/standards/*.
30. Pat Kossan, "State Deems Failing Grades Good Enough to Pass AIMS," *Arizona Republic*, May 13, 2005, *http://www.azcentral.com/arizonarepublic/news/articles/0513scores13.html*.
31. From Carey, "Hot Air," 8.
32. Kevin Rothstein, "Minority Dropouts Sky-High in Mass," *Boston Herald*, Feb. 26, 2004; Diana Jean Schemo and Ford Fessenden, "Gains in Houston Schools: How Real Are They?" *New York Times*, Dec. 3, 2003; Sarah Garrecht Gassen and Jennifer Sterba, "State Talks Tweak for AIMS Test," *Arizona Daily Star*, Sept. 3, 2003.
33. James Salzer, "Teachers Find Flaws in State Test's Science Part," *Atlanta Journal-Constitution*, June 3, 2001.
34. Derrick DePledge, "Educators Check Tests for Errors," *Honolulu Advertiser*, May 6, 2004.
35. Diana B. Henriques, "Rising Demands for Testing Push Limits of Its Accuracy," *New York Times*, Sept. 3, 2003, *http://performanceassessment.org/articles/pa_rising.html*.

36. Kevin Rothstein, "Two Rights Better MCAS Scores," *Boston Herald*, Dec. 9, 2003.
37. Michael Gormley, "Multiple Choice Question in 4th Grade Test Flunks," Associated Press, Mar. 6, 2003.
38. James Middleton, "Analysis of the Mathematics Portion of the Arizona Instrument to Measure Standards (AIMS) High School Form A Released Items," *Electronic Collaborative for Excellence in the Preparation of Teachers* (2001).
39. James A. Middleton, "Critique of Released Items on the Arizona Instrument to Measure Standards—Mathematics Portion of the 2004 Administration" (Tempe: Arizona State University, College of Education, 2004).
40. "FCAT Failures," *Orlando Sentinel* (editorial), Mar. 19, 2003, *http://www.orlandosentinel.com/news/opinion/orledped191031903mar19,0,4532284.story?coll=orl%2Dopinion%2Dheadlines.*
41. The full report is by Kathleen Rhoades and George Madaus, *Errors in Standardized Tests: A Systemic Problem* (Boston: Boston College, National Board on Educational Testing and Public Policy, 2003).
42. Henriques, "Rising Demands" (2003).
43. From Vicki Lee Parker, "Measurement Inc. Slips Down a Notch: After a Goof on Ohio Students' Tests, Company Loses—No Errors, Bragging Rights," *Raleigh (NC) News & Observer*, Dec. 21, 2005, taken from Thomas Toch, *Margins of Error: The Education Testing Industry in the No Child Left Behind Era* (Washington, DC: Education Sector, 2006), *http://www.educationsector.org/usr_doc/Margins_of_Error.pdf.*
44. Robert Brodsky, "Testing Their Patience—Citywide Third-Grade Exams Riddled with Errors," *Queens Chronicle*, May 20, 2004.
45. Michael Winerip, "Standardized Tests Face a Crisis Over Standards," *New York Times*, Mar. 22, 2006.
46. Karen W. Arenson, "Colleges Say SAT Mistakes May Affect Scholarships," *New York Times*, Mar. 26, 2006.
47. Arenson, "Colleges Say" (2006).
48. Paul Goodsell, "State Education Department Offers Apologies to Seven Schools," *Omaha World-Herald*, May 1, 2002, 2B.
49. Rhoades and Madaus, *Errors in Standardized Tests* (2003).
50. Government Accountability Office, *No Child Left Behind Act: Improvements Needed in Education's Process for Tracking States' Implementation of Key Provisions* [GAO-04-734] (Washington, DC: United States Government Accountability Office, 2004).
51. Steve Geissinger, "State Board Penalizes Company for Errors on School Tests," Associated Press, Aug. 3, 1999.
52. Brodsky, "Testing Their Patience" (2004).
53. Derrick DePledge, "Standardized Tests Checked for Errors," *Honolulu Advertiser*, May 6, 2004.
54. Karen W. Arenson, "Nobody's Perfect: Neither Is the Test," *New York Times*, Apr. 2, 2006.

5. WHAT HAPPENS TO VALIDITY

1. American Federation of Teachers, *Smart Testing: Let's Get It Right, How Assessment-Savvy Have States Become Since NCLB?* [AFT Policy Brief no. 19] (Washington, DC:

American Federation of Teachers, 2006), *http://www.aft.org/presscenter/releases/2006/smarttesting/Testingbrief.pdf.*

2. Wayne J. Camara and Gary Echternacht, "The SAT I and High School Grades: Utility in Predicting Success in College," *College Board Research Notes,* RN-10 (July 2000), *http://www.collegeboard.com/research/pdf/rn10_10755.pdf.*
3. Annapurna Ganesh and David Berliner, "What Do Positive High Correlations of Teachers' Ranking with Students' Actual Standardized Test Scores Mean?" paper presented at the annual meetings of the American Educational Research Association, San Francisco, Apr. 2006.
4. See Gene Glass, "Standards and Criteria Redux (2003 Revision)," Arizona State University, *http://glass.ed.asu.edu/gene/papers/standards.*
5. For example, see M. Gail Jones, Brett Jones, and Tracy Hargrove, *The Unintended Consequences of High-Stakes Testing* (New York: Rowman & Littlefield, 2003).
6. U.S. Department of Education, "Spellings Hails New National Report Card Results," *http://www.ed.gov/news/pressreleases/2005/07/07142005.html.*
7. This is a point Jay Mathews made in his article in the *Washington Post* arguing that teaching to the test is not outright "bad." Jay Mathews, "Let's Teach to the Test," *Washington Post,* Feb. 20, 2006, A21.
8. Damian J. Troise, "'No Child' Rules Bring Problems," *Union Leader,* June 23, 2003, B1.
9. Lorrie A. Shepard and Katharine Cutts Dougherty, "Effects of High-Stakes Testing on Instruction," paper presented at the annual meetings of the American Educational Research Association, Chicago, Apr. 1991, and the National Council on Measurement in Education, Chicago, 1991.
10. Peter Simon, "This Is a Test . . . and Yet Another Test . . . and Still Another Test," *Buffalo News,* Dec. 11, 2005, A1.
11. M. Gail Jones et al., "The Impact of High-Stakes Testing on Teachers and Students in North Carolina," *Phi Delta Kappan* 81 (1999): 199–203.
12. Public Agenda, "Reality Check 2001," *http://www.publicagenda.org/specials/rc2001/reality.htm.*
13. Public Agenda, "Reality Check 2002," *http://www.publicagenda.org/specials/rcheck2002/reality.htm.*
14. Mary Lee Smith, "Put to the Test: The Effects of External Testing on Teachers," *Educational Researcher* 20, no. 5 (1991): 8–11; Mary Lee Smith, "Meanings of Test Preparation," *American Educational Research Journal* 28, no. 3 (1991): 521–42.
15. George Perreault, "The Classroom Impact of High-Stress Testing," *Education* 120, no. 4 (2000): 705–10, cited in Jones, Jones, and Hargrove, *Unintended Consequences* (2003).
16. Smith, "Put to the Test," 8–11; Smith, "Meanings of Test Preparation," 521–42.
17. LaKisha Ladson, "Year of Preparation Faces Test Next Week," *Dallas Morning News,* Feb. 19, 2004.
18. Linda Blackford, "The Testing Dilemma: Should Students be Coached for a Standardized Test?" *Charleston Gazette,* July 30, 1995.
19. Linda Blackford, "Coaching Improves Test Scores," *Charleston Gazette,* May 23, 1996.
20. Peter Sacks, *Standardized Minds: The High Price of America's Testing Culture and What We Can Do to Change It* (New York: Perseus, 2001).

21. Ruma Banerji Kumar, "Making Cash, not the Grade," *Commercial Appeal*, Mar. 6, 2006, A1.
22. Kumar, "Making Cash, not the Grade," A1.
23. Linda McNeil and Angela Valenzuela, "The Harmful Impact of the TAAS System of Testing in Texas," in *Raising Standards or Raising Barriers? Inequality and High-Stakes Testing in Public Education*, ed. Gary Orfield and Mindy L. Kornhaber (New York: Century Foundation Press, 2001), 134.
24. McNeil and Valenzuela, "Harmful Impact," 133.
25. Jones, Jones, and Hargrove, *Unintended Consequences* (2003).
26. Alfie Kohn, *The Case Against Standardized Testing: Raising the Scores, Ruining the Schools* (Portsmouth, NH: Heinemann, 2000), 325, cited in Jones, Jones, and Hargrove, *Unintended Consequences* (2003).
27. Karen Mitchell, "What Happens When School Reform and Accountability Testing Meet?" *Theory into Practice* 36, no. 4 (1997): 263, cited in Jones, Jones, and Hargrove, *Unintended Consequences* (2003).
28. Lucy Calkins et al., *A Teacher's Guide to Standardized Tests: Knowledge Is Power* (Portsmouth, NH: Heinemann, 1998), 2, cited in Jones, Jones, and Hargrove, *Unintended Consequences* (2003).
29. Grace Taylor et al., *A Survey of Teachers' Perspectives on High-Stakes Testing in Colorado: What Gets Taught, What Gets Lost* [CSE Technical Report 588] (Los Angeles: University of California, 2003).
30. Harold Wenglinsky, "Closing the Racial Achievement Gap: The Role of Reforming Instructional Practices," *Education Policy Analysis Archives* 12, no. 64 (2004), *http://epaa.asu.edu/epaa/v12n64/*. See also a critique of Wenglinsky's work: Sarah Thuele Lubienski, "Examining Instruction, Achievement and Equity with NAEP Mathematics Data," *Education Policy Analysis Archives* 14, no. 14 (2006), *http://epaa.asu.edu/epaa/v14n14/*.
31. Nancy Trejos, "Time May Be Up for Naps in Pre-K Classes," *Washington Post*, Mar. 14, 2004, A1.
32. "Class Requirements Cut into Recess Time," *Waltham (MA) Daily News*, Feb. 27, 2004, *http://www.dailynewstribune.com/news/local_regional/walt_recess02272003.htm*.
33. Alexa Aguilar, "Many Illinois Districts Opt Out of PE Requirement," *St. Louis Post-Dispatch*, Sept. 28, 2004.
34. Jennifer Booher-Jennings, "Below the Bubble: 'Educational Triage' and the Texas Accountability System," *American Educational Research Journal* 42, no. 2 (2005): 255.
35. "Leave Time for Recess," *Seattle Post-Intelligencer*, Sept. 21, 2004.
36. Personal communication from a teacher who wishes to remain anonymous.
37. Claus Zastrow and Helen Janc, *The Condition of the Liberal Arts in America's Public Schools: A Report to the Carnegie Corporation of New York* (Washington, DC: Council for Basic Education, 2004).
38. Benjamin Barber, *An Aristocracy of Everyone: The Politics of Education and the Future of America* (New York: Oxford University Press, 1994).
39. Anand Vaishnav, "Art Teachers Fade in Bay State: Educators Cite Shifting Focus," *Boston Globe*, July 24, 2005.
40. Sherry Posnick-Goodwin, "Is It Curtains for the Arts in California's Public Schools?" *California Educator* 9, no. 9 (2005), *http://www.cta.org*.

41. Center on Education Policy, *From the Capital to the Classroom: Year Four of the No Child Left Behind Act* (Washington, DC: Center on Education Policy, 2006), *http://www.cep-dc.org/nclb/Year4/CEP-NCLB-Report-4.pdf.*
42. Taylor et al., *Survey of Teachers' Perspectives* (2003).
43. Brett Jones and Robert Egley, "Voices from the Frontlines: Teachers' Perceptions of High-Stakes Testing," *Education Policy Analysis Archives* 12, no. 39 (2004), *http://epaa.asu.edu/epaa/v12n39/.*
44. Gregory Marchant and Sharon Paulson, "The Relationship of High School Graduation Exams to Graduation Rate and SAT Scores," *Education Policy Analysis Archives* 13, no. 6 (2005), *http://epaa.asu.edu/epaa/v13n6/.*
45. Kathleen Kennedy Manzo, "Graduates Can't Master College Text: Study Finds Students Fall Off Track After 10th Grade," *Education Week* 25, no. 25 (2006).
46. ACT, *Reading Between the Lines: What the ACT Reveals About College Readiness in Reading* (Iowa City, IA: ACT, Inc., 2006), *http://www.act.org/path/policy/pdf/reading_report.pdf.*
47. See pages 16–17 from ACT, *Reading Between the Lines.*
48. Richard Rothstein, "Testing Our Patience: Standardized Tests Have Their Uses, but Current Federal Law Uses Testing to Destroy Learning," *American Prospect* 15, no. 12 (2004), *http://www.prospect.org/print/V15/2/rothstein-r.html.*

6. HOW HIGH-STAKES TESTING UNDERMINES EDUCATION

1. "Tears and Joy Fill One School," *Daily Hampshire Gazette,* June 28, 2000.
2. W. Edwards Deming, *The New Economics for Industry, Government, Education,* 2nd ed. (Cambridge, MA: MIT Press, 2000).
3. Laura Blumenfeld, "Margaret Spellings: In Her Own Class," *Washington Post,* Jan. 26, 2006, A23.
4. Erika Hobbs, "Schools Entice Kids with Cash, iPods, Cars and More: Facing Pressure to Boost Student Performance, Many Educators Say They'll Do Whatever It Takes," *Orlando Sentinel,* Mar. 1, 2006.
5. Matt Chittum, "Teachers Feeling More Pressure," *Roanoke (VA) Times,* Apr. 24, 2006, A1.
6. Leo Rigsby and Elizabeth DeMulder, "Teachers' Voices Interpreting Standards: Compromising Teachers' Autonomy or Raising Expectations and Performances?" *Education Policy Analysis Archives* 11, no. 44 (2003), *http://epaa.asu.edu/epaa/v11n44.*
7. Tracy Dell'Angela, "School Says Exam Leaves Unfair Mark: Controversial Test Brings 'Failing' Tag," *Chicago Tribune,* Oct. 31, 2003.
8. Pedro Noguera, "It Takes More Than Pressure to Help Struggling Schools," *Motion Magazine,* Oct. 2005.
9. Monte Whaley, "Colorado Schools Battle Attrition at Top: Record 30 Percent of Superintendents in State New This Year—Job Pressures Cited," *Denver Post,* Aug. 24, 2003, B1.
10. M. Gail Jones, Brett Jones, and Tracy Hargrove, *The Unintended Consequences of High-Stakes Testing* (New York: Rowman & Littlefield, 2003).
11. Daniel Koretz et al., *Final Report: Perceived Effects of the Maryland School Performance*

Assessment Program [Center for the Study of Evaluation Technical Report 409] (Los Angeles: National Center for Research on Evaluation, Standards and Student Testing, Graduate School of Education, University of California, 1996), cited in Jones, Jones, and Hargrove, *Unintended Consequences* (2003).

12. M. Gail Jones et al., "The Impact of High-Stakes Testing on Teachers and Students in North Carolina," *Phi Delta Kappan* 81, no. 3 (1999): 199–203, cited in Jones, Jones, and Hargrove, *Unintended Consequences* (2003); Joyce Elliot, "NCAE Issues Recommendations to Improve ABCs Accountability Plan," North Carolina Foundation for Public School Children, 2003, *http://www.ncae.org/news/000717pr.shtml*.
13. Mary Alice Barksdale-Ladd and Karen F. Thomas, "What's at Stake in High-Stakes Testing: Teachers and Parents Speak Out," *Journal of Teacher Education* 51, no. 5 (2000): 390 (cited in Jones, Jones, and Hargrove, *Unintended Consequences*, 2003).
14. George Perrault, "The Classroom Impact of High-Stress Testing," *Education*, no. 4 (2000): 707 (cited in Jones, Jones, and Hargrove, *Unintended Consequences*, 2003).
15. Barksdale-Ladd and Thomas, "What's at Stake in High-Stakes Testing," 392 (cited in Jones, Jones, and Hargrove, *Unintended Consequences*, 2003).
16. Tracie Lynn Yarbrough, "Teacher Perceptions of the North Carolina ABC Program and the Relationship to Classroom Practice" (PhD diss., University of North Carolina at Chapel Hill, 1999), 86.
17. All quotes come from pages 26, 27, and 49 in Taylor et al., *Survey of Teachers' Perspectives* (2003).
18. "Teachers Feel Stress of High-Stakes Testing: Results Can Make or Break Some Educators' Careers," *CNN.com Education News*, May 7, 2002, *http://cnnstudentnews.cnn.com/2002/fyi/teachers.ednews/05/07/testing.pressure.ap/*.
19. Michael Gormley, "School Mental Health Services Stressed Amid Tests, Violence Fears," Associated Press State and Local Wire, Apr. 1, 2001.
20. From David Herzenhorn and Elissa Gootman, "City Tests Loom, and Third Graders Feel the Heat," *New York Times*, Apr. 19, 2004, cited in R. Murray Thomas, *High-Stakes Testing: Coping with Collateral Damage* (Mahwah, NJ: Erlbaum, 2005).
21. From Herzenhorn and Gootman, "City Tests Loom" (2004).
22. Sandra L. Foster, "How Latino Students Negotiate the Demands of High Stakes Testing: A Case Study of One School in Texas" (PhD diss., Arizona State University, Dec. 2005).
23. William Bender, "In-Depth: Grading Our Schools—How Delco Fared on PSSA Test," *Delco Times*, Mar. 8, 2004.
24. Vivian Toy, "Elmont's School Success Is a Lesson to Others," *New York Times*, Jan. 1, 2006, 14L, p. 1.
25. Pam Belluck, "And for Perfect Attendance, Johnny Gets a Car," *New York Times*, Feb. 5, 2006; Kathleen Conti, "High Schoolers May Find Class Leads to Cash, Officials Will Pay $100 for Perfect Attendance," *Boston Globe*, July 24, 2005; Rebecca Piro, "Student Winners Are Laptop Losers," *Lowell (MA) Sun*, May 5, 2005.
26. Hobbs, "Schools Entice Kids" (2006).
27. Edward Deci and Richard Ryan, *Intrinsic Motivation and Self-determination in Human Behavior* (New York: Plenum Press, 1985); Edward Deci, Richard Koestner, and Richard Ryan, "A Meta-Analytic Review of Experiments Examining the Effects of Extrinsic Rewards on Intrinsic Motivation," *Psychological Bulletin* 125, no. 6 (1999): 627–68;

Edward Deci, Richard Koestner, and Richard Ryan, "Extrinsic Rewards and Intrinsic Motivation in Education: Reconsidered Once Again," *Review of Educational Research* 71 no. 1 (2001): 1–28.

28. Thomas Tobin and Melanie Ave, "Teachers Troubled with Job, Poll Says," *St. Petersburg Times*, May 14, 2006, 1A.
29. Patricia Delawder, "MSPAP Costs Far Outweigh the Benefits," *Maryland Gazette*, Mar. 13, 2002, A14.
30. Debbie Cenziper, "North Carolina Teachers Denounce ABC Testing, Pulses," *Charlotte Observer*, Aug. 12, 1998.
31. Alfie Kohn, *The Case Against Standardized Testing: Raising the Scores, Ruining the Schools* (Portsmouth, NH: Heinemann, 2000), 27.
32. Whaley, "Colorado Schools Battle Attrition at Top," B1.
33. Sharon Nichols and Tom Good, *America's Teenagers—Myths and Realities: Media Images, Schooling, and the Social Costs of Careless Indifference* (Mahwah, NJ: Erlbaum, 2004).
34. Jonathan Kozol, *The Shame of the Nation: The Restoration of Apartheid Schooling in America* (New York: Crown, 2005).

7. ALTERNATIVE SYSTEMS OF ACCOUNTABILITY

1. This statement is available online: American Educational Research Association, "High-Stakes Testing in Pre-K-12 Education," *http://www.aera.net/policyandprograms/?id=378.*
2. The Education Trust, *Missing the Mark: An Education Trust Analysis of Teacher-Equity Plans* (Washington, DC: Education Trust, 2006), *http://www2.edtrust.org/NR/rdonlyres/5E2815C9-F765-4821-828F-66F4D156713A/0/TeacherEquityPlans.pdf.*
3. See report by Gail L. Sunderman and Jimmy Kim, *Teacher Quality: Equalizing Educational Opportunities and Outcomes* (Cambridge, MA: Civil Rights Project at Harvard University, 2005), *http://www.civilrightsproject.harvard.edu/research/esea/Teacher_Quality.pdf*; see also Phyllis McClure, Dianne Piché, and William L. Taylor, *Are States and the Federal Government Up to the Challenge of Ensuring a Qualified Teacher for Every Student?* (Washington, DC: Citizens' Commission on Civil Rights, 2006), *http://www.cccr.org/DaysofReckoning.pdf*; Education Trust, *Missing the Mark* (2006).
4. Caroline Chauncey, "Proficiency for What? A Wyoming Standards-Setting Panel Weighs the Impact of Its Decisions," *Harvard Education Letter*, July/Aug. 2006, *http://www.edletter.org/inthenews/wyoming.shtml.*
5. Audrey L. Amrein and David C. Berliner, "High-Stakes Testing, Uncertainty, and Student Learning," *Education Policy Analysis Archives* 10, no. 18 (2002), *http://epaa.asu.edu/epaa/v10n18/.*
6. Commission on Instructionally Supportive Assessment, *Building Tests to Support Instruction and Accountability: A Guide for Policy Makers* (Arlington, VA: American Association of School Administrators, 2001), *http://www.aasa.org/files/PDFs/Policy/Building_Tests.pdf.* Also available through the commission's other sponsors: National Association of Elementary School Principals, National Association of Secondary School Principals, National Education Association, and the National Middle School Association; Ellen Forte and W. James Popham, "Red Light, Green Light: Wyoming's New

Accountability Tests Provide 'Traffic Signals' to Help Teachers Improve Instruction," *Harvard Education Letter* 22, no. 2 (2006): 6–8.

7. Ann Harlow and Alister Jones, "Why Students Answer TIMSS Science Items the Way They Do," *Research in Science Education* 34, no. 2 (2004), *http://www.springerlink.com/content/v81027uh63m74227/fulltext.pdf*.
8. Julian Elliott, "Dynamic Assessment in Educational Settings: Realising Potential," *Educational Review* 55, no. 1 (2003): 15–32; Julian Elliott and Carol Lidz, eds., *Dynamic Assessment: Prevailing Models and Applications* (New York: Elsevier, 2000); Robert Sternberg and Elena Grigorenko, *Dynamic Testing: The Nature and Measurement of Learning Potential* (New York: Cambridge University Press, 2002).
9. Lev S. Vygotsky, *Mind in Society: The Development of Higher Psychological Processes*, ed. Michael Cole et al. (Cambridge, MA: Harvard University Press, 1978); Lorrie A. Shepard, *The Role of Classroom Assessment in Teaching and Learning* [CSE Technical Report 517] (Los Angeles: Center for the Study of Evaluation National Center for Research on Evaluation, Standards, and Student Testing, 2000).
10. Paul Black et al., *Working Inside the Black Box: Assessment for Learning in the Classroom* (London: King's College London School of Education, 2002).
11. Black et al., *Working Inside the Black Box* (2002).
12. OFSTED, *The OFSTED Handbook: Guidance on the Inspection of Nursery and Primary Schools* (London: Stationery Office, 1995); see also Swedish National Agency for Education, "Inspection for Improvement," *http://www.skolverket.se/sb/d/397*; Goethe-Institut, "Identifying Strengths and Weaknesses—External Assessments of Schools in Germany," *http://www.goethe.de/wis/sub/thm/en144816.htm*.
13. W. Edwards Deming, *The New Economics for Industry, Government, Education*, 2nd ed. (Cambridge, MA: MIT Press, 2000).
14. See David C. Berliner, "Our Impoverished View of Educational Reform," *Teachers College Record* 108, no. 6 (2006): 949–95, *http://www.tcrecord.org*; Richard Rothstein, *Class and Schools: Using Social, Economic and Educational Reform to Close the Black-White Achievement Gap* (Washington, DC: Economic Policy Institute, 2004).
15. Marshall Johnson, "What's the Matter with Rural Education?" *Teachers College Record*, Aug. 07, 2006, *http://www.tcrecord.org*.
16. John H. Bishop et al., "The Role of End-of-Course Exams and Minimum Competency Exams in Standards-Based Reforms," *Cornell University Digital Commons*, Center for the Advanced Human Resource Studies Working Paper Series, 2000, *http://digitalcommons.ilr.cornell.edu/cgi/viewcontent.cgi?article=1087&context=cahrswp*.
17. For more information, see *http://www.mdk12.org/mspp/high_school/what_is/index.html*.
18. Edward Deci and Richard Ryan, *Intrinsic Motivation and Self-Determination in Human Behavior* (New York: Plenum Press, 1985); Edward Deci, Richard Koestner, and Richard Ryan, "A Meta-Analytic Review of Experiments Examining the Effects of Extrinsic Rewards on Intrinsic Motivation," *Psychological Bulletin* 125 (1999): 627–68; Edward Deci, Richard Koestner, and Richard Ryan, "Extrinsic Rewards and Intrinsic Motivation in Education: Reconsidered Once Again," *Review of Educational Research* 71, no. 1 (2001): 1–28.
19. See, for example, Pamela A. Moss, "Shifting Conceptions of Validity in Educational Measurement: Implications for Performance Assessment," *Review of Educational Research* 62, no. 3 (1992): 229–58.

20. Deborah Meier, *The Power of Their Ideas: Lessons for America from a Small School in Harlem* (Boston: Beacon Press, 2002).
21. For information on this model, go to *http://www.essentialschools.org/*.
22. Richard Rothstein, "A Worthwhile Substitute for the Regents Exams," *New York Times*, Feb. 21, 2001; also available at the Education Column Archives at the Education Policy Institute website, *http://www.epinet.org/content.cfm/webfeat_lessons20010221*.
23. Howard Gardner has been a strong critic of testing that fails to represent the important ideas derived from the disciplines. His thoughts about the power of the disciplines to illuminate ideas like truth, beauty, and goodness are given in *The Disciplined Mind: Beyond Facts and Standardized Tests, the K–12 Education That Every Child Deserves* (New York: Simon & Schuster, 1999).

ABOUT THE AUTHORS

Sharon L. Nichols is an assistant professor at the University of Texas at San Antonio. She is also a consulting editor for the *Journal of Experimental Education,* and for the last three years she has served as chair of the Adolescence Special Interest Group of the American Educational Research Association. Nichols's current work focuses on how the pressure of high-stakes testing affects novice and veteran teachers. She previously received a postdoctoral fellowship from the Educational Policy Studies Laboratory at Arizona State University to engage in research on high-stakes testing. There she was instrumental in producing technical reports on the impact of high-stakes testing on teachers, students, and schools. She earned a bachelor's degree in psychology from Bucknell University and a master's and doctorate in educational psychology from the University of Arizona in Tucson. Her doctoral studies focused on adolescent motivation in middle school contexts. Nichols has authored over a dozen publications related to youth development and motivation and educational policy. She is coauthor of *America's Teenagers—Myths and Realities: Media Images, Schooling, and the Social Costs of Careless Indifference* (with T. L. Good).

David C. Berliner is a Regents' Professor of Education at Arizona State University. Berliner spent much of his career studying teaching and teacher education, and his current research interest is in educational policy. His research has won him the Brock International Prize for educational research; the distinguished contributions award and the best book award from the American Educational Research Association; the E. L. Thorndike Award for lifetime contributions from the American Psychological Association; the Friend of Education award from the National Education Association; and the Medal of Achievement from the University of Helsinki. He is a fellow of the Center for Advanced Study in the Behavioral Sciences; a member of the National Academy of Education; and past president of the American Educational Research Association and the Division of Educational Psychology of the American Psychological Association. He was previously dean of the Mary Lou Fulton College of Education at Arizona State University. Berliner earned his bachelor's degree from UCLA, his master's from California State University at Los Angeles, and his doctorate from Stanford University; he also holds a doctorate in humane letters, *honoris causa.* His recent authored and edited works include *The Manufactured Crisis* (with B. J. Biddle), *Educational Psychology* (6th ed., with N. L. Gage), *Putting Research to Work in Your Schools* (with U. Casanova), and *The Handbook of Educational Psychology* (with R. C. Calfee). Recent journal articles have appeared in *Teachers College Record; Educational Policy Analysis Archives; Bulletin of Science, Technology, and Society;* and *Educational Researcher.*

INDEX

Note: Page numbers in italic type indicate material presented in text boxes.

Index